Operation Crusader and the Desert War in British History and Memory

Operation Crusader and the Desert War in British History and Memory

'What Is Failure? What Is Loyalty?'

Alexander H. Joffe

BLOOMSBURY ACADEMIC
LONDON • NEW YORK • OXFORD • NEW DELHI • SYDNEY

BLOOMSBURY ACADEMIC
Bloomsbury Publishing Plc
50 Bedford Square, London, WC1B 3DP, UK
1385 Broadway, New York, NY 10018, USA
29 Earlsfort Terrace, Dublin 2, Ireland

BLOOMSBURY, BLOOMSBURY ACADEMIC and the Diana logo
are trademarks of Bloomsbury Publishing Plc

First published in Great Britain 2020
This paperback edition published in 2022

Copyright © Alexander H. Joffe, 2020

Alexander H. Joffe has asserted his right under the Copyright, Designs and
Patents Act, 1988, to be identified as Author of this work.

Cover design by Terry Woodley
Cover image: FLHC 1E / Alamy Stock Photo

All rights reserved. No part of this publication may be reproduced or
transmitted in any form or by any means, electronic or mechanical, including
photocopying, recording, or any information storage or retrieval system,
without prior permission in writing from the publishers.

Bloomsbury Publishing Plc does not have any control over, or responsibility for,
any third-party websites referred to or in this book. All internet addresses given
in this book were correct at the time of going to press. The author and publisher
regret any inconvenience caused if addresses have changed or sites have
ceased to exist, but can accept no responsibility for any such changes.

Every effort has been made to trace copyright holders and to obtain their
permissions for the use of copyright material. The publisher apologizes for any errors
or omissions and would be grateful if notified of any corrections that should be incorporated in
future reprints or editions of this book.

A catalogue record for this book is available from the British Library.

Library of Congress Cataloging-in-Publication Data
Names: Joffe, Alexander H., author.
Title: Operation Crusader and the desert war in British history and memory: "What is failure?
What is loyalty?" / Alexander Joffe.
Description: London ; New York, NY : Bloomsbury Academic, 2020. | Includes bibliographical
references and index.
Identifiers: LCCN 2020019752 (print) | LCCN 2020019753 (ebook) | ISBN 9781350132870
(hardback) | ISBN 9781350132887 (ebook) |
ISBN 9781350132894 (epub)
Subjects: LCSH: Operation Crusader, 1941. | Great Britain. Army. Army, Eighth. |
World War, 1939-1945–Campaigns–Africa, North. | World War, 1939-1945–Campaigns–Africa,
North–Historiography. | World War, 1939-1945–Influence. |
Nationalism and collective memory.
Classification: LCC D766.82 .J63 2020 (print) | LCC D766.82 (ebook) | DDC 940.54/2312–dc23
LC record available at https://lccn.loc.gov/2020019752
LC ebook record available at https://lccn.loc.gov/2020019753

ISBN:	HB:	978-1-3501-3287-0
	PB:	978-1-3502-0261-0
	ePDF:	978-1-3501-3288-7
	eBook:	978-1-3501-3289-4

Typeset by Integra Software Services Pvt. Ltd.

To find out more about our authors and books visit www.bloomsbury.com
and sign up for our newsletters.

For Bruce Galloway.
My friend.

Contents

Figures		viii
Acknowledgements		ix
Introduction		1
1	Reconstructing *Crusader*	5
2	23–26 November: Breakdown and Insubordination	27
3	History Takes Shape after 26 November	43
4	The Path towards Rehabilitation and the Genesis of History	57
5	The Evidence of Other Voices	73
6	History and Memory in an Era of Commemoration and Forgetting	93
7	*Crusader* and the Desert War in the Public Eye	147
8	*Crusader* between History and Memory	189
Notes		201
Bibliography		236
Index		250

Figures

1	Portrait of Claude Auchinleck, 21 November 1940	7
2	Portrait of Alan Cunningham, 21 November 1941	9
3	Portrait of Alexander Galloway, September 1942	10
4	Alan and Andrew Cunningham, October 1941	11
5	Map of the Crusader battle	27
6	Claude Auchinleck with Alexander Galloway, Arthur Coningham, Neil Ritchie and Captain Grantham, naval liaison officer, December 1941	36

Acknowledgements

How this book came to be is an unusual story best told elsewhere. But an important early highlight was when a Scottish genealogist suggested I contact the association for retired Rhodesian policemen. My email to Berwick-upon-Tweed was followed by a message to Zimbabwe, which prompted one to Edinburgh and then another to New York. Within a few minutes I was talking on the phone to Bruce Galloway, son of Sir Alexander Galloway, one of the key figures discussed in this book. This book would not have been possible without the kindness and friendship of Bruce, as well as that of Sally Galloway, granddaughter of Sir Alexander.

All books represent journeys among people. The support of Richard Mead and Kenneth Startup has been invaluable. Correlli Barnett also offered important early encouragement. Wm. Roger Louis of the University of Texas deserves special mention, as do Glyn Harper and Rachael Bell of Massey University in Wellington, New Zealand. Sadly, several scholars who offered support did not survive to see its completion, namely the late Robin Higham and Jeffrey Grey.

I also acknowledge the kind permission to cite and quote documents from the Trustees of the Liddell Hart Centre for Military Archives, the University of Manchester, the National Army Museum, the Churchill Archive Centre, Archives New Zealand (Wellington), the Christ Church Library and the Imperial War Museum. Materials from The National Archives in Kew, Her Majesty's Stationary Office are used under Crown copyright. I express thanks to Mr Chas Bazeley for permission to quote from James Blewitt's documents. Efforts to locate other copyright holders have been made.

Thanks also go to Angus Gordon, Nigel Hamilton, Major Alexander and Shirley Greenwood, Fred, Elizabeth and Christopher Catherwood, Christopher Andrew, Gill Smith, Brigadier Ian Dobbie, the late Zara Steiner, Harold Winton, Lavinia Greacen, Harold Raugh, Owen Humphrys, Tim Severin, Ian Martin, Philip R. Grant, Major Ian Farquharson, Barrie Duncan, Simon Robbins, Gill Smith, Nina Hadaway, Diana Manipud, Ian van der Waag, David Katz, Evert Kleyhans, Dewald Nel, Gerald Prinsloo, Lester Crook, Hilary Battye, and finally Myra Johnson, the genealogist whose wisdom put me in touch with Bruce Galloway.

I am grateful to them all, and to my family, especially my wife Rachel, who accepted our house being garrisoned by the British Army for over a decade.

Introduction

Why do we remember the things that we do? How do certain narratives come to be accepted as standard or authoritative? How then do we come to believe those things as 'history', and incorporate them into ourselves, helping to form our identities? And how does this vie with memories, the fabric of our experience, to form the larger realities of society, its culture and character? What is included or elided, why or by whom? And how does one episode illuminate a larger whole, the pattern of remembering and forgetting?

German Chancellor Otto von Bismarck is famously (if inaccurately) quoted as having said that the two things one should never see being made are laws and sausages. To this we should perhaps add the process of writing history.

The Desert War has a particular place in the history of the Second World War. From 1940 to 1943 hundreds of thousands of British and Commonwealth soldiers confronted equal and larger numbers of Italians and Germans in battles across half the width of the Mediterranean. These battles were crucial to the course of the war and included notable successes at a time when the British military was reeling elsewhere.

For the most part historical focus on this theatre of the war, however, does not begin before the summer of 1942 and the appointment of Bernard Law Montgomery as commander of British forces prior to the famous second and third battles of El Alamein. Why did the British popular narrative, and those of many professional historians, begin here and not earlier? Part of answer is found not only in Montgomery's relentless self-promotion but also in the pattern of military success and then reverses that prevailed before August 1942, a series of command and operational failures, and how they were selectively recalled. But what exactly was remembered and what was forgotten, by whom and why?

This book tells three stories: what happened on a North African battlefield in late November 1941; how that event was remembered by participants, historians and journalists; and what it all meant, or didn't mean, to the British people.

The first is an unusual story of commanders on a battlefield, about events and decisions – including mental breakdown and acts of insubordination – that quietly shaped the outcome of battle and possibly the Second World War as a whole. The second is the story of how history is written of Official Historians and their governmental minders in competition (and collusion) with journalists and memoirists. And the third is about Britain after the Second World War, how events of enormous wartime gravity resonated for a shrinking number of people, largely within the Establishment and with an ageing cadre of retired military leaders, while society's interests as a whole simultaneously moved away from history and towards sentimental representation. Ultimately, it is about choices to remember, commemorate and forget the war.

It is therefore, hopefully, an interesting story about an important military episode early in the Second World War, which had political ramifications that persisted within Britain and the Empire after the war concluded. But it is also a microcosm of how events, at once concrete and evanescent, are translated into history – written documents – and then into memory, the informal textures of people's lives and behaviours. As such, this work cannot be easily categorized: it is military history, based on operational documents; historiography, based on documents from archives as well as books such as memoirs and histories; and it is social history, a portrait of the fabric of memory, reconstructed from books, newspapers and other evidence. Through these various historical methods, the book tries to connect individual but consequential events with broad if intangible social phenomena.

The question the book ultimately asks is why do we remember what we do? Put another way, in the words of one of the participants, 'what is failure and what is loyalty?' Why do we assess something as failure; indeed, what is failure in a military sense? Is it measured by the gain or loss of territory, or by casualties accrued? Or is failure also a matter of learning, to operate with new technologies and new doctrines, to predict and respond to adversaries? Who defines failure and success? Is failure to be defined in the moment or in retrospect? And what is the role of loyalty, to comrades and commanders, in the past, present and future? How does loyalty shape perceptions and thus history at the individual or societal levels? Should it? In a sense, loyalty – allegiance and obligation – is at the root of a sense of connectedness with the past, creating closeness and sympathy. But that sense of loyalty is never complete or even. What do we remember and what do we forget?

Operation *Crusader*, in November–December 1941, was the third and final British attempt to relieve the siege of the Tobruk fortress and break the German and Italian forces in North Africa. After tough initial fighting, the British made important gains, only to be countered by a stunning breakthrough overseen personally by Lt General Erwin Rommel. As the British situation teetered, the commander of the 8th Army, Lt General Alan Cunningham, was relieved of duty by his superior, General Claude Auchinleck. This decision changed the direction of the battle and perhaps the war itself. Why and how Cunningham was relieved has been the subject of commentary and speculation since it occurred.

Operation *Crusader* was the largest British military operation in North Africa to that date, and on that basis it would have been ensured mention in history books. But the circumstances under which Alan Cunningham was relieved of duty have given it unique significance. Rarely is a military commander relieved of command at the height of battle. Rarer still is that commander the brother of an unambiguously admired figure, in this case Admiral Andrew B. Cunningham.

With so much invested, the circumstances of Cunningham's dismissal became an internal military and then political problem. At the same time, the fortunes of the 8th Army quickly wavered yet again under Cunningham's replacement, Lt General Neil Ritchie, and by early 1942 moderate British gains had been reversed. Worse yet, in June 1942 the fortress of Tobruk fell and the Germans were again at the borders of Egypt. While Auchinleck managed to stem the German advance, the result was that in August 1942 Prime Minister Winston Churchill removed him from command of the Middle East theatre. With Auchinleck's replacement by General Sir Harold Alexander, and the promotion of Lt General Bernard Law Montgomery to command the 8th Army, a new era of British successes began in North Africa, along with a largely positive – if sometimes ambivalent[1] – reflection in British history and memory, constructed in no small part by Churchill and Montgomery.

The pressures to situate the extraordinary events of November 1941 began a complex historiographic saga lasting several decades. Why was Cunningham relieved? Had he become 'defensively minded' or in fact had he suffered a mental breakdown? What, or who, prompted Auchinleck's decision to relieve Cunningham? And to what extent was Cunningham's supersession the result of an act of insubordination by his Brigadier General Staff (BGS) Alexander Galloway? But parallel with this was the process of creating popular memory of *Crusader* and the Desert War, generated by newspaper reports, journalistic accounts, and by films and commemorations, such as the annual Alamein Reunion. These two broad strands ran in different if not opposite directions.

Understanding Operation *Crusader* and its ramifications, both in November 1941 and across the next quarter century, helps situate Britain's memory of the

Desert War, in which *Crusader* and preceding operations of great improvisation and daring were relegated to the background. Understanding the construction of history also situates Cunningham's career, which, after several years in relatively unimportant administrative postings, in late 1945 saw him appointed High Commissioner for Palestine, one of the most fraught assignments in the Empire. These questions, so different in scale, were both immensely consequential for Britain.

The world in which *Crusader* and the war were written about was dramatically different from that in which they had taken place. The rise of the Labour Party to power in the summer of 1945 drew a de facto dividing line between the Empire and the age of decolonization. Class structures that had defined Britain were also changing, as were relations with Commonwealth nations. What sort of history would be written, particularly about an ambiguous episode in the desert marked by command failures and seemingly pointless sacrifices, especially by Commonwealth nations? How would it be received in a society wracked by slow and awkward demobilization of soldiers and their haphazard reintegration into British society, and a British economy that was on its knees?

Cleavages between Official History, written by and to an extent for the Establishment, and unofficial histories, written by individual including soldiers of all ranks, illustrate not only different genres of writing but the nature of growing social divisions and openness. When juxtaposed against contemporary journalism, various types of histories highlight the ways in which postwar Britain and the Commonwealth came to grips with success, failure and sacrifice, in a formal, intellectual sense, and socially, in terms of what the 'people' wanted to remember. The world of class deference and Commonwealth deference had begun to end with the 'People's War', and a new age, initially led by the Labour Party, would chart a path to a new Britain, one that still had to comprehend success, failure and sacrifice. The story of *Crusader* is thus a microcosm of remembrance, commemoration and forgetting, the processes of both history and memory, which underpinned the New Britain of the late 1940s and thereafter.

1

Reconstructing *Crusader*

Operation *Crusader* as a problem in historiography

One of the perennial problems of history writing is drawing lines between periods and types of evidence. What are primary documents that bear directly on events and what is secondary evidence, individual representations or interpretations of the original events? How can very different types of evidence, from laconic operational documents, private correspondence, to prolix memoirs, be measured and meshed? What are the boundaries of the contemporary and what is the meaning of proximity to an event when assessing source texts? What is being said and left unsaid, using what voices or rhetoric? In military history, as Michael Howard has pointed out,[1] eyewitnesses and written records demand particular scepticism, but they may at least have the advantage of chronological priority. Memoirs by participants or observers may offer welcome details or colour but are by definition self-interested, if not self-serving.

The unusual category of 'Official History', however, written or supervised by military or political institutions, is pulled three ways, variously described as historiography, memorialization and didacticism,[2] the need to 'inform, persuade and defend',[3] or, more cynically, between 'history, amnesia and selective memory'.[4] All tend to blur contemporary observations with later judgements. The goal of writing history is also never strictly understanding the past, but shaping the present and/or the future. Official Histories may thus be intended for a broader audience of educated readers or a narrower one of historians and other specialists, themselves frequently involved in the production of history or policy. Indeed, the planners of the British Official History series discussed the project in just these terms.[5]

When addressing Operation *Crusader* we must distinguish between the documents of 23–26 November 1941, when the primary concern of participants was command of the battle itself, generated as part of the unfolding offensive. Next are documents originating in the immediate aftermath of Alan Cunningham's supersession, roughly December 1941 through 1945, where individual agendas and perceptions were advanced with only a limited view towards personal legacy or the 'judgment of history'.

This discussion therefore proceeds from a large-scale discussion of *Crusader* in its military and political settings, to finely detailed analyses of operational documents and correspondence with a bearing on the specific issues surrounding Cunningham's supersession and, finally, a more broadly framed look at the writing of *Crusader* history.

History writing about Operation *Crusader* actually began shortly after the event, with the publication of early official accounts of the 8th Army and those of war correspondents, including Eve Curie, Alan Moorehead, Alaric Jacob and Alexander Clifford. The later period saw two other major historiographic streams, military memoirs by participants at various removes from *Crusader* and the construction of Official Histories, most importantly in Britain, South Africa and New Zealand, the principal Commonwealth nations involved in the battle.

All streams were interconnected: the official processes necessarily involved inquiries with participants and the reverse. But relationships between various Official Historians were important for acquiring information and interrogating individual narratives, a process in which preeminent military historian Basil H. Liddell Hart played multiple roles behind the scenes. In Britain writing history also entailed navigating powerful forces, including the interests of the government, represented by the Cabinet Office, and two towering, almost cult-like figures, each with a passion for constructing their own self-images, the former 8th Army commander and later Chief of the Imperial General Staff, Field Marshal Bernard Law Montgomery, and the once and future Prime Minister, Sir Winston Churchill.[6]

November 1941: The military and political situations

The correlation of forces and personalities

The British Army in Egypt had been engaged in operations against the Italians since August 1940.[7] The initial Italian advance was checked and then decisively repulsed, and by February 1941 British forces had advanced as west as Benghazi. But the introduction of a German expeditionary force under Erwin Rommel, and the redeployment of Commonwealth forces in March to an ill-fated defence of Greece, changed the situation completely.[8]

Spring was a season of disasters. By March 1941 the British had been forced back to within 100 miles of the Egyptian border. A Commonwealth garrison in the Libyan port of Tobruk was besieged, and two subsequent British offensives failed to regain the territory. In April a German invasion of Greece forced the British expedition to evacuate with the loss of all their equipment. This was quickly followed in May by the German occupation of Crete. British forces also had to be diverted from Egypt in May to contain a pro-German coup that had overthrown the Iraqi monarchy and besieged British installations there, a move that led to the British capture of all of Iraq and Syria in June and July. In August and September, Iran was occupied by British and Soviet forces.

Figure 1 Portrait of Claude Auchinleck. Portrait by Bassano Ltd, 21 November 1940. Courtesy of the National Portrait Gallery. NPG x85320.

Since the outset of the war General Archibald Wavell, Commander-in-Chief of Middle East Command, had been engaged on multiple fronts, including North Africa, East Africa, Greece, Iraq, Syria, Lebanon and Iran. But after the reverses of early 1941 Wavell was relieved in June and replaced by General Claude Auchinleck,[9] one of three command figures central to *Crusader* (Figure 1).

By 1941 Auchinleck had already had a long and distinguished career in the Indian Army. He had helped develop imperial defence strategy and thus became known to many British officers, relationships that had deepened during his commands in Britain and Norway in the first years of the Second World War. His initiative in dispatching Indian troops to Iraq had permitted Wavell to reluctantly organize the relief of British garrisons there and the eventual capture of Syria. But like virtually all the military officers of the era, Auchinleck had no experience in armoured warfare.

Auchinleck's strategic situation was as complex as Wavell's, only with growing concerns regarding the success of Germany's invasion of the Soviet Union in June, and the possibility of war in the Far East with Japan. Political pressure for a successful British offensive in North Africa from Prime Minister Winston Churchill was also growing. With a steady increase in manpower and supplies, especially tanks, flowing to British forces, Operation *Crusader* was conceived as means to destroy Rommel's recently introduced Afrika Korps and lift the siege of Tobruk.

Appointed command of the newly formed 8th Army in August 1941 was Lt General Alan Cunningham (Figure 2),[10] who had previously commanded East Africa Force. Cunningham's rapid defeat of much larger Italian forces in Somaliland and Ethiopia during April and May had been a rare victory in an otherwise bleak string of British defeats. It was hoped that the tactical cleverness and daring that Cunningham had displayed in the mountainous highlands of East Africa would be repeated in the desert. But he had even less experience, and possibly appreciation, of armoured warfare than Auchinleck, and certainly less than his new subordinates.

Cunningham was a Royal Artillery officer who had briefly commanded several divisions in Britain prior to being assigned to East Africa Command. While he was mostly unknown to the British officers who had fought in the desert, his brother, Commander-in-Chief, Mediterranean Fleet Admiral Andrew B. Cunningham, was one of Britain's most famous military figures. Cunningham's Mediterranean fleet was critical for keeping supplies flowing to Egypt, ensuring the survival of the colony at Malta, and for control of the Suez Canal and the route to India. By the fall of 1941 Cunningham had already led the

Figure 2 Portrait of Alan Cunningham, 21 November 1941. Imperial War Museum, E 006661. Courtesy of the Imperial War Museum.

fleet to important victories over the Italians at Taranto and Cape Matapan, and had facilitated the rescue of tens of thousands of British soldiers from Greece and Crete.

The third figure in question was Alexander 'Sandy' Galloway, assigned as Brigadier General Staff (BGS) of 8th Army (Figure 3). Earlier in 1941 Galloway had commanded the 23rd Brigade, which had a relief role in the brief campaign against Syria. Galloway had previously served as Lt General Henry Maitland 'Jumbo' Wilson's BGS in the expeditionary force in Greece and played a key role in organizing its subsequent evacuation. Prior to that he had been BGS when Wilson commanded British troops in Egypt and had

Figure 3 Portrait of Alexander Galloway. Portrait by Walter Stoneman, September 1942. Courtesy of the National Portrait Gallery. NPG x164368.

helped plan Lt General Richard O'Connor's December 1940 victory against Italian forces, Operation *Compass*.

Unlike Cunningham (Figure 4), Galloway's experience with desert warfare stretched back to the Sinai and Gaza campaigns in the First World War, and from 1932 to 1934 he had been Brigade Major to Frederick Alfred (Tim) Pile in the Canal Brigade in Egypt (one of whose battalions was commanded by Bernard Montgomery). Both figures would later have hidden roles in shaping the story of *Crusader*.

With the increased flow of supplies to British forces in Egypt, and pressure from Churchill growing for an offensive, a plan was developed. The Western Desert Force was reorganized into 8th Army, consisting of 13 Corps, under Lt General

Figure 4 Alan and Andrew Cunningham, October 1941. Imperial War Museum, E 3550e. Courtesy of the Imperial War Museum.

Alfred Reade Godwin-Austen, and 30 Corps, under Lt General Willoughby Norrie. Both formations included British and Commonwealth forces but 30 Corps was allocated most of the heavy 'cruiser' tanks while 13 Corps comprised infantry and light tanks. The final plan for Operation *Crusader* envisioned the 30 Corps crossing the Libyan border and then swinging north to engage and defeat German armour at Gabr Saleh, a point in the desert between the two primary east–west roads. The 13 Corps would pin down Italian forces closer to the coast and then push through towards Tobruk once the German armour threat was eliminated.

The separation of armour and infantry conformed to British doctrine that was predicated on the fanciful notion of a decisive desert tank battle on the analogy of a naval engagement at sea. The *Crusader* plan also called for British armour to cross mostly flat and featureless terrain towards an arbitrary point with the hope of encountering and then destroying Rommel's armour forces, which operated on a combined arms concept, calling for close cooperation between infantry, armour, artillery and air support.[11]

Compounding British difficulties were an inadequate and fragile communications network,[12] weaker anti-tank weapons and tactical underestimation of German anti-tank capabilities,[13] a propensity to retreat into 'leaguers' (from the Afrikaans *laager*) at the end of the day rather than to secure the battlefield, and general overconfidence. A longstanding official mindset that celebrated amateurism, martial spirit, regimental tradition and lack of coordination over professionalism and cooperation was about to be tested, along with the sweeping and disconnected metaphors of Britain's armoured warfare advocates.[14]

The British intelligence and air power situations were more positive. Substantial amounts of Italian and German communications traffic were being decoded, and as of the fall of 1941 the Commander-in-Chief of the 8th Army was included as an *Ultra* recipient.[15] These sources gave access to frank German assessments regarding their own supplies and a fairly accurate picture of German capabilities and intentions. This included plans for a German attack on Tobruk that affected the timing of the British offensive. Complex deception operations were thus developed to confuse the Germans regarding the timing and axis of the British offensive. Intelligence sources also gave Auchinleck a detailed view of the German order of battle and logistics that would be critical to his decision to continue the battle and to relieve Cunningham.[16]

Air power was another area where the British had a narrow advantage, in terms of numbers of aircraft, support and infrastructure, command and control, and a nascent approach to close air support.[17] Finally, British medical services were far more advanced than the Germans, as were the general hygiene levels of British forces.[18] Using Cairo, Alexandria, the Canal Zone and the Nile Delta as a base, connected to British territories in Palestine and ultimately to India, was another immeasurable help. In preparation for *Crusader* rail lines were extended west and large supply dumps were established to support the offensive.

But the British military situation was again offset by Axis advantages, including better tactics and anti-tank weapons, their own field and signals intelligence,[19] and intercepted intelligence reports from the American military attaché in Cairo.[20] While the British had overall superiority in numerical terms (e.g. 724 tanks versus Rommel's 414),[21] serious misunderstanding of German anti-tank capabilities led to overconfidence that was shattered during the course of *Crusader*. Superior numbers would mean little when the range and striking power of German guns meant that British tanks could be destroyed before their own guns could even reach the enemy. Finally, unquantifiable factors, like morale, weather, and not least of all the skills and temperaments of commanders, were to weigh heavily on the course of the battle. But despite last minute objections from British Corps commanders regarding the vagueness of the plan – the very nature of which would become a historiographic controversy – *Crusader* went forward.[22]

The politics of Crusader

Overlying the military preparations for *Crusader* were complex politics and personalities,[23] as well as constant political pressure from – and on – Churchill himself. Military success or failure was critical to political success. Neville Chamberlain had faced what was effectively a vote of no confidence over the ill-fated offensive in Norway in May 1940. A dramatic attack by Sir Roger Keyes, retired Admiral of the Fleet, who portrayed himself as speaking on behalf of the Navy, as well as by Conservative politician Leo Amery and former Prime Minister Lloyd George, was key to Chamberlain's fall and Churchill's rise. The failure of the Greek expedition in May 1941 had resulted in a vote of confidence for Churchill but there was growing criticism of his government, the war effort and Churchill himself.[24] But by the end of the year, during the latter phases of *Crusader*, Churchill was forced to reshuffle his cabinet. And indeed, as the military situation in the Middle East deteriorated further after the fall of Tobruk so too did Churchill's political position; a vote of no confidence would be held in July 1942 in which the issue of Cunningham's supersession was raised.[25]

For political reasons, and from pure warlike instinct, Churchill had thus begun pressuring Auchinleck to launch an offensive from the moment the latter assumed command in July, his communications employing, as Auchinleck's biographer described it, 'The overpowering sense of urgency, the abruptness, the passion for detailed and absolute control, and the misunderstanding, all garnished with compliments, and served in the grand manner'.[26]

In a private letter General John Dill, Commander of the Imperial General Staff (CIGS), warned Auchinleck of these pressures and their deleterious effects, noting 'the fact is that the Commander in the field will always be subject to great and often undue pressure from his Government: Wellington suffered from it: Haig suffered from it; Wavell suffered from it. Nothing will stop it'.[27]

But unlike Wavell, Auchinleck had the advantage of the newly appointed Minister of State for the Middle East, Oliver Lyttelton (later Lord Chandos), and the new Middle East Defence Committee (MEDC)[28] to provide some relief from crushing administrative tasks and political insulation from Churchill.

Still, after a stream of inconclusive communications Churchill demanded Auchinleck visit London for face-to-face consultations. Auchinleck complied and believed he had made his case for Alan Cunningham and for delaying *Crusader* until the fall. By his own later account, however, Churchill was less than fully convinced.[29]

The appointment of Alan Cunningham to head 8th Army also had a political background. In April 1941 Miles Lampson, British Ambassador to Egypt, cabled Foreign Secretary Anthony Eden and suggested Cunningham command the upcoming offensive in Libya. But this suggestion had even more unexpected roots: 'The Egyptian Prime Minister impressed on me this morning the urgent need for appointing someone to command in the West who would appeal to the public imagination. I only wish that we could have had dear Jumbo [Wilson] here, but that is no doubt impossible. You, may, however, think it just worth considering whether the appointment of Cunningham might not justifiably be considered?'[30] Egypt's Prime Minister, Hussein Sirri Pasha, was likely familiar with Cunningham only through the Ethiopian campaign and his famous brother. Why he was so captivated by Alan Cunningham is unclear, but a note on the document in Eden's files indicates the recommendation was forwarded to the CIGS, Dill, and that no action was taken.

Within months, however, Cunningham's appointment came to pass at Auchinleck's request,[31] in part because he judged Churchill's first choice, General Henry Maitland 'Jumbo' Wilson, too old for the task. The other primary candidate to command 8th Army, Lt General Richard O'Connor, who had directed the successful Operation *Compass*, had been captured by the Italians in April 1941.[32] Characteristically, the gadfly Irish-British officer Eric Dorman-Smith, who would become Auchinleck's deputy in 1942, later claimed to Basil Liddell Hart that it was he who suggested Cunningham be appointed to command the 8th Army.[33]

More likely it was South African Prime Minister Jan Smuts who advocated for Cunningham. Recently appointed a British Field Marshal, Smuts had developed a close relationship with Cunningham during the East Africa campaign and had also pushed Churchill for Auchinleck's appointment. The same day he cabled his choice to Churchill, Auchinleck reported to Dill that he had met Cunningham with Smuts and that 'from what I have seen of him and heard of him, I feel that he ought to fill the bill very well as G.O.C.-in-C. Western Desert. The South Africans who will be under him know him well and think a lot of him, which cannot fail to help. He will bring a fresh brain to problems which I feel are getting a bit stale and fishlike'.[34]

In London, the launch of *Crusader* was also juxtaposed with the intersection of command and political pressures. After months of clashing with Churchill, John Dill had prepared to resign as CIGS upon reaching the mandatory retirement age of sixty in November, which coincided with the launch of *Crusader*. The search for his successor quickly focused on Alan Brooke, chief of Home Forces. Churchill offered the position to Brooke on 16 November, only two days before the offensive began, and on 18 November he informed Dill of the decision.[35] Brooke assumed the position on 1 December and was instantly confronted by the vast global scope of Britain's war. As if reflecting the unsettled command structure, Brooke barely mentioned *Crusader* in his diary,[36] while Dill appears to have been disengaged from the battle.

The Cunningham brothers were also enmeshed in broader military-political contexts that affected Churchill. Andrew B. Cunningham, known as 'ABC', was one of Britain's few unequivocal military heroes, with a public reputation as a fighting sailor and whose broad strategic and diplomatic experience was acknowledged within the government. The Royal Navy also had enormous cachet, especially after the evacuation at Dunkirk.

But Churchill's own relationship with the navy was fraught. For decades he had clashed with the Admiralty regarding the threat posed by Japan and the appropriate scale of naval shipbuilding.[37] Churchill had also clashed directly with Cunningham on naval operations in the Mediterranean in late 1940 and early 1941, characteristically demanding more aggressive action and directly criticizing Cunningham and his subordinates for their alleged 'lack of offensive spirit'.

Cunningham, like all Churchill's commanders, had to endure the criticism and push back against his ill-conceived schemes, such as the proposal to capture the island of Pantelleria or block the harbour of Tripoli, as well as argue ceaselessly but in vain for aircraft to support naval operations. He was especially horrified when ordered to destroy the French fleet at Oran in July 1940 and rankled at being constantly called upon to support what he regarded as unnecessary ground operations, such as the Greek offensive or the maintenance of Tobruk.[38] Moreover, Cunningham also had a poor relationship with Auchinleck, whom he regarded, in the words of a biographer, as 'ignorant of naval warfare and unappreciative of the navy's efforts to support Tobruk and the "Crusader" offensive in November'.[39]

Cunningham's reputation and influence with other senior commanders in 1941 and 1942 cannot be minimized. Nor can the Mediterranean naval situation be ignored as a significant source of crisis for military and political commanders: the loss of the aircraft carrier *Ark Royal* on 13 November 1941, the eve of *Crusader* was followed by the sinking of the battleship *Barham* on 25 November, at the very height of the battle.

The question of politics also applies to Alan Cunningham's relationship with the British Army's power structures. The Royal Artillery had a respectable social standing and Cunningham belonged to its most fashionable branch, the Royal Horse Artillery.[40] Along with the Royal Engineers, gunners had the best technical educations in the army. But how networks of military officers exercised political power is unclear. The formal command structures, the Chiefs of Staff and Army Council, had the ability to shape military decisions and appointments and, to a point, contest those by political authorities. But political power was also exercised informally by serving and retired officers and through the class, regimental and school systems, and it was in part through these ties that Cunningham sought restitution after his supersession.

Another important but overlooked example of how political pressures intruded on military decisions, and one with a bearing on the unfolding of *Crusader*, the relief of Cunningham and subsequent interpretation of these events, were Churchill's efforts to have the head of the RAF Middle East Command, Air Marshal Arthur Tedder, relieved of command before the battle.[41]

In mid-October Tedder had indicated the number of aircraft the RAF projected to employ for *Crusader*. The figure had caused Churchill 'considerable disappointment' as well as 'acute political difficulty' with the prime minister of New Zealand, who had sought Churchill's assurances regarding air superiority during the upcoming offensive. The Tedder affair was resolved in a tense exchange between Churchill, Air Chief Marshal Portal, Vice Chief of the Air Staff Sir Wilfrid Freeman and Auchinleck, who, with Oliver Lyttelton, Minister of State in the Middle East, expressed their complete confidence in Tedder. But that Tedder was almost removed suggests that the idea of relieving a senior officer was not a radical proposal, not even before – or during[42] – a major operation.

More consequential military and political pressure from Commonwealth leaders bore down on Churchill prior to the operation, particularly after the Greece and Crete disasters, which Churchill then projected onto his commanders.[43] During the lead up to *Crusader* (August to October) no less than three successive Australian prime ministers had demanded that their troops at Tobruk be relieved.[44] Pressures on Auchinleck came not only from Churchill but from national leaders and from Commonwealth commanders in the field, such as Lt General Bernard Freyberg, commander of the New Zealand

Expeditionary Force, and Major General Frank Theron of the South African Union Defense Force, who had dual political and military responsibilities. They were charged with defending their national interests, including protecting their forces, while at the same time acting as field commanders. The manner in which Commonwealth units were used by British commanders and their uneven performance during *Crusader* helped shape subsequent history writing from those quarters, particularly in South Africa and New Zealand.

In the broadest sense, however, the year 1941 itself shaped *Crusader* and later memories. The misallocation of personnel within the army had reached a crisis, to the point where it was necessary to appoint a committee under Sir William Beveridge to investigate. Resentment was also widespread in the military regarding men who were not being drafted because they were in reserved professions necessary for war industries.[45] Despite Beveridge's recommendations it would take over a year before reforms, which included psychological and vocational testing instituted by the Adjutant, General Sir Ronald Adam, to show results.[46] But the image of military disorganization would be difficult to expunge.

More importantly, the general atmosphere in Britain was turning negative. Over 50,000 soldiers were killed during 1941, primarily in the Mediterranean theatre. Stories of waste and profiteering, real and imagined, spread along with shortages and black marketeering. Delays in urban clearance and reconstruction after air raids were the public face of governmental disorganization. More damaging to the war effort were delays in munitions productions, the result in part of the dispersal of factories away from urban areas, the piecework approach where countless subcontractors provided components for complex weapons systems, unrealistic production targets, the proliferation of management structures and analysts, and labour shortages. Recriminations were inevitable, with the left wing blaming owners and capitalists and the right wing blaming trade unions and the working class.[47]

As labour shortages became menacing, the conscription of women was introduced in December 1941. To compound the discomfort, food rationing had been extended that fall and then deepened in 1942, with more foodstuffs added to the scheme. To add insult to injury, soap and chocolate were rationed, and more items of clothing were restricted, available only by the redemption of coupons. Production of household items was progressively restricted, to the point where in August 1942 only twenty-two types of furniture, with strictly prescribed wood content, were allowed. Most toys were banned.[48]

The upper and lower classes felt these restrictions differently: with more savings and higher wages, the former were obviously more resilient. At the same time, some areas of the country suffered greatly under German bombardment while others were peaceful and even experienced a measure of prosperity. Farming expanded immensely and farmers enjoyed price subsidies, but coal miners remained tied to the pits with strikes as their primary recourse. Many production and administrative schemes were tried in these and other sectors, especially war materiel such as aircraft. One result was massive bureaucracies, but the successful realization of strategic plans came only in 1943 and then with the implementation of mass production techniques that were the descendants of those used in the First World War.[49]

In short, the home front was anything but a happy place during 1941 and 1942: arguably, production and morale reached their lowest ebbs. Though difficult to quantify, these unhappy memories had an inevitable impact on later perceptions, including history writing. But in a sense the British Army in the field paralleled the situation at home. As an emanation of British society and wholly a product of British culture, the army was subject to many of the same problems that manifest on the home front with respect to strategy and planning, the reorganization of industrial design and production, and large-scale social structures such as consumption. The military was a microcosm of society. Units were split-up piecemeal and badly coordinated, a function of specific traditions regarding amateurism or craft-like specialization. Communication and morale were poor, and larger and larger administrative structures grew rapidly as means to control the entire enterprise. Few fundamentals were rethought until a series of failures made the shortcomings unavoidable.

Eventually, in later 1942 and 1943, the fumbling but ultimately successful reorganization of wartime production paralleled the equally awkward reorganization of the British Army during the same period, both on the basis of planning and control rather than dramatic conceptual or technological innovations. Personnel were studied and properly allocated for the first time, and overall educational levels were systematically raised. Battlefield tactics in which economies of scale could be applied were relearnt: larger formations rather than smaller ones, and sheer firepower – in terms of the size of guns and the thickness or armour – were the keys to success. And commanders were chosen on the basis of their tactical and administrative skills rather than adherence to tradition or even daring and flair.

These lessons were necessary and perhaps inevitable, but the failures from which they were learnt also contributed to a perception that the period of 1941 and 1942 was unhappy for Britain both at home and on the battlefield. And, as will be suggested below, these perceptions of failure were in turn connected to the perception that postwar Britain had failed to capitalize on the lessons learnt and may have contributed to the influential thesis of British 'decline'.

Crusader and the contexts of command: Class and comportment

Two further contexts to *Crusader* must be discussed. One is British command philosophy; the second are the class-based expectations of command. Both in a sense are behavioural norms that reflect abstractions of 'national character', martial virtues and masculinity.[50]

David French has pointed out that the interwar period saw British high command learning the lessons of the Great War and articulating a combined arms strategy of infantry, armour and air cooperation. At the same time, after 1919 the military laboured under the 'ten year rule', which stated that a major continental war would not occur in the next decade, as well as stunning budget cuts that thwarted plans for mechanization and prevented realistic exercises from being conducted. Most commanders had no experience with armour, little with large-scale manoeuvres, and were subject to severe restrictions on promotion. The mechanization of the army proceeded slowly, with deep resistance from the entrenched cavalry, and with equally slow gains in vital branches such as communications and intelligence. Innovative minds languished in a shrunken and sclerotic force that had largely retreated to its default role of imperial policing. Then, as during the war, the Royal Air Force was the technological service that attracted the best recruits and projected the most glamour.

Nonetheless, a fundamental tenet of strategy and practice was to prevent the same appalling bloodshed that had characterized the Great War and which had so deeply scarred the British officer corps and the British public. This produced both formal doctrine and a command mentality that encouraged attack but not exploitation, and which relied on massive artillery barrages to suppress enemy activity while advancing. Lower-ranking commanders and non-commissioned officers were discouraged from exercising personal initiative and from tactical improvisation. Written orders were the rule and plans were to be adhered to until alterations were authorized, usually in writing, while utterly inadequate wireless communications networks shackled individual units and commanders of larger formations. The British Army could, in a sense, only proceed in one direction, forward, and was unprepared to either advance further or retreat even if initial objectives were met.[51]

The regimental system, with its rigid social rankings, also conditioned operational capabilities as well as the functioning of the army as a social enterprise. Though perhaps adequately adapted to the military's default purpose, imperial policing, the regimental system was woefully inadequate for large-scale combined arms warfare. Regiments adhered to traditional infantry weapons and tactics, celebrated history rather than innovation and often lacked the capability (and practical experience) of combined arms and large-scale operations. Promotion was almost exclusively on the basis of seniority rather than merit.

French also stressed the social and behavioural conformity demanded from both military regulations and daily practice. Formality in dress and comportment, rituals and ceremonies, an atmosphere of enforced conformity in speech and behaviour, created identity, *esprit de corps,* and a prevailing fear of deviancy which then reproduced itself as intolerance.[52] Even for regiments that were not socially prestigious, officers had to abide by a code. 'To deviate from acceptable codes of behaviour was to risk ostracism or worse.'[53]

Officer training comprised both formal education and socialization into a series of accepted norms, the virtues and limitations of which are still subjects of debate.[54] French emphasized how in officer education 'organized team games, which taught boys not only how to channel their aggression and to work as part of a team, but also made them physically fit and taught them how to make decisions quickly and to disregard their physical safety. They also inculcated their students with a code of gentlemanliness, which stressed honor, bravery, loyalty, generosity, self-sacrifice, and a concern for the welfare of their subordinates'.[55]

But to complement this picture of chivalrous gentlemen, Correlli Barnett has stressed the inculcation of amateurism in professional officers: those who took military studies seriously were exceptions. Despite the fact that in the public schools 'it was the army classes, with their emphasis on science, geography and modern history, that were least remote from the contemporary world',[56] in the officer class itself 'cleverness, push, ruthlessness, self-interest and ambition were considerably less prized than modesty, good manners, courage, a sense of duty, chivalry and a certain affectation of easy-going non-professionalism'.[57] As Keith Douglas, armour officer, poet and Desert War chronicler, put it regarding a fellow officer who came up through the ranks in the Royal Tank Regiment, 'his curious origins, accounted for the disapproval of the majority of the officers whose origins and ideas were beautifully standardized'.[58]

These gentlemanly attributes, the essence of late Victorian middle-class respectability, must be set within the larger shifting notions of British 'national character', which in the interwar period focused on popular self-conceptions of the Englishman as 'something decidedly kindlier, gentler, more relaxed, more cooperative, more domesticated, if anything a rather shy and timid sort', the 'Little Man', 'an imaginative compound of the City gent and the "man in the street"'[59]

Ultimately the crucible of war brought ruthlessly professional officers like Alan Brooke and Bernard Montgomery to the forefront and then to the highest position in the army, Chief of the Imperial General Staff, along with scores of lower-ranking officers. But there is no doubt that early in the war easy-going and heroic amateurism and inspirational battlefield leadership were prized as much or more highly than military professionalism. The years 1941 and 1942 mark the end of an era, a dividing line between two ethos in the British Army's social and battlefield cultures.

Dress, deportment and drill were the foundations of the officer corps both before and even after the First World War, when the service academies expanded their general curricula.[60] Mathematics, geography, language and engineering prevailed over strategy, history and tactics, particularly for officers in specialty branches such as artillery. Leadership skills as such were not taught but rather assumed to be implicit in the character of well-bred officers who were sportsmen and gentlemen. The actual levels of British military amateurism and professionalism, as well as technical competence, both before and after 1918 may be debated but the role of officer comportment cannot.

Drawn as they were almost exclusively from public schools,[61] future officers at military academies and Staff College could be expected to share similar outlooks and behavioural norms based in the first instance in class. These attributes would be even more pronounced in the military's 'inner elite, that is, the staff and high command'.[62] The Staff College was the first opportunity for officers to interact as professionals, create trusted friendships and inculcate similar worldviews regarding politics and strategy among future commanders.[63] It also exposed dissenting or innovative attitudes to criticism from peers and the military hierarchy. The famous incident of Eric Dorman-Smith publicly burning his notes at the end of his Staff College course as a sign of disdain for the education he had received under the leadership of Bernard Montgomery permanently marked him as a deviant within a closed society.[64]

The question of the 'public school values' such as 'group loyalty, deference and obedience to the accepted hierarchy, an opposition to politics and intellectual matters, and an emphasis on self-assurance and character', and the tension between the 'two concepts of war in the Edwardian period – the traditional, gentlemanly, amateur ideal and the technical, functionally competent, professional ideal'[65] also comes into play when analysing the decisions and behaviour of principal figures in Operation *Crusader*, namely Auchinleck, Cunningham and Galloway.

On the surface Cunningham, an artilleryman, appears to stand on the technical side of the professional divide, while the infantrymen Auchinleck and Galloway stand on the other. But the reality was more complicated. For one thing Cunningham and Galloway were British Army officers, while Auchinleck spent his entire career before 1940 in the Indian Army, engaged in irregular warfare and planning for mechanization. The record also suggests that despite Cunningham's technical education as a gunner, both Auchinleck and Galloway ultimately grasped combined arms warfare better, if only to a point and after considerable exposure.[66] And all three served in command, staff and other positions before the Second World War and thus had a grasp of the political realities of higher command.

There are also age and educational contrasts. Although all three were middle-class Scots, Auchinleck and Cunningham (born 1884 and 1887, respectively) were Edwardians commissioned into the army long before the First World War, while Galloway (born 1895) joined at the beginning of the First World War. Only Auchinleck came from a military family: Cunningham's father was a prominent physician and Galloway's a minister. All, however, experienced brutal combat in the First World War and had witnessed both strategic failure and success at close range. Galloway's experience is perhaps instructive: as a junior officer his first posting found him in 1915 mired in the immense failure and waste of Gallipoli,[67] and then later as part of Allenby's army that brilliantly defeated the Ottomans in Palestine. One was utterly ill-conceived and wasteful, if heroic in the sense of personal behaviour, including his own, while the other was, despite being meticulously planned and executed, a hard-fought series of battles.

The educational backgrounds of each were also factors. All attended public schools, but Auchinleck was a graduate of Sandhurst, Cunningham graduated from Woolwich, while Galloway had no little formal military training before the First World War. After the war Auchinleck and Galloway graduated from and were later instructors at Staff College while, unusually, Cunningham was a graduate of the Royal Naval College and the Imperial Defence College. All these experiences, however, may have been more important not simply for military education and promotion but for integrating them into the social enterprise of higher command.

In the absence of full biographies of Cunningham and Galloway, much must be left to speculation regarding the role of their personalities and personal experiences, although some available information will be introduced below. But the larger context of the cultural and behavioural expectations that came with being British officers and respectable gentleman cannot be neglected when analysing the events of November 1941 and thereafter.

The final dimension of comportment and behavioural expectations is understanding when these defining personal characteristics are lost. Throughout the Second World War any number of British generals were wounded and killed in action, but it is unclear how many became psychological casualties. Here the experience of the First World War with 'shell shock' arises along with the development of British military psychiatry. All wars create psychological casualties, but the vast industrial brutality of the First World War did more than any other to focus military and popular attention on this problem. Great resources were expended to address psychological casualties, solutions to which ranged from rest to therapeutic methods to threats of the death penalty for 'malingers'.[68]

The causes of psychological casualties were at once both obscure, sought in the innate intelligence or character of soldiers, and glaringly obvious, particularly in the colossal scale of often impersonal and mechanized death and destruction brought about by trench warfare, artillery and gas attacks. Soldiers' reactions ranged from irritability to paralysis, but the precise physical and psychological mechanisms were unclear. 'Neurasthenia', a purported disease of the nervous system that produced sudden physical weakness and even collapse, was a nineteenth-century diagnosis that continued to be used until the beginning of the Second World War, despite its utter vagueness, particularly after the term 'shell shock' was ruled unusable in February 1917.[69] 'Shell shock' and its successors – which today might be called combat stress reaction – also had particular cultural significance to the generation of soldiers who had experienced the First World War, including future commanders.

Military psychiatry in the British Army generated a considerable literature during the First World War and after, primarily with respect to officer selection, morale and treatment of psychiatric cases. But the military's medical infrastructure for psychological support that had been largely dismantled by the early 1920s had to be quickly reinvented when the Second World War began. Many of the same forward psychiatric observation mechanisms and interim treatment techniques pioneered during the First World War were rediscovered, particularly the principles of what came to be known as 'PIE' – proximity, immediacy and expectancy – wherein traumatized individuals were quickly withdrawn from the line for a few days of rest and relative normalcy before being returned to combat, as they knew they would be.[70]

During the Second World War the terms 'shell shock' and 'battle stress' were again put out of use, along with others that emphasized the psychological nature of the injury. Instead, by the fall of 1942 'in the retreat to Alamein the term "exhaustion" was adopted for psychiatric casualties'.[71] This was an important therapeutic innovation that emphasized the temporary nature of the injury and the promise of restoration, as well as the apparent inevitability of returning to combat. As a semantic innovation it removed some of the stigma from psychiatric casualties, but in doing so may also be fairly understood as a form of understatement.

As Harrison put it, close examination of psychiatric cases showed that

> Combat neuroses – of which 9,000 cases were recorded in the British Army in the Middle East during 1942 – manifested themselves in a number of ways, including panic reactions such as screaming, laughing, or crying; hysterical fits; stupor or coma; gross tremors; and staring cataleptic states. These symptoms could appear before, during, and even some time after a battle. Those reactions that occurred during a battle were likely to be simple psychological responses to fatigue, fear, and danger, and could usually be treated quickly with rest and reassurance. Post-battle reactions were usually more complex, being related not only to fear but also to guilt over killing. They manifested themselves in a variety of ways, such as the so-called 'campaign neurosis', a form of mild, chronic anxiety state indicated by tremor and loss of appetite; or what were known as 'personality reactions', including mild hysteria, alcoholism, and delinquency.[72]

But the problem of breakdowns in the military, the majority of whom were found to be 'mentally defective' and 'dullards' as one psychiatrist put it in the 1950s,[73] is not discussed with regard to high commanders. The question of mental health for commanders also links to the problem of officer comportment.

In his classic book *Anatomy of Courage*,[74] Churchill's personal physician Lord Moran discussed the question of courage in commanders, primarily from the standpoint of officer selection. His perspective is especially useful since he was a military physician whose experience began during the First World War and he thus reflects the received knowledge at work during and after that conflict. Moran's notion that each man had a capital reserve of courage that was progressively drawn down by combat experience is well known. But his views on leadership are of particular relevance. 'The art of command is the art of dealing with human nature,' Moran states, adding that 'apart from all the rest, alone in its influence over the hearts of men I place phlegm – a supreme imperturbability in the face of death which half amused them and half dominated them – the ultimate gift in war'.[75] Judging these attributes, Moran adds, becomes more difficult in the case of high command, particularly the further removed it is from the battlefield and subject to political interference.

But throughout, character was more important than capacity or creativity. He quoted Jan Smuts on the matter: 'Men of action,' he said, 'live on the surface of things, they do not create.'[76] This implied that action and reaction, not the depths of introspection, and certainly not self-doubt, are key attributes of command. And while on the one hand, 'the strain on mind and body is such that we must do what can be done to lighten the load. If it is necessary to keep a vigilant eye on the fitness of our Generals, it may be as necessary to keep them out of harm's way. On the other hand, men's hearts go to the leader who is ready – as Wellington and Marlborough were – to risk his life'.[77] Commanders who lost heart, whether they project amateurism or professionalism, put the entire enterprise of war at risk.

Ultimately, these cultural and psychological factors, rarely spoken about explicitly by military historians or memoirists at the level of high command, may have considerable explanatory power when considering the case of Operation *Crusader* and the supersession of Alan Cunningham, as well as how they were regarded later in British history and memory.

2

23–26 November: Breakdown and Insubordination

Towards battle

Operation *Crusader* began on 18 November (Figure 5). As the weather became stormy, 30 Corps crossed into Libya and, largely unopposed, quickly reached their initial objectives. But the next day this armoured force was split up, with some elements heading towards Tobruk and others going in search of opponents. The divided British forces then collided in the west with Italian defences and engaged German armour moving down from the north.

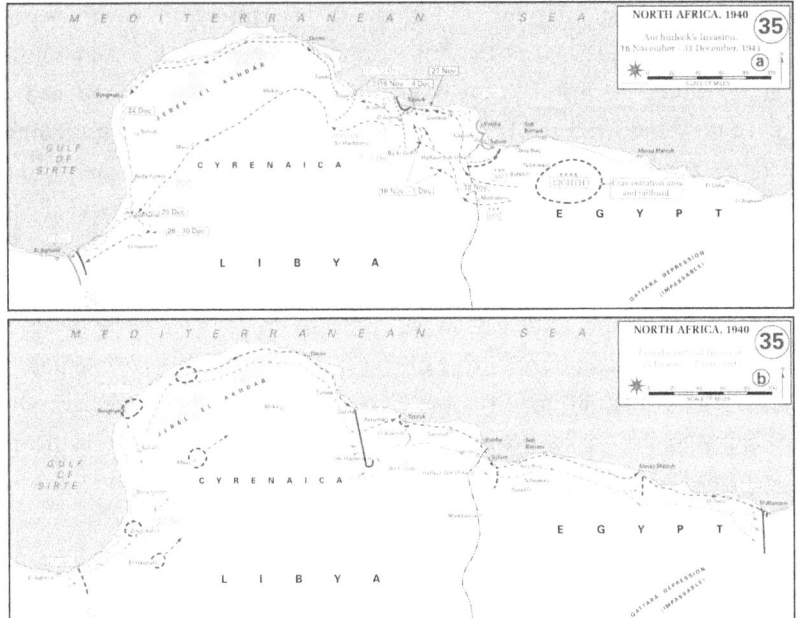

Figure 5 Map of the Crusader battle. Courtesy of the Department of History, United States Military Academy.

The battles that ensued were remarkable for their confusion,[1] movement and misperception by commanders on both sides. Initially British forces pressed forward towards Tobruk, whose garrison had begun to break out from its long perimeter southeast towards the airfield at Sidi Rezegh. But as Rommel and his commanders discerned the British plan, they shifted German forces west, away from the Egyptian frontier, a move interpreted by the British as a general withdrawal.

Thanks to poor communications (including a massive army-wide communications breakdown late on 19 November) British commanders at 8th Army headquarters also had a poor appreciation of just how badly their armoured forces were being mauled. Instead, after an initial period of concern, they were largely optimistic, and on 21 November Cunningham ordered 13 Corps to begin its attack, pinning down German frontier forces at Bardia and manoeuvring west towards Tobruk. In reality, however, the battle was not going well for the British.

Engagement and crisis

On 22–23 November British forces approaching Tobruk from Sidi Rezegh had suffered substantial losses including the entire 5th South African Brigade, the headquarters of the 4th Armored Brigade (which compromised communications security), most of the 7th Armored Brigade and half the tanks of the 22nd Armored Brigade. The battle had degenerated into countless individual confrontations among intermingling forces that could barely identify one another amidst the smoke and confusion. British forces to the east had fared somewhat better, besieging the German and Italian frontier forces, moving towards Tobruk and the main battlefield at Sidi Rezegh.

But on 22 November, the day on which British forces were being savaged at Sidi Rezegh, the perception at 8th Army headquarters appears to have positive. From the following day, however, the picture had changed dramatically. These two days were crucial for Alan Cunningham, the direction of the battle, and subsequent historiography. And it is on 22–23 November that the threads of various accounts must be disentangled and then rewoven.

During the opening phases of the operation, Cunningham had accompanied Norrie at 30 Corps headquarters but returned to his own Advanced Headquarters at Fort Maddalena on 20 November. The true condition of British armoured forces was unknown at either the Corps or Army level.[2] He had apparently remained with Norrie for several hours while British positions in the west were smashed repeatedly.

Early on 23 November Cunningham flew to Godwin-Austen's headquarters.[3] Shortly after his return news of the various disasters began to arrive at his headquarters. At this point several events took place that brought *Crusader's* key participants together.

Cunningham, distressed at the situation, contacted Auchinleck in Cairo and asked him to come to the Advanced Headquarters.[4] At the same time or before, however, Galloway contacted Brigadier John ('Jock') Whiteley, BGS at General Headquarters Middle East in Cairo.[5] The precise details of this call are unknown, although different accounts appeared in publications and correspondence after the war. These sources (discussed below) agree that Galloway insisted a senior officer come to the front. Almost simultaneously, Air Vice Marshal Arthur ('Mary') Coningham, Air Officer Commanding Western Desert Air Force, called Air Marshal Arthur Tedder and told him to come to the front.[6]

Auchinleck then flew with Tedder[7] to the front on a plane allocated to Brigadier Eric John Shearer, Director of Military Intelligence (DMI) at GHQ Middle East, who accompanied them.[8] Shearer was obviously well informed regarding the operation, and both he and his wife[9] played a role in later accounts of Cunningham's supersession.

Prior to Auchinleck's arrival, a third important event took place, a mid-day Corps level conference between Galloway, Godwin-Austen and Major Michael Carver, who represented Norrie.[10] In later years this conference was much discussed, not least of all by future Field Marshal Carver, who wrote several accounts, but the original War Diary is laconic: 'After discussion between B.G.S. Army and Comdr 13 Corps, it was decided that the present battle must go on under present arrangements as there was no other option.' The conference agreed that withdrawal might be necessary and agreed on fallback positions, but after consulting with Godwin-Austen by radio who said 'he was quite sure that Gen Norrie, in view of what he said, was perfectly able to deal with the situation for the rest of the day',[11] it was decided the battle would go forward.

Critically, later accounts make it clear that Galloway had pressed the Corps commanders to continue the battle and that Cunningham had or was prepared to order a withdrawal. In 1950 Godwin-Austen reported Galloway had stated that Rommel's moves had 'given the Commander 8th Army grave apprehensions regarding the safety of his railhead. If this went, a most serious situation would arise. So serious indeed, that there was a question as to whether it would be wise to continue the battle'.[12] Godwin-Austen replied 'I was horrified' and that he would 'not dare to confront my Divisional Generals with such a dreadful and unnecessary alternative'. He also reported, 'Galloway seemed gratified by my views.'

The question of orders to withdraw was to become an important ambiguity. No orders for either a full withdraw of the army or a limited redeployment rearward of the Advanced Headquarters appear to have been preserved in 8th Army records. But later writers were clear regarding these, as well as Galloway's efforts to stall movement of the headquarters pending the arrival of Auchinleck.

There is, however, contemporary evidence regarding orders to withdraw. Renowned British journalist Alexander Clifford of the *Daily Telegraph* arrived at the Advanced Headquarters on 25 November and recorded in his diary 'the chaos had been complete the night before and the camp had been told to pack up ready to leave at half hours notice'.[13] If Clifford's sequence of events was correct, these orders would have been issued on 24 November, at which point Auchinleck was already at headquarters. They do not speak of possible earlier orders to withdraw prior to the summoning and arrival of Auchinleck. Clifford's account is inconclusive but either way, points to unsettled conditions at 8th Army headquarters.

Auchinleck arrived late on the 23rd and then conferred privately with Cunningham and Galloway. A typed record of that conversation was preserved in Auchinleck's documents[14] and in the War Office's file on Cunningham's succession,[15] but *not* in Cunningham's own papers on *Crusader*.[16] The document itself is short, only four paragraphs:

> G.O.C.-in-C 8th Army told C-in-C that as a result of our losses in Cruisers and American tanks during the past five days, the enemy was now probably superior to us in fast tanks which enabled him to attack and over-run our infantry without interference from our tanks.
>
> This gave rise to a situation in which it might be possible to turn the southern flank of our forces in the SIDI REZEGH area and cut them off from their base. As the Army Comdr had by this time practically nothing in reserve, this meant that there might be nothing to oppose an enemy advance into EGYPT.
>
> In these circumstances General CUNNINGHAM had thought it his duty to ask the C-in-C to visit his H.Q. so that he might learn the situation at first hand, and decide whether it was necessary to break off the battle and adopt a defensive attitude or continue the offensive with the object of destroying the German

armoured forces. The Army Commander pointed out that a continuation of the offensive might result in our having no fast tanks left at all.

The C-in-C replied that he had no doubt whatever that our only course was to continue our offensive with every means at our disposal, and that he wished the Army Commander to act accordingly.

As the junior officer present it was Galloway's responsibility to take notes that were then transcribed. The narrative structure suggests a faithful if laconic report of the conversation, consisting of (1) a situation report, (2) Cunningham's explanation of the request for Auchinleck to come forward, (3) two possible courses of action, (4) emphasis on possible defeat and (5) Auchinleck's decision to continue the battle. It is also significant to note that Auchinleck's initial response was concise and direct. The memorandum also proves that withdrawal was discussed.

But the next day, 24 November, Auchinleck's perceptions began to shift. That morning, while Cunningham visited the front, Auchinleck sent a telegraph to Churchill regarding his visit to Advanced Headquarters. He stated that 'on arrival found Cunningham perturbed at situation owing to very small number of our tanks reported still in running order',[17] described the battlefield situation and reiterated his orders to continue the offensive.

At mid-day Auchinleck issued a long and detailed order to Cunningham again recounting the two courses of action, this time stating 'there is no possible doubt that the second is the right and only course', and issuing detailed orders regarding operational objectives.[18] For whatever reason, Auchinleck felt it necessary to reiterate and sharpen his orders to Cunningham. This document, which appears in the War Office file, was distributed to both the CIGS and Air Officer Commanding-in-Chief Tedder, demonstrating that Auchinleck's concerns were known both up the chain of command and outside of the army.

But that day was to prove especially trying for the 8th Army and for Cunningham personally. In a remarkable turn, on the morning of 24 November Rommel elected to change his offensive strategy and, gathering his forces, headed east towards Egypt. Rommel's famous 'dash to the wire' took German armoured forces 'in succession through the headquarters of the 30 Corps, 7th Armoured Division, 1st South Africa Division, 7th Support Group and 7th Armoured Brigade, mostly caught basking in the sunshine of a brilliantly fine and warm day'.[19]

The chaos of 24 November was described simply in an intelligence report by an American journalist accompanying military attachés in the field, 'And then came the big rout'.²⁰ Hundreds of British vehicles began chaotically speeding east to escape the advancing Germans, who covered some 60 miles during the course of the day. In another sign that the British believed their position was collapsing, hundreds of aircraft were redeployed from landing zones near the frontier to positions further east.²¹

Rommel's sudden move nearly swept up Cunningham personally. That morning Cunningham had flown to confer with 30 Corps commander Norrie, who at the time was at 7th Armoured Division headquarters. But as Germans began to shell the headquarters and then the landing ground, Cunningham was rushed back to his plane, which just missed striking a truck on takeoff.²² During the flight Cunningham observed columns of German armour heading east.²³ Upon his return to headquarters in the late afternoon Cunningham met again with Auchinleck. It is unclear whether Auchinleck's longer order to Cunningham was issued before or after the latter's visit to 30 Corps.

As he prepared to leave the advanced headquarters on 25 November, Auchinleck issued a famous statement to be transmitted to the entire 8th Army.²⁴ In it he reiterated his instructions but added a comment – informed by *Ultra* intelligence – on Rommel's offensive:

> His position is desperate and he is trying by lashing out in all directions to distract us from our object, which is to destroy him utterly. We will NOT be distracted and he will be destroyed. Hang on and bite deeper and deeper and hang on till he is finished. Give him NO rest. The general situation in NORTH AFRICA is EXCELLENT. There is only one order ATTACK AND PURSUE. ALL OUT EVERYONE.

Late in the day Auchinleck returned to Cairo on Brigadier Shearer's plane. Tedder returned with him while Shearer appears to have returned later the same day. The precise circumstances under which Auchinleck made his decision to relieve Cunningham are described in later memoirs but the timing is clear. Only hours after his departure from the front, Auchinleck acted; Cunningham was relieved the next day. But his precise motives, and Cunningham's condition, remained to be established.

25 November 1941: The historiographic morass begins

Reconstructing the military progression of *Crusader*, the movements of forces and the outcomes of battles is difficult but ultimately the results were clear, if perhaps not their significance. After much fighting, and after additional reverses, the British forces pushed Rommel back, Tobruk was relieved and by January Cyrenaica had been captured. But at the end of that month, Rommel regained the initiative and pushed the 8th Army back to the Gazala line. There the situation remained largely static until renewed German offensives at the end of May and the first of the epic series of battles that culminated at El Alamein.

The same cannot be said for the battle for history surrounding the supersession of Cunningham. From 25 November onwards different participants felt it necessary to document and defend decisions, as well as to attack decisions made by others. The initial writing of letters, and their selective preservation in official and unofficial files, became the foundations for decades of subsequent debates. These finely grained data are not uniformly informative but certain exchanges are revealing of the key questions: Alan Cunningham's condition during Operation *Crusader*, Alexander Galloway's role and the construction of subsequent narratives.

At 22:00 on the night of 25 November, 8th Army rear headquarters received a signal from Lt General Neil Ritchie, Auchinleck's Deputy Chief of Staff, saying he would arrive at Fort Maddalena the next day. This information was forwarded to the advance headquarters by telephone.[25]

Thirty-five minutes later Middle East Command Chief of Staff, Lt General Arthur Smith, sent a cable on behalf of Auchinleck[26] to the CIGS stating 'as result my two days visit am convinced CUNNINGHAM no longer fit to conduct intensive offensive required'. After announcing Ritchie's appointment Auchinleck added, 'CUNNINGHAM most loyal but in my opinion has lost spirit of offensive and consequently I have lost confidence in him.'

But another cable,[27] signed by Smith for Auchinleck, addressed to Prime Minister Winston Churchill, introduced ambiguity by saying that

> I have telegraphed to CIGS to say that I have decided to replace General CUNNINGHAM temporarily by General RITCHIE my present DCGS (.) This is not rpt not on account of any misgiving as to present situation in my mind but because I have reluctantly concluded that CUNNINGHAM admirable as he has been up to date has now begun to think defensively instead of offensively mainly because of our large tank losses (.)

Auchinleck's subtexts cannot be reconstructed but communications with the CIGS and Churchill were inevitably political, and were thus likely to differ subtly in phrasing, tone and emphasis. Importantly, Auchinleck's initial statement to Churchill mentioned Cunningham's 'fitness' but then pulled back, perhaps since this issue could reflect on both Cunningham and Auchinleck himself. It also implied the possibility that Cunningham's relief would be temporary, an improbable prospect. But there was also no mention of Cunningham's hospitalization or of future public announcements. These issues would emerge over the next few days.

At almost precisely the same time that Auchinleck cabled Churchill, however, the prime minister received a message from the Minister of State for the Middle East, Oliver Lyttelton.[28] To Auchinleck's laconic statements Lyttelton added that he had also spoken to Tedder and Shearer and that 'Cunningham, it appears, is shaken and now thinking in terms of withdrawal and defense'. He added that as a member of the War Cabinet, he took full responsibility for Cunningham's supersession. 'Shaken' was a new level of seriousness regarding Cunningham, and 'withdrawal' a new level of specificity beyond 'defensively'. Only much later did Lyttelton provide his own account of how the decision in Cairo came about.

Newly appointed 8th Army Commander, Lt General Neil Ritchie, arrived at 8th Army advanced headquarters on the morning of 26 November 1941, along with Lt General Arthur Smith, bearing two letters from Auchinleck relieving Cunningham of command. The primary letter is dated 25 November, showing that Auchinleck had made his decision soon upon arriving back in Cairo. That letter also introduced another note of ambiguity regarding Auchinleck's assessment of Cunningham's condition:[29]

1. With the greatest regret I have to tell you that, after most anxious consideration, I have decided that I must relieve you of the command of the 8th Army.
2. During my recent visit to your Advanced Headquarters, you asked me to give a decision as to whether we should continue the offensive or abandon it. After due consideration of the reasons for and against each course, I gave my decision that an offensive must be pressed relentlessly, regardless of loss.
3. You loyally accepted this decision and at once gave order to give effect to it.
4. I have formed the opinion, however, that you are now thinking in terms of defence rather than offence, and I have lost confidence in your ability to press to the bitter end the offensive I have ordered to continue.
5. I have decided, therefore, to replace you as Commander of the 8th Army by A/Lt Gen N.M. Ritchie. I request you to hand over your command to him on receipt of this letter.
6. You will realize, I hope, that this is an extremely painful decision for me to make. It is all the more painful because I realize that I owe you a deep debt of gratitude for the conduct of the battle up to this moment.

Auchinleck's personal letter to Cunningham[30] reinforced the ambiguity. Auchinleck was apologetic regarding his decision, telling Cunningham

> It is no use, I am afraid, telling you how I hate to have had to do this thing, but I must act according to my belief and I have done so. It is most painful to me because I like and respect you a great deal, and I never thought that I should have to act in this way towards you. I can only assure you that I do so because I honestly feel that it is necessary to ensure the total defeat of the enemy in the shortest possible time.

But later Auchinleck stated:

> I realize that this supersession must be a most bitter blow to you, and that I am not entitled to ask favours of you. In the public interest, however, I do ask you to agree to being placed on the sick list and to go to hospital for a period. I know that this will be against all your instincts, and that you will hate doing it. All the same, I think you should agree to this suggestion of mine, and if I may say so, I think the strain under which you have been working for the last three months, and the last few days in particularly, does provide justification for a rest.

This may be read as either sympathetic understatement of Cunningham's condition or as a request for him to participate in a cover story. Auchinleck's true beliefs are not clearly stated.

This undoubtedly sympathetic letter does appear in both Auchinleck's and Cunningham's private files, but it was *not* part of the official CIGS file on the supersession. This file, as will be discussed below, was assembled between December 1941 and 1944 on the basis of materials Cunningham provided himself, and included a detailed 1944 War Office analysis of the supersession. Subtly shaped before the war's end and transferred to the Cabinet Office Historical Section in 1949, it is the seed of Britain's Official History of *Crusader*.

Although the letter is not preserved, Auchinleck also evidently wrote to Andrew Cunningham, who replied on 26 November,[31] 'Naturally I am most distressed about Alan but you must undoubtedly do what you think the right thing + he will I am sure accept it in the right spirit.' He concluded by thanking Auchinleck 'for being frank with me', but without the original it is unclear which direction this frankness took. That neither Auchinleck nor Andrew Cunningham preserved the letter is suspicious.

Subsequent exchanges between Auchinleck and the Cunninghams went on into December and involved Arthur Smith. Smith's appearance in the narrative is critical. He had observed Cunningham personally, and his comments to both Cunningham's aide de camp, James Blewitt, and Cunningham himself regarding

Figure 6 Claude Auchinleck with Alexander Galloway, Arthur Coningham, Neil Ritchie and Captain Grantham, naval liaison officer, December 1941. Imperial War Museum, E 006998. Courtesy of the Imperial War Museum.

the latter's mental state must be squared with the competing narratives of 'defensive-mindedness' and 'exhaustion'.

After delivering Auchinleck's letters, Smith accompanied Cunningham back to Cairo. The command change barely registered in the 8th Army's war diary and communications records, much less at the front, but another war had already begun (Figure 6).

23–26 November 1941: Overlooked evidence

Outside of operational records there are few documents that may be dated precisely to 23–26 November 1941 and the question of Alan Cunningham's succession. But two thus far overlooked pieces of evidence deserve close attention, Alan Cunningham's personal diary and the diary and letters of his aide de camp, James Blewitt.

The Cunningham diary

Cunningham's diary, preserved in his collection at the National Army Museum,[32] is written on thin sheets of paper, some of which have the letterhead of the 'Conservo della Somalia Italiano'. They reveal both his perceptions of *Crusader* as it unfolded, and, to some extent, his condition.

> 22nd
> Went up to talk to Willoughby-. He was fully aware of necessity of putting a firmer hold on the El Rezegh escarpment and was doing all he could to get 5th S.A. Bde. Up. I said I hoped he would be able to use both brigades.
>   Stressed Tank recovery and asked that everything should be done to put back tanks.
>
> 23rd
> Went over to see Godwin Austen re reorganization of Tobruk perimeter attack-
>   On return heard of tank situation and troubles on Willoughby's front. Sent up Sandy to say that if a withdrawal had to take place I would reluctantly accept it as did not want to have S.A. Div. cut off. Sandy on return from Conference at which Godwin present told me they would hold on. Am trusting to New Zealand attack from East to turn tide.
>
> Chief arrived at my request: I told him tank situation and situation on map. I said that being practically without tanks, should the enemy put in a tank concentration cf. their 120 tanks on my left flank a serious situation would arise and I would have great difficulty in extricating S.A. Div. I would not entirely certain of the [Ch's?] tank situation but had every indication very few left.
>
> Chief appreciated the critical situation but said in view of known enemy difficulties attack should go on. Front was reorganized and 13 Corps told to push on. + Tobruk. I envisioned this gamble but justifiable if all what intelligence said about the enemy were true.
>
> 24th
> Day after attack on 5th S.A. Inf Bde had made it possible for enemy to ___ and to ___ on ___. Gave order WN.- Assist left of N.Z. Div.

Destroy Tanks
Protect immediate front.

Visited him and found him clear and confident. __ attacks in his area took place during my return, and enemy appeared at Sheferzen (Witnessed by me ___ when I visited 13th Corps_.

C.inC. was in camp. I rather diffidently tried to point out ___ of situation, but was met always the argument that the forward policy was the thing-Withdraw nothing. I was apprehensive, and although always clear that the attack of the New Zealand Division if successful would completely turn the tables, was not so confident of this as ___ that Rommel ___ ___ ___ ___ small forces forward which would run dry and be able to open ___ ___. The manner in which my suggestion as made to the effort was met made it impossible for me to pursue it, ___ ___ ___ was on & stated definitively that the ___ of the operation further caused on to gamble and depended on the capture of Tobruk – I felt that in defense of this a withdrawal might have to take place – I could not ___ this view again in face of the attitude taken up- it need be recalled that I had already told CinC that the last chance of withdrawal PTO with safety was night ?

25th
This day opened with the enemy ___ sent a column to Sheferzen and through the ___ there.

I could not believe the column was large. They had appreciated the potentialities after(?) CinC unmoved. I felt that if it pressed the damper I wanted to ___ as heavy(?) of our morale(?) and ___ ___ when on a___ for everything I accepted the "forward policy" again. In fact and could do nothing else. It seemed to me that the ___ of the enemy supply lines was not at that time the vital need. I sent my B.G.S. to ___ and W.N. to make whatever arrangements he could to this effect. W.N. had sent in dispositions which concerned the ___ area and which ___ to a certain extent interfered wit the enemy supply by raiding. I was anxious that our attack should be made in Sheferzen but in view of the ___ ___ over which the corps was working, and the ___ that out BGS was already engaged, the splitting up of the ___, W.N. told(?) B.G.S. he was not in a position to carry it out. I sent the L.O. Kisch(?) to say that any thing which ___ the ___ attack ___ ___ area and the supply columns must be undertaken.

Cunningham's own account thus supports most of the accepted narrative regarding the days in question. The tactical situation was serious, and on 23 November he had asked Auchinleck to the front. Cunningham had suggested a withdrawal of some magnitude might be necessary but this was rejected.

Their discussion had continued on 24 November after Cunningham's visit to 13 Corps. Of particular note are Cunningham's description of his own suggestion as 'diffident', Auchinleck's forceful rejection of the suggestion and the indication that Cunningham felt constrained about mentioning it again. While the exchange cannot be reconstructed, it appears Cunningham was rebuffed and that his self-described sense of apprehension may have been visible to Auchinleck. The diary entry for 25 November mentions a German attack but Cunningham notes that he 'could not believe the column was large'. This may be read as an expression of either genuine shock or mere suspicion.

One piece of evidence for understanding Cunningham's state of mind is his handwriting, which deteriorated visibly from the 22 November through the final entry on the 25th. The circumstances under which he wrote, and the very writing surfaces he found available, may account for some of the deterioration, but the shaky and uneven script suggests intense stress. But it must be noted that when he initially proposed withdrawing his forces to Auchinleck on 23 November, his handwriting is clear. If Cunningham's handwriting is to be giving any weight, his state deteriorated between 23 and 25 November, precisely the period when the battle was turning against him and when Auchinleck was present at his headquarters.

Interestingly, Cunningham makes no mention in his diary of any private conferences between Auchinleck and Galloway, as he would later. Nor does he display any suspicion that Galloway had independently contacted Auchinleck and delayed retreat of 8th Army Advanced Headquarters.

The James Blewitt evidence

James Blewitt was Cunningham's aide de-camp (ADC) in East Africa and the Western Desert, serving under him for some two years. Blewitt also came from a long family of Royal Artillery officers. His grandfather, Major General William E. Blewitt, had passed away in 1939 and both his father Ralph and uncle Guy had served with distinction during the First World War. Ralph Blewitt, a good friend of Cunningham, had retired in 1921 but returned to service during the Second World War, commanding a small coastal supply vessel.

At the suggestion of Brigadier Otto Marling Lund, then Deputy Director of Military Operations at the War Office, Cunningham had approached Ralph Blewitt in 1940 to arrange for James to serve as his ADC[33] and the two corresponded throughout the war. In his letters to Ralph, as well as to James,

Cunningham expressed avuncular concern for James and his career. Young Blewitt's wartime diary and letters to his family in England, sent by hand without censorship, provide a unique first-hand view of Cunningham.

James Blewitt's diary suggests he saw little amiss during *Crusader*. Blewitt noted that Auchinleck had come to headquarters in the afternoon of 23 November, had spoken with Cunningham until 1:30 the next morning and was 'very gloomy to + from his camp'. He also noted laconically: 'The battle has become v. bloody + tougher than was expected it was 1st day or so. AGC rather rattled yesterday but CinC expressed wonderful feeling of calm + things this morning look better.'[34]

Blewitt's account of the 24th began with the sad news of a friend killed. He added, referring to Cunningham's near catastrophe departure from 30 Corps, that 'AGC worried by battle but rattled by flight + take off etc'. His daily entry concludes, however, 'Slightly more optimistic'. His description of the 25th was equally positive: Auchinleck had returned to Cairo and 'AGC preoccupied but bearing up wonderfully well'.

November 26 was an entirely different matter. Blewitt crisply recounted that Neil Ritchie and Arthur Smith had arrived in camp: 'Letter tells AGC he is sacked for "being defensively minded" and AGC is whisked off to No 64 General Hospital Alex. I am left uncertain as to his state of health. A. Smith stating categorically he is ill "poor chap tho he doesn't know it." Shattering evening.' Smith's words show that a narrative of mental breakdown already existed by the 26th.

Blewitt followed Cunningham to Alexandria, where his impressions of the situation became more complicated, as on 28 November when he noted: 'A.G.C. appears the best of health ... whole thing a complete secret + he is there incognito. Strain + needs 6 or 8 weeks rest. Doctor was told he had a nervous breakdown. Diagnosed by A Smith?' Smith appeared in Blewitt's diary again on 1 December: 'A Smith again asks as whether I think A.G.C. was ill or not. "Quite clear" he says.' Blewitt's answer to Smith, however, remains unknown. Blewitt then spent a few more days visiting Cunningham and attending parties and dinners before putting him on a plane for England.

Most of Blewitt's letters to his family were chatty and filled with discussions of his duties and travels, and more inappropriately, battle plans, locations and other details. A few also confirm statements found in conventional accounts. For example, on 29 October he wrote:

> Our health remains excellent tho A.G.C. has been suffering from some white spots in front of his eyes which his oculist says is nicotine poisoning and he

thinks is ___. As a result he has had to give up smoking completely which he seems have done quite easily but his temper is not quite so equitable + I stopped a raspberry or two yesterday. However later in the evening I was successful in fishing for a word of praise.

Blewitt's odd mention of 'our health' and 'stopping a raspberry or two' suggests he had come to view himself and Cunningham as a single unit, with Blewitt acting as a kind of superego.

But another letter demonstrates that within days of the affair efforts were underway to communicate another version, although to whom is not clear. On 3 December Blewitt wrote that 'A.G.C. says 1) this is ok, 2) you must realize that it is strictly for your personal information, 3) there is no question of him having been sacked, 4) the bearer of this will get in touch at the 1st possible opportunity (so Uncle O will not be able to help)'. He concluded the letter with a PPS, 'You will realize that the fact that there even is a mystery must be kept secret.' The identity of 'Uncle O' is not clear but likely refers to Otto Marling Lund. While the letter was addressed to Blewitt's parents, the message appears intended for others.

James Blewitt's worshipful tone and genuine shock at Cunningham's supersession suggest he may have been too close to notice issues that were apparent to others. And despite his momentary expression of uncertainty regarding Cunningham's mental state, his loyalty never flagged. Blewitt would go on and serve as Cunningham's Personal Secretary in Palestine from 1946 to 1948.[35]

3

History Takes Shape after 26 November

For Britain, 7 December entailed the construction of a formal alliance with the United States, but at the same time it meant confronting its own war in the Pacific. This quickly saw the Japanese invasion of Hong Kong and Malaya, the shocking loss of two British capital ships, HMS *Repulse* and HMS *Prince of Wales*, and growing threats to Burma and Singapore. Events in the desert assumed new proportions, at once larger but also smaller as the new global war began.

In the weeks following Cunningham's supersession there was a flurry of communications in which the question of Cunningham's mental condition was both elaborated and denied. Although paramount for Cunningham himself, for others this was framed in terms of command responsibilities and public opinion. The larger issue, even as the battle continued, was whether *Crusader* was a success or failure, a triumph or an embarrassment. But the medical issue was never far from the forefront.

Auchinleck's accounting to London

In his initial cable to the CIGS Auchinleck did not mention Cunningham's condition. But on 27 November another cable from Auchinleck to the CIGS[1] and signed by Smith[2] complicated the story further.

> CUNNINGHAM took blow very well and consented to go to hospital ALEXANDRIA where he is now incognito (.) He is NOT repeat NOT really ill but his eyes have troubled him and he admits being tired (.) Because of eye trouble he recently gave up smoking which may have had something to do with it (.) He can NOT repeat NOT remain indefinitely in hospital incognito and I shall be grateful if you will order him home (.) Am asking him how he would like to travel (.) I hope he may be fit for further employment later (.)

Blewitt's evidence showed that Cunningham's eye trouble existed in late October. Arthur Smith, not Auchinleck, was in contact with Blewitt and seems the likely source for the information on Cunningham's eyes, which later circulated widely. But Smith had pressed Blewitt to affirm that Cunningham was indeed sick. The fact that the 27 November cable was *not* composed by Smith but rather by Auchinleck himself may therefore be significant.

Regardless, Dill appears to have either misread Auchinleck's message or received information separately regarding Cunningham's health:[3] 'Extremely sorry to hear of CUNNINGHAM's illness. He has had a long and strenuous inning and it seems clear he should now be sent home to recuperate when fit to travel.' Whether Dill was speaking of the emerging cover story regarding Cunningham's condition or something more is unclear. There is no indication how Dill came to this conclusion, especially since Brigadier John Noble Kennedy, then Director of Military Operations and Plans, reported in his memoir that by 27 November Dill was no longer active as CIGS but 'still came to the War Office most days, to talk about the war'.[4]

Although disengaged on the verge of his retirement, Dill's slim involvement was an important step in medicalizing Cunningham's supersession. Consistent with this emerging narrative (and in contradiction to his telegram of two days previous) a cable from Auchinleck to the CIGS on 29 November then emphasized his medical condition: 'Doctors say CUNNINGHAM suffering from exhaustion and will need two or three months to recover (.)'[5] The next day Auchinleck's communication with Churchill emphasized the narrative of Cunningham's medical condition still further, 'When I realized Cunningham was not fit I considered very carefully whether I myself should take his place in command 8th.'[6]

A medical interpretation of Cunningham's supersession was thus in place by 29 November, ready to be drawn upon by later commentators. This early use of the term 'exhaustion', a year before the 8th Army adopted it formally as a gentler euphemism for 'shell shock', is medically ambiguous. But these specifics of command and fitness were quickly overshadowed by the political question of making the supersession public. A week of intense exchanges followed, in which Churchill sought clarification regarding Cunningham's condition and the political implications.

Churchill cabled Auchinleck on 30 November to warn: 'I may have to make a statement to House on Tuesday on information received to that date, especially if events continue to take a favourable turn. I think it would then be proper, unless you see objection, to disclose the change in Command which will by then be more than a week old, and the reason.' Churchill then described a draft statement regarding Cunningham, claiming his 'proposed dispositions were not in accord with the principle of relentless offensive at all risks and at all costs'.[7]

But on 1 December Auchinleck replied to Churchill to 'strongly urge therefore that your announcement should be postponed especially as enemy does not (repeat not) know and when he does hear of change is bound to make capital of it'.[8] Auchinleck then noted: 'CUNNINGHAM at my urgent request and much against his will agreed to go on sick list and enter hospital at Alexandria INCOGNITO where he still is. Specialist report says that when admitted to hospital he was suffering from exhaustion and strain and that he will need a month or so to recuperate.'

Auchinleck added laudatory remarks about Cunningham but also two pointed comments: 'I asked him to go sick for the general good. At that time I did not (repeat not) realize he was ill though in actual fact he was,' and 'Dispositions and plans were all right but I had not (repeat not) confidence that in his then state of mind he could carry out the operation with the resolution that was essential.' Auchinleck's changing narrative, that Cunningham had become 'defensive minded' and that he, Auchinleck, had not realized until *after* the supersession that Cunningham had a medical condition of 'exhaustion', was subtle and protected both him and Cunningham from accusations of incompetence or malfeasance.

Churchill followed up on Auchinleck's cable the next day saying, 'Of course disclosure change of Command must be postponed till decision in battle I reached. Will discuss actual form with you later.'[9] But as if taken aback by Churchill's laconic reply, Auchinleck sent another cable to Churchill to clarify that his decision to remove Cunningham 'does not (repeat not) mean that operations have been mishandled up to date'.[10] Nevertheless, Churchill's scepticism increased during the week. On 7 December he cabled Auchinleck again with a list of issues that included a request for estimates of South African and New Zealand casualties, defective radio sets, the Russian front and the prospect of Japan coming into the war.[11]

The final and longest item dealt with Cunningham:

> Although General Cunningham is arriving home almost immediately and there will certainly be much talk behind the scenes, I do not intend to make any announcement until your news is decidedly good. Let me know the moment when you feel the idea has definitely turned. I should find it difficult to make out that he was superseded on health grounds because that was not the reason which you gave me in your original telegram which I imparted to Cabinet.

Churchill went on to describe Cunningham's medical condition as 'serious overstrain' but added that 'it would seem to me wrong in the interests of the

Army that the classical severity of your action, which was greatly admired here, should be marred by explanations which many people know would not square with the actual facts'. Churchill, then, appears to have accepted the 'defensive minded' explanation but suspected the medical explanation to be a post hoc rationalization. In any case, he admired the 'classical severity' of relieving Cunningham, against whom he would nurse a grudge for almost a year.

The actual facts were becoming more and more obscure, but on 12 December Churchill cabled Auchinleck to say that the Australian press had reported Cunningham's supersession and that he could make a statement based on his previous telegram.[12] Auchinleck responded quickly and endorsed the narrative.[13]

In fact, Churchill had addressed Parliament on 11 December[14] at length regarding *Crusader*. In his speech he defended the optimistic statements of the Military Spokesman in Cairo and, before describing the battle itself, noted:

> The Libyan offensive did not take the course which its authors expected, though it will reach the end at which they aimed. Very few set-piece battles that have to be prepared over a long period of time work out in the way they are planned and imagined beforehand. The unexpected intervenes at every stage. The willpower of the enemy impinges itself upon the prescribed or hoped-for course of events. Victory is traditionally elusive. Accidents happen. Mistakes are made. Sometimes right things turn out wrong, and quite often wrong things turn out right.

Churchill's specific comments regarding Cunningham were a masterful combination of airy contextualizing, fulsome praise and subtle misdirection:

> All the troops have fought all the time in every circumstance of fatigue and hardship with one sincere, insatiable desire, to engage the enemy and destroy him if possible, tank for tank, man to man and hand to hand. And this is what has carried us on. But behind all this process working out at so many different points and in so many separate combats has been the persisting will-power of the Commander-in-Chief, General Auchinleck. Without that will-power we might very easily have subsided to the defensive and lost the precious initiative, to which, here in this Libyan theatre, we have for the first time felt ourselves strong enough to make a claim.

> The first main crisis of the battle was reached between 24th and 26th November. On the 24th General Auchinleck proceeded to the battle headquarters, and on the 26th he decided to relieve General Cunningham and to appoint Major-General Ritchie, a comparatively junior officer, to the command of the 8th Army in his stead. This action was immediately endorsed by the Minister of State and by myself. General Cunningham has rendered brilliant service in Abyssinia and

is also responsible for the planning and organisation of the present offensive in Libya, which began, as I have explained, with surprise and with success and which has now definitely turned the corner. He has since been reported by the medical authorities to be suffering from serious overstrain and has been granted sick leave. Since 26th November, therefore, the 8th Army has been commanded, with great vigour and skill, by General Ritchie, but during nearly the whole time General Auchinleck himself has been at the battle headquarters. Although the battle is not yet finished, I have no hesitation in saying that for good or ill it is General Auchinleck's battle.

The responsibility for the supersession was thus firmly shouldered by Churchill and Auchinleck, and 'loss of initiative' ultimately explained as the result of 'serious overstrain'. But having presented Cunningham's 'serious overstrain' in Parliament, an 'official' medical explanation was being offered to the highest nation's political echelon, against a background of suspicion and relief.

Finally, on 12 December Auchinleck cabled the new CIGS,[15] Brooke; articulated a non-medical reason for relieving Cunningham, 'loss of confidence'; and emphasized that 'my conviction that he was taking counsel of his fears was shared by TEDDER and CONYNGHAM AOC Western Desert as well as by ARTHUR SMITH and other competent observers'. Cunningham was 'distracted and perturbed by enemy threats against his rear areas' and had to go. If anything, Cunningham taking 'counsel of his fears' and losing the confidence of senior commanders, without the benefit of a medical condition, could be read as an even more serious statement regarding his fitness. As if aware of this, Auchinleck ended with a warning that Cunningham 'apparently intends to appeal to the Army Council'.

Two explanations had thus reached London in the last weeks of 1941. But what was Cunningham's actual medical condition?

The medical reports

Both Cunningham's December 1941 report on *Crusader* and the 1944 CIGS analysis on his supersession state that upon his arrival to Cairo on 26 November he was examined by a medical officer.[16] Neither report, however, indicates the name of the physician or precise diagnosis of this examination.[17] But on 29 November at his brother's insistence Alan Cunningham was examined by the consulting physician to the Middle East Forces, William Denton Douglas Small, at Number 64 General Hospital in Cairo.[18]

In his report[19] Small's noted:

> I was informed that when he was admitted to hospital, on the evening of November 26th, he was exceedingly tired and showed signs of strain. His long and heavy responsibilities had culminated in a period of about a week with practically no sleep. He voice was weakened. When speaking he tended to break off in the middle of sentences. He showed a marked tremor of the hands.

But beyond his 'long and heavy responsibilities' Small had another explanation: 'It appears that about a month ago he consulted an ophthalmologist, who found a scotoma affecting the right eye. He was advised to stop smoking, and did so. It is to be noted that sudden cessation of tobacco in a heavy smoker often produces marker irritability and unrest.'

Blewitt had previously noted that smoking had affected both Cunningham's eye and his temper. But after several days of rest Small observed that Cunningham had slept well, 'and that all signs of strain had disappeared except a slight general increase of his deep reflexes. His general physical state is good. His voice is normal. The tremor has disappeared. He is composed, and very alert and mentally active. There is no evidence of any "nervous breakdown."' Small's diagnosis was 'severe physical exhaustion' and he recommended a month of rest before Cunningham was returned to duty. Small's report is likely to have been the source of Auchinleck's comment to the CIGS on 29 November regarding Cunningham's exhaustion. Curiously, no other observer had mentioned a tremor.

But Small was not an impartial observer. Small had received his medical degrees at the University of Edinburgh in 1907 and 1914.[20] Alan Cunningham's father, the distinguished physician Daniel John Cunningham, was professor of Anatomy at Edinburgh from 1903 until his death in 1909: it is highly probable that Small had been Daniel Cunningham's student. He could not have been unaware of Alan Cunningham's parentage.

Beyond this direct conflict of interest is the context of medicine in Edinburgh as a whole. Daniel Cunningham's oldest son Lt Colonel John Cunningham was also a physician who had returned to Edinburgh in 1929 after a distinguished career in the Indian Medical Service to run a hospital,[21] and his daughter Elizabeth had married prominent Edinburgh surgeon Edwin Bramwell.[22] With the exception of military service during the world wars, Small's entire career was spent in Edinburgh.

Given a context in which the extended Cunningham family loomed so large, it is unlikely that Small would have officially declared that Alan Cunningham had suffered a nervous breakdown. Small's medical report therefore cannot be considered authoritative. Andrew Cunningham's recommendation of Small also appears suspect.

Cunningham's complaints to Ralph Blewitt that the medical board at South East Command to which he had been summoned in December after his return had graded him 'D'[23] may have more accurately assessed his condition, both then and by extension, in November.

The Cunningham–Auchinleck letters

Even as *Crusader* was still being fought, Auchinleck continued to address questions from London regarding Cunningham's supersession. But he also had to deal with letters from both Cunningham brothers.

On 25 November Auchinleck had asked Cunningham to 'be placed on the sick list and go into hospital for a period'. But on 27 November Auchinleck wrote again to Cunningham, beginning a short but intense exchange.[24]

Addressing Cunningham as 'My dear Alan', Auchinleck stated:[25]

> I want to thank you very much for the way in which you accepted my decision, and for your great loyalty and public spirit in agreeing to go into hospital against your will.
>
> I ask for forgiveness for having inflicted this indignity on you, and I know very well how you disliked having to pretend that you are sick when you are not. I would not have done it had I not thought it essential to the conduct of the battle and in the public interest generally all over the World. I repeat that I am most grateful to you. I know you loathe your present position and are longing to be your own master again. I would like to ask you to bear it for another two or three days until I can see how things go at the front. I have cabled the C.I.G.S. asking him to summon you home.

Auchinleck went on to propose various routes by which Cunningham might return to Britain but then returned to the question of health:

> I know you do not think you are ill and you don't look ill, but are you sure that you are really as fit as you think you are?
>
> It occurred to me that perhaps you suddenly giving up smoking may have affected you more that is apparent to you? Don't think I am impertinent please, I only ask these things because I am desperately anxious that you shall become your old self again and play your part. We need you.

Auchinleck stated clearly that Cunningham was *not* sick and then questions whether he was in fact 'unfit' as a result of his ceasing to smoke. But was

Auchinleck trying to simultaneously reassure Cunningham about his health and introduce doubts, or was he expressing his own confusion? Only Auchinleck's warmth seems certain.

This note and Auchinleck's early letter of 25 November prompted two separate replies from Cunningham on 28 November.

Cunningham began his longer response on an equally conciliatory note[26]: 'It is my earnest desire not to embarrass you with personal matters at this critical period.' But his real concern quickly came into view, namely that 'At the same time it cannot be ignored that through no fault of my own my name has received certain publicity in England and America. So drastic a step as my removal in the middle of a battle may well, at some future date, whether near or distant, bring in its train both official and public notice.'

Then, 'for purposes of record', Cunningham answered Auchinleck's specific criticisms. He accepted 'that as you had lost confidence in my ability to carry out your wishes you had no other course open to you'. At the same time he could 'not accept the statement that latterly I was thinking more in terms of defense than offense'. He cited the perception that the 'superiority in tanks had disappeared' and that the 'enemy might be in a position to round my left flank and raid Egypt'. And he insisted that 'the only purely defensive measures taken by me at any time were to direct that the Army rear areas should be organized against raid and that the security of the railhead must be ensured'.

Cunningham concluded with a magnanimous wish that the 'offensive should succeed and if my removal is necessary to ensure that end I accept the situation uncomplainingly'.

With this letter for the 'record' Cunningham also responded to Auchinleck's second note.[27] After stating that he preferred to return to Britain as quickly as possible, Cunningham noted:

> You ask whether I am not ill – Here they tell me I am tired – I won't [?] hate to admit to anything else, and to the need for more than a few days rest.
>
> My brother tells me they are sending down a consultant tomorrow + he can say. I suppose there are advantages in labeling it a medical case much as I dislike it.
>
> Perhaps you would be good enough to let me know what recommendation you have made to the C.I.G.S. I must seriously consider whether I am to stay on as a major general or whether it is time to leave altogether and do what I can to help on the war on other lines.

Indeed, Cunningham relinquished the rank of Lieutenant General on 15 December. Cunningham's rank and hence pay would continue to be an issue until he was again promoted to Lieutenant General in October 1943.

To complicate matters, on 28 November Andrew Cunningham also wrote to Auchinleck saying that he had seen his brother and that while[28] 'he himself says that though he is certainly tired there is nothing the matter with him + I must from my personal observation I don't think there is. It may be however that medical reasons are best from all points of view + I know he is seriously taking this into consideration'.

Auchinleck replied separately to both Cunningham brothers the next day. To Andrew[29] he merely stated that the RAF had arranged Alan's transportation back to Britain.

Auchinleck's responses to Alan were much more detailed. In the shorter of the two[30] he noted that the RAF had arranged transportation back to Britain. Regarding what he had told the CIGS, Auchinleck noted: 'I told him that the doctors say you are suffering from exhaustion, and that you may need two or three months to recover,' and that 'I had an answer from him to say that he was extremely sorry to hear of your illness.' Here Auchinleck honestly related his own report and Dill's response invoking 'illness'.

Auchinleck's other reply was much longer[31] and in a tone that was generous but no longer warm; he addressed each of Cunningham's points, the most salient being 'the fact that you even considered the possibility of breaking off the offensive and standing on the defensive seriously perturbed me'.

Auchinleck noted that his directive of 24 November was intended to 'relieve you of part of the burden of that responsibility and to remove the fears you felt as to the results which might accrue from the continuation of the offensive'. He added that he had prolonged his 'stay at your headquarters in order to give myself an opportunity of seeing whether my hopes would be justified' but had returned to Cairo and 'finally decided that that I could no longer have confidence in you to prosecute the offensive as single-heartedly as I wished to see it prosecuted. Having made reached this decision I had no alternative but to ask you to relinquish your command'.

Auchinleck concluded: 'Whether I was right or wrong is, and must remain, a matter of opinion,' but regardless, the responsibility for that decision and the outcome of the battle was his. Cunningham's strategic judgement, not mental state, was the basis of the problem.

Despite Auchinleck's cooler tone, Cunningham pressed yet ahead, again writing two letters. In one he was more combative, saying that Auchinleck had implied[32] 'that I suggested the offensive should be called off, I am afraid I must write again and say this was not so'. But he added a small and telling concession: 'Admittedly the defensive was the only alternative, but I considered this decision was yours.' In the second, he made another concession:[33] 'I note that I am to go home sick' and adds that 'there seems no way of hiding my arrival home'.

Auchinleck did not reply and there is no record of the two communicating again for the twenty-five years.[34]

Arthur Smith communicates with Cunningham

Lt General Arthur Smith, Auckinleck's chief of staff, had come to 8th Army Advanced Headquarters with Ritchie to relieve Cunningham on 26 November and escorted him back to Cairo. But this did not end his involvement with the Cunningham affair.

On 29 November Smith wrote to Cunningham to say, 'I have been thinking so much about you, + write to thank you for making my task easy last Wednesday.'[35] But Smith added:

> You know Alan you are not well, + for that reason were not able to do yourself justice. I know you will refuse to admit that you are not well – so we must leave it at that! Nevertheless I am going to see (in due course) that people realize your going to hospital was not mere camouflage: in fairness to yourself.

A follow-up on 1 December acknowledged Auchinleck's receipt of notes from Cunningham, repeated the idea that 'sick leave is no camouflage' and stated that the latter would definitely return to Britain. Smith even offered Cunningham the use of his flat in Cairo as he waited for details of his return.

Cunningham wrote to Smith on 30 November, thanking him for his note, acknowledging Smith's difficult position[36] ('I was only too sorry for you in a task which I knew must have been horribly distasteful to you') and conceding his situation; 'Well, apparently whether I like it or not I am to be sick. I admit I did not foresee the doctors would say so, and cannot bring myself to believe them.'

He then asked Smith to make arrangements for Blewitt's further employment, stating that 'one lesson I have learnt and that is to keep my mouth shut', and expresses 'so many thanks continual help and sympathy. An oasis in this dreary desert which I find myself around me at present'.

But over the next five days Cunningham's attitude changed dramatically, as demonstrated by a remarkable letter from Smith to Auchinleck on 4 December.[37]

> I have just come back from an extraordinarily awkward interview with Alan Cunningham. I think it best to record it at once.
>
> Alan opened by saying "You know, I am not going to take this lying down. It may mean the end of my career but I dont care."

Thinking he might be going to tell me fully of his intentions I at once reminded him that I would have to report our conversation to yourself, but he replied that he had no objection.

He then added that he considered, after due reflection, that he had been very badly treated. He had never been given an adequate reason for his removal, except the state of his mind – "but I ought to know the state of my mind better than anyone." He was emphatic that he was not ill, and stated that he had discussed the matter with the doctors who he was sure in their heart of hearts knew he was not ill. He said that Small (I think he is the specialist) obviously realized that he was not ill, but he had backed up the junior MOs and would not let them down after they had said he was ill.

He complained (perhaps that is too strong a word) that you had never given him an inkling that you doubted his ability to carry on efficiently in command when you were up at Adv HQ 8 Army. He had shown the amber light, and in view of the subsequent events of the battle he had obviously been right. He had realized the importance of relieving Tobruk, but had urged the danger to his L of C etc.

He asked me strongly to represent the impossible situation he was in while this secrecy about the change of command lasted. He asked the reason, and I explained it. He asked when the secrecy ban would be lifted, and I said that you would ask the PM to lift it at the earliest possible moment that you felt safe in the public interest. He asked the terms of the announcement and I told him that the PM had telegraphed to say he would consult you first. I added that in view of the difficulty of secrecy once he reached the War Office, I hoped it would soon be made public. He asked that the date of the change should be announced.

He remarked on more than one occasion that he was only too willing to play as regards secrecy and anything in the 'public interest' but from other remarks it is clear that he is going to appeal for the case to be investigated, presumably to the Army Council.

He also said that examination by a doctor was thrust upon him and had he refused to go to hospital he would never have been classified as sick. He went voluntarily at your request but obviously feels that a medical overhaul was not part of this bargain.

So much for our talk.

Now my reactions. I suggest the first thing is to convince him that your decision was right. On this point (I forgot to mention it before) I told him that I myself could see he was suffering from strain, and that in my opinion there was ample reason for you to have had lack of confidence in his being able to carry out efficiently the duties of an Army Commander. He agreed that if you lacked confidence in him, you were right to remove him but "it was done in the wrong way."

> I know you want no outside support to prove you were right, for the sole responsibility rests with you. On the other hand if Alan is not convinced, then he will talk and it must do harm. Therefore would it be wise to tell him that your misapprehensions were shared by five offices of the rank of Brigadier and upwards – Conyngham, Sandy, Neil, Nares and myself – without mentioning names? Also John Shearer – six.
>
> Next point is the announcement. Is it time to fix up with the PM the exact wording? I enclose your suggestion and the PM's. Also I remind you of your statement to the CIGS, for feel it is important that the PM does not say anything contrary to this, of which Alan is aware.
>
> I am sorry you should be bothered about all this just now, specially as I KNOW your decision was right.

Smith interviewed Cunningham after the latter's examination by Small. This apparently helped convince Cunningham that he was not ill, and indeed to have emboldened him. But Smith also confirmed that senior officers, including Coningham, Galloway, Ritchie, Shearer and Brigadier Eric P. Nares, Deputy Adjutant and Quartermaster General on the staff of Tom Riddell-Webster, PAO Middle East, all had 'misapprehensions' regarding Cunningham on the basis of personal observation.

Cunningham was only one of the countless issues Auchinleck had to deal with. Writing to Smith on 6 December[38] Cunningham is the sixth of twelve matters addressed. Auchinleck apologized for Smith having been 'dragged into this very awkward controversy'. But Auchinleck's growing frustration is evident:

> I am grateful for all you have done to help me in the matter, and I am sure that Alan Cunningham will be too when he has time to think matters over quietly.
>
> So far as I can see, he has said nothing which I had not said to him already, and admitted to be true. As regards the method of his removal and the allegation of unfair treatment, there is no answer but that I held my hand till the last possible moment, hoping against hope that action would not be necessary. As for giving him an inkling as to my doubts about him, I never had any doubts till he sent for me to visit him. In any event, one does not treat an Army Commander like a junior subaltern and tell him not to do it again! The issues are too great!
>
> I agree that he is at present in a difficult though not impossible position, but he will have to lump that until it is safe to announce the change without doing harm to our cause. Surely he can stand that?
>
> I hope he will not appeal to the Army Council. If he does, he will have the humiliation of hearing that he had lost confidence not only of his own service,

but of the Air Force as well. As to telling him this, I am not so sure. If he takes his removal quietly he need never know, and may regain his self-esteem. Once he does know, he will never be able to have confidence in himself again. At least that is how I see it. Perhaps I am wrong.

I have no shadow of doubt that I did the right thing. My only regret is that I did not do it before, as apparently I was blind where other people, including Tedder, were not. I enclose a telegram for the P.M. on the subject of the announcement. If today's battle goes well, we may be able to release the news in a day or two now.

Auchinleck continued to be concerned with Cunningham's self-esteem but he had a new element of self-criticism, namely that he should have made the decision to relieve Cunningham *earlier*, as Tedder had apparently counselled.

One more letter from Smith to Cunningham, from July 1942,[39] muddies things still further. Smith was responding to a now-missing communication from Cunningham, but after an initial pleasantry, he got to the heart of the matter:

At no lecture have I ever referred to your removal from 8 Army: I have only spoken appreciatively of your work.

When actually asked about the change in command I have said you were unwell. Yes: I know you had a letter from Gen Auk thanking you for going into hospital. But Gen Auk: did not know till a day or so after you had gone to hospital that the medical specialist had reported you were suffering from nervous exhaustion (not a breakdown).

I don't know the workings of the Medical Directorate, but I do know for absolute certain that Gen Auk was not party to any intrigue or camouflage.

I now hear that I am reported to have behaved badly over the affair! My conscience is clear, it does not disturb me in the least!!

You will believe me when I regret, more than I can say, what you have gone through.

God bless you Alan

Blewitt's diary shows that Smith had remarked on 26 November that Cunningham was ill and that by 28 November the 'nervous breakdown' narrative was already circulating. But he had also told Dill on behalf of Auchinleck on 27 November that Cunningham was *not* ill? What then did Smith actually believe?

Arthur Smith is a little commented upon officer.[40] Commissioned into the Coldstream Guards, Smith spent his career as a staff officer with assignments in Britain, Egypt, Persia and, finally, as commander of British forces in India and

Pakistan prior to partition. Also notable, however, was Smith's deep Christian faith: from a devout family, throughout his career Smith ran Bible study groups for soldiers and wrote the *100 Days Bible Study* which abstracted Biblical lessons for military personnel. After his retirement he became chairman of the British Evangelical Alliance and the World Evangelical Fellowship.[41] On this basis it seems improbable that he would deliberately lie.[42]

Did Smith have a change of heart or was the idea of Cunningham's illness being used to triple effect, to explain the change of command to Auchinleck, London and Cunningham himself? What would be the purpose: to confirm Auchinleck's strategic decision, manufacture a cover story for Churchill and the War Office or spare Cunningham's feelings? Perhaps more important is that by July 1942 rumours had reached Cunningham that Smith and others had been publicly discussing the supersession and that a counter-narrative of Smith having wronged Cunningham had been generated. This must also be set into the larger contexts of growing dissatisfaction with Auchinleck's direction of the theatre after the fall of Tobruk and resulting parliamentary debates in which Cunningham's supersession became an issue.

Given Smith's proximity to Cunningham and the events of 26 November and later, his letters have considerable weight. But their obvious contradictions cannot be easily resolved. If nothing else they point to the 'impossible situation' generated by Cunningham's supersession and the evolution of a medical cover story that, true or not, was proving impossible to clarify or expunge.

4

The Path towards Rehabilitation and the Genesis of History

Cunningham's efforts to restore his reputation began before he had even left Egypt and returned to Britain. Initially this entailed contacts with military and political figures to relate his version of *Crusader*, but it quickly changed into an effort to shape and reshape the writing of history.

Cunningham's report to Alan Brooke

In early December Cunningham returned to Britain by air and on 22 December had been reviewed by a medical board at Aldershot, which graded him 'D'. Cunningham also visited the new CIGS, Alan Brooke, at the War Office. Whether in response to the medical review, his interview with Brooke or simply to put his own account on the record, Cunningham then submitted a file to Brooke. Cunningham's selection of documents and editing were critical to his case and the British Official History.

From the beginning Cunningham's cover letter adopted an unctuous tone, simultaneously stating to Brooke that he did 'not wish to cause embarrassment and am loathe to intrude personal matters at this critical time', but adding that 'I feel however that for the sake of the future I should ask that my story be recorded and given consideration'.[1] He perceived that his public reputation was under attack, noting 'From remarks in the Press and from other sources I have gathered that some accusations are being made against me that are far from the truth.'

But these allegations, 'a wish to go on the defensive', were secondary to the real crux of the matter:

> When I saw you in the War Office I gathered you thought I really had had a breakdown. As you will see from the account given my reputed illness was

a pretence to which I was asked to agree. I was ordered to appear in front of a Medical Board the other day and was classified "D" which I feel is carrying the pretence too far.

Cunningham's report on *Crusader* from 18 to 26 November is exculpatory but introduced several new elements. The battle had begun according to his plan and on the basis of available information appeared to be proceeding well. But he complained: 'During this period I had no knowledge in my desert headquarters of the communiqués being issued in CAIRO or of the activities of the CAIRO spokesman. Indeed, I head nothing of the accusations of premature optimism on the latter's part until I had been relieved.'[2] Prior to Cunningham's report, overly optimistic press releases and coverage had not been mentioned in any official source. Raising the issue with Brooke inserted doubt regarding the background of Auchinleck's decision.

Cunningham then recounted the tactical reverses but presented his decision to ask Auchinleck to come to the front in an almost neutral tone:

As the primary condition of a preponderance of tanks was no longer present, I therefore felt it my duty to ask Gen. AUCHINLECH to come down to my headquarters so that I could place the position before him. It was apparent to me that a continuance of the offensive was going to entail a considerably greater expenditure of men and material than had been foreseen.

At this point Cunningham stated that he made a 'note for the record' about this meeting but quoted his diary entry of 23 November that 'chief arrived at my request. ...' He then proceeded to cite this private document as evidence that he had *not* proposed to go on the defensive saying 'I feel the above extract which is given verbatim shows that this is not the case'.[3] Citing his own diary as a 'note for the record' is at best careless and at worst mendacious. Shaping of evidence still further, Cunningham also failed to mention the short orders Auchinleck issued immediately after this meeting on 23 November, namely the directive to continue the offensive, even though he included them in the collection of papers.

The remainder of the report was equally selective. Cunningham claimed that the only reorganization of forces he had proposed was 'to move some troops up from the rear to protect the railhead and to organize the defence of the rear areas with the troops already there'. He also claimed that he had persuaded Auchinleck to return to Cairo. Upon his relief, he was examined by a medical officer

who I heard later reported that I was suffering from "exhaustion." There was no question of breakdown, having been sent into hospital the M.O. had to find something wrong (he was not informed of the real facts) and I contend my condition was quite consistent with that of any other commander in 8th Army who had been through the same period.[4]

The documents Cunningham provided along with his report included Auchinleck's shorter and longer orders to continue the offensive, and his formal letter relieving Cunningham but not the accompanying private letter. Small's medical report was included along with a Cunningham's commentary in which he reiterated that the 'young doctor who examined me had no idea why I was there and very naturally assumed I must be ill' and that 'General Auchinleck's wire to the C.I.G.S. was clearly sent as a result of the young M.O.'s report'.[5] He then reiterated Dr Small's findings.

Cunningham had written to Auchinleck twice on 28 November but included only his first, longer letter, omitting the shorter note. Similarly omitted is Auchinleck's shorter reply of 29 November in which he noted that 'I told him that the doctors say you are suffering from exhaustion, and that you may need two or three months to recover,' and that 'I had an answer from him to say that he [Dill] was extremely sorry to hear of your illness.'[6] The notes Cunningham and Auchinleck exchanged on 30 November are similarly omitted, as are all those with Arthur Smith.

Brooke's reply, however, addressed only one issue:[7]

> I am so sorry not to have answered your letter of the 1st instant sooner. But I have been very rushed lately and I also had the report of our medical board sent for to see whether as you said the matter of "pretence had been carried too far." I could see no case of pretence about it, but a genuine report that you required rest. I should hate you to think that any instructions had been issued to this board with a view to keeping up some form of pretence.

He informed Cunningham that the papers would be collected 'so that a complete record may exist'. That appears to be the last official comment Brooke made on the matter of *Crusader*. Early the next month Cunningham submitted his last official statement on *Crusader*, a fourteen-page operational report that stressed the soundness of the plan but criticized the inadequacy of British tanks, guns and tactics.[8] This too would become a major line of argument for Cunningham, his defenders and among historians.

The transmission history of these files is critical. Cunningham's and Brooke's original letters and reports cannot be located: the earliest file contained copies of Cunningham's cover letter to Brooke, dated 1 January 1942, the multi-page report on the execution of *Crusader*, and excerpted correspondence between himself and Auchinleck.[9] Copies of letters between Cunningham and the

Assistant CIGS, Major General John Kennedy, and the Military Secretary, Lt General Colville Weymss, were added in 1944 regarding the question of using the documents when writing the official history of *Crusader*. A note from Kennedy to Brooke, however, asked whether the documents should first be handed to Colonel Robertson of the Records Section for analysis before being given to the Historical Section. This was done and evidently received Brooke's approval.

But Brooke was not especially interested in the issue and according to an annotation, the folder sat in a steel cupboard, open and unsealed, until it was resealed on 12 December 1946. Another annotation 'seen' by 'M of A', that is, Montgomery of Alamein, then CIGS Field Marshal Montgomery, was dated 29 March 1948. Later, in August 1946 Montgomery used the file to argue against the Colonial Office appointing Cunningham as High Commissioner in Palestine.[10] Two copies were retained in the CIGS safe.

The file was duly transmitted to the Historical Section and was labelled CAB 106/655. Thus shaped by Cunningham's selection of documents, the CIGS and Historical Section presented a one-sided version in which Cunningham's strategy was largely vindicated, the question of his health elided and his prudence reaffirmed. His supersession was largely recast as a matter of Auchinleck's subjective judgement. In a sense, Cunningham's version was cemented, at least within the Establishment.

Discussions between the Cunningham brothers

Though no longer in close proximity, Alan Cunningham appears to have kept his older brother informed of developments after his return to England, including with copies of letters to others. These provide a few clues regarding Alan's efforts to exonerate and rehabilitate himself. On 1 January Alan wrote to Andrew noting:[11]

> I got back here on 11th to hear on the wireless that night the P.M.'s brutal statement on my removal, and to see the gutter press headlines "Cunningham sacked"!

> I saw Brooky at once was as usual very kind, though told me the P.M. was rampant and he could do nothing for me while he was in that mood. I cannot make out what he was told, so wrote enclosed to Brooky. I suspect O.L. [Oliver Leese, in pencil] of embroidery. Now I am on leave and have a feeling that I am being ostracized. No one has suggested that my experiences might be of some value and are worth hearing! I suppose everyone frightened of Winston. I hear

murmors[?] that Shearer has made a statement that plans for Libya have been in no way affected since the beginning. Rumors have it that the question was asked why & was never cared [?], and confusion reigned.

Why Alan Cunningham suspected that acting Major General Oliver Leese, commanding the recently formed Guards Armoured Division, had been 'embroidering' against him is completely unclear but speaks to both his state of mind and swirls of intra-service gossip that were recorded only in passing. Andrew responded to Alan on 14 February,[12] calling the note to Brooke 'dignified & public spirited' and describing Churchill's speech regarding the supersession as 'absolutely damnable'.

A later communication, however, is more informative.[13] Likely dated 4 April 1944, it began mysteriously with reference to Andrew's inquiries regarding 'your lady friend'. It continued with a reference to 'that army book about 8th Army' but added that 'as you know the War Office disclaimed responsibility'.

The identity of the 'lady friend' is unknown but other ladies figured in Cunningham's narrative, at least privately. The book in question is likely *The Eighth Army*, a pamphlet published by the War Office in 1944. As will be shown below, Cunningham's concern over his representation in nascent forms of historical writing would be persistent for over a decade.

Cunningham to Smuts

On 5 December, apparently only hours before he left Cairo, Cunningham wrote to South African Prime Minister Jan Smut to inform him of the supersession.[14] Cunningham opened apologetically, saying that he did 'not wish to weary you with the circumstances which brought this about'. He was 'extremely anxious for you to know that Gen. Auchinleck has made a special point of telling the C.I.G.S that there had been no mishandling of the battle prior to my relief', since 'it would be a matter of great distress to me if I thought you felt I had let the South African troops down'.

Cunningham added several curious details. His 'whole plan was based on a preponderance of tanks that would enable me to use a comparatively small number of infantry'. But 'it was not foreseen that, mainly through superiority of equipment and natures of tanks, the Germans would be in a position to cause, for a period, an actual superiority in tank strength on our side'. This emphasis on the superiority of German tanks and artillery, and the inferiority of British equipment, was a significant theme for Cunningham and later historians alike.

> But another of Cunningham's themes was more painful.
>
>> I talked to several witness of the attack on 5th S.A. Bde. The German tanks came on in mass and charged straight through to Brigade position. Every where have I heard tales of the gallant manner in which the brigade stood their ground and fought back with the [?] execution. It will be an epic of South African war history, and will I am sure prove in the end to be one of the cornerstones on which our future success will be built.

This statement may be read both as self-interested and as reassurance to a Commonwealth leader whose forces had been destroyed in the battle.

Smuts's response was supportive but laconic.[15] He noted that he had heard of the change of command from Frank Theron, General Officer, Administration to the Union Defense Force's Middle East Force, but he did not describe Theron's comments, which were hardly admiring regarding Cunningham. Still, Smuts added sympathetically, 'However you might feel – your nerves were overtaxed by this continued heavy strain.'

Cunningham's response to Smuts, dated 10 February 1942, expressed appreciation for[16] 'the generous and kindly things you say arriving as they do at a time when I have had to put up with some vilification and criticism which has not always been correctly informed' and that the 'Prime Minister himself is very much against me'. But Cunningham had 'a clear conscience and complete peace of mind helped so largely by many letters from old friends who have served with me with me in the past and asked to do so again'.

Cunningham quickly turned to broader issues, including the 'restlessness' and 'spirit of extreme nationalism in the country', the entrance of the United States into the war, and the need for an 'imperial war council', in which he hoped Smuts would participate. These show that Cunningham was capable of looking beyond his own predicament in a thoughtful way, and that he could project interest in larger wartime political affairs to an interlocutor deeply involved in such issues. Overall, the exchange is intriguing for what it implies that Cunningham thought Smuts's influence would be helpful in his rehabilitation. He would be proved correct.

Cunningham reaches out to other gunners

After his supersession Cunningham quickly turned to several fellow gunners with his predicament.

The Blewitt family was at the centre of the Royal Artillery and the Army. Major General William E. Blewitt had been Commandant of the School of Gunnery, Director of Artillery at the War Office, and commander of South Coast Defenses and the Portsmouth Garrison.[17] His son Ralph, of the Royal Field Artillery, had been decorated in the First World War and after his retirement had helped start the Royal Artillery Yacht Club in 1933. Another son, Guy, had also been highly decorated and retired as a Lt Colonel from the Oxfordshire and Buckinghamshire Light Infantry. And it was at the suggestion of Otto Marling Lund, shortly to become head of Royal Artillery for the Home Forces, that in 1940 Alan Cunningham had reached out to his friend Ralph Blewitt to recruit James Blewitt as his ADC.

Cunningham confided in the elder Blewitt before and after *Crusader*. On 26 December 1941 shortly after his return to Britain, Cunningham responded to several of Blewitt's letters, which are not preserved.[18] Cunningham was 'ashamed that I have not answered your letters before, more particularly as they were the first I had', but appreciative of the 'friendship and good feeling that exist in this topsy turvy present day world, and to say as one does ones best, and is not treated like a criminal by everyone'!

His gratitude and magnanimity, however, were short-lived. 'Actually I am afraid that I cannot feel like one or by anything but quite ___, any only resentful of the lengths even the highest in the land are prepared to go to save their faces. If further employment depends on following similar courses, I will gladly step out.' Cunningham explained he would accept the medical board rating of 'D' despite being 'quite convinced that could get the best civilian medical advice to say there was nothing the matter, if it suited me'. In effect, William Denton Douglas Small had already done so.

Another, better-positioned gunner contacted immediately by Cunningham was General Sir Robert Hadden Haining, Vice Chief of the Imperial General Staff and Colonel-Commandant of the Royal Artillery. Churchill had appointed Haining to the position of 'Intendant-General', effectively the chief supply officer for the theatre, in May 1941.[19] Nearing 60, Haining was at the very end of his career.

Haining wrote to Cunningham on 1 December responding to an earlier note that is not preserved.[20] Haining began by answering what must have been Cunningham's request for information: 'I never heard anything, except that R: had gone to your HQ,' and went on to state 'I am astonished: and dismayed beyond words.' The identity of 'R' is unknown.

That Cunningham complained to Haining regarding the mental breakdown narrative is also clear from the latter's reply: 'I know your sanity of outlook, and that you did not subscribe to an easy victory over the Boche. You are a victim of political expediency, brought about by insane overestimation and lack of logical forecast, at home: and weak-kneed wobbling here.'

Haining next wrote on 5 December and showed a network of gunners being put into action on Cunningham's behalf.[21]

> I have written Otto [Marling Lund] a few lines – to emphasize my views – so that I hope he'll appreciate the background without too much explanation. Remember, you must not be labeled a scapegoat: you have Auck's denial: + you have his statement re: the illness. Put the straight plain talk to a paper, + let Otto see it – + Alan Brooke.

Finally, Haining noted to Cunningham that he was 'still doing the same game of seeing various people'. But the purpose of the letter was to return a copy of Cunningham's report to the CIGS on the *Crusader* plan, which Haining praised for its 'soundness'.[22]

Haining's significance went beyond his roles during 1941 and 1942, when he finally retired. He had succeeded Wavell as General Officer Commanding British Forces in Palestine and Transjordan in 1938, was a member of the Army Council in 1941 and Colonel of the Royal Artillery from 1938 until 1950. He was well situated to exercise influence behind the scenes.

But if Haining was appalled by Cunningham's situation and strove to be helpful, the most important gunner, CIGS, Alan Brooke, took a different approach. Taking command of the military on 1 December, Brooke was confronted by a rapidly expanding war, in which Cunningham's predicament did not loom large. Cunningham's report to Brooke and its cover letter have already been described. Brooke's diary noted on 7 December that he had met with the Secretary of State, presumably Secretary of State for War David Margesson, 'to put him in the picture and discuss with him advisibility of letting Cunningham down as easily as possible on his return from the Middle East, PM being include to hold up the dismissal as an example'.[23] He also noted a meeting on 12 December with Cunningham 'very depressed and hard to comfort'.[24]

Thereafter the Cunningham matter was a persistent if sporadic concern. On 1 March Brooke noted a conversation with Duncan Sandys, the Financial Secretary of the War Office, regarding Cunningham's future employment and a Parliamentary question on the matter, a 'painful interview' with Cunningham himself on 10 March, and another on 24 April with 'poor Alan Cunningham, who wishes his case judged definitely on way or another'.[25]

Whatever Brooke wished to do for 'poor Cunningham', his diary makes it clear that Churchill was the ultimate source of opposition to Cunningham's reappointment. Brooke had met with Brooke on 18 May and 'refused to consider reemployment of either Cunningham or Godwin-Austen',[26] who had resigned in January in protest over an order countermanded by Ritchie. On 27 May Brooke met with Cunningham 'to inform him of lack of success both Grigg [the new Secretary of State for War] and I had with PM as regards his future employment'.[27] Coincidentally, Brooke's next meeting that day was with Galloway, regarding his new position as Director of Staff Duties at the War Office.

After another meeting on 28 July Brooke did not mention Cunningham until October when he noted: 'I again approached Smuts and asked him to assist me with reference to Cunningham and Godwin-Austen. I that that at last we may overcome Winston's objections to employing them again.'[28] A note Brooke appended later added: 'According to him [Churchill] these officers had failed in action, had proved themselves deficient of offensive spirit, should never be employed again and could indeed consider themselves lucky they were not being made a public example of as in the case of Admiral Byng.' Cunningham's rehabilitation, however, would come later at the hands of Brooke and another old ally, Smuts.

The evidence shows Cunningham reaching out to a network of gunners who went on to make inquiries and press his case, ultimately centring on his reappointment. But before his efforts were successful, behind the scenes Cunningham was also moving through other avenues. The most notable was Parliament, where Cunningham became part of a more broad effort aimed at Churchill and the direction of the war.

Debates in Parliament, 1942

The Cunningham supersession was raised several times in Parliament. The first was on 8 January 1942 when Richard Stokes, representing Ipswich, spoke during a lengthy debate on the war situation. Clement Atlee spoke in Churchill's place, and the modest successes in the desert were balanced against unfolding collapse in the Far East. The strategy behind the allocation of British forces prior to 1942 loomed large during the debate, as it would in later historical analyses.

Stokes expressed his anger at the 'complacency with which old men of the Cabinet who have had no real experience of fighting a war, who have never indulged in the filthy business of killing – and any one who has killed a man knows it is filthy'.[29] He criticized Churchill's absence, the campaigns in Norway and Greece, and then Libya:

> Do not let anybody think for a moment that I do not recognise the terrific efforts made by all officers and men everywhere and the magnificent and brave show they put up in the various theatres of war in which they are engaged. But my anxiety is whether they are really getting a square deal. I take Libya particularly. The Prime Minister, when speaking on 11th December, backed the military spokesman in Cairo as having made a reasonable anticipation of what was going to happen and said that, on the whole, he thought he was right. But does not the House recollect that within the last few days there has been a report in the newspapers to the effect that General Cunningham, just before the attack started, said that the fight would be hazardous and that, while it might end quickly, it would be a very risky proceeding having regard to the forces which he knew would be against him. It is an astonishing thing that, after having given that warning, General Cunningham is apparently now at home ostensibly because he is sick, though I did not seem to notice any particular frailty about him when I saw him walking about the other day. The point I want to put to the House out of fairness to the soldiers in Libya is: What might anybody expect from what was said in this country about the Libya offensive?

Stokes went on to criticize Churchill's claims regarding the quantity and quality of British equipment, the release of information on those matters, and specifically questioned the 'armour and in gun-power and range' of British tanks. Stokes then turned to the situations in Hong Kong, Malaya and Singapore and mentioned specifically the relief of Air Chief Marshal Sir Robert Brooke-Popham, Commander-in-Chief of Far East Command.

The case of Brooke-Popham has curious similarities to Cunningham's. Brooke-Popham was relieved of duty on 27 December 1941 during the battle of Malaya and was replaced by Lt General Henry Pownall. His relief came after a secret letter to Churchill from Resident Minister at Singapore Duff Cooper complained that Brooke-Popham was 'very much an older man than his years warrant and sometimes seems on the verge of collapse'.[30] Cooper had stated earlier to Secretary of State for War David Margesson in October that Brooke-Popham was 'damned near gaga'.[31]

Stokes raised the issue of Cunningham again later in January, asking Margesson 'how soon it is intended to appoint Lieutenant-General Sir Alan Cunningham, recently relieved of his command in Libya, to a new post; and whether he will state the nature of that post?'[32] Margesson replied that 'Lieutenant-General Sir Alan Cunningham is at present on sick leave, and the question of his re-employment will not arise until he is once again passed fit for duty'. But Stokes pressed the matter: 'Has the Minister himself seen Sir Alan Cunningham since he came home, and is he satisfied that he has been placed in the correct medical category?' Margesson tactfully responded: 'That is not really for me to decide.' Stokes's questions regarding Cunningham came on the verge of a three-day parliamentary debate on a no confidence motion, which Churchill won.

In early February, as if to take another tack, Stokes raised Cunningham in a question to Lt Colonel Edward Grigg, Parliamentary Undersecretary for War, asking 'whether the original plans and dispositions prepared by Sir Alan Cunningham for the relief of Tobruk were carried out; and whether General Auchinleck expressed complete satisfaction with them?'[33] Grigg declined to answer but was pressed by Stokes, who complained: 'Is it not a fact that General Cunningham's anticipations of the probable course of the battle were far more accurate than those of the military spokesman in Cairo or of the Minister of Defence in London?' These comments reflected Cunningham's talking points.

Cunningham was raised twice in March, the first time by Stokes to Duncan Sandys, Financial Secretary to the War Office: 'Why an announcement was made on 25th February that Lieutenant-General Sir Alan Cunningham was in a military hospital in the South of England, as in fact he had been passed Grade A some days previously?' Sandys, Churchill's son-in-law, replied that no such official announcement had been made and that press reports had been denied. This prompted Stokes to assert:

> Arising out of that reply, is my hon. Friend aware that the Press Association said that this was an official statement, and is it not a fact that General Cunningham has never been ill and that all this unfortunate affair has been used to cover up the over-statements made in this country by the Minister of Defence about the Libyan Campaign?

Sandys did not respond.

Sir Thomas Moore also raised the issue with Sandys, asking 'what is the present position of General Sir Alan Cunningham; and when his medical advisers anticipate that this distinguished soldier will be able to return to duty?'[34] Sandys replied: 'This officer on his return to this country was examined by a medical board and classified as temporarily unfit for service. He has recently been reexamined and has now been passed as fit. There is at present no suitable appointment in which he can be employed.'

After March, as the Britain's situation deteriorated globally, in the desert and the Far East, the issue of Alan Cunningham receded. It would be raised in the House of Commons only one more time, in July, in what was its fullest airing. The larger debate surrounded a motion 'that this House, while paying tribute to the heroism and endurance of the Armed Forces of the Crown in circumstances of exceptional difficulty, has no confidence in the central direction of the war'.[35] Tobruk had fallen less than two weeks earlier.

The debate was wide-ranging and there was intense criticism of Churchill and his government's direction of the war. But it was also framed by idiosyncratic demands from Sir John Wardlaw-Milne, who had brought the motion, for the Duke of Gloucester to be appointed the commander-in-chief of the British Army. Wardlaw-Milne's comments regarding Libya were more pointed, 'an inquiry into what it is that causes us always to be behind the enemy. What is wrong with our plans, our strategy or our production which puts us into this inferior position?' He conceded that 'it may be that we have to give credit where credit is due and say that we were out-generalled' but quickly turned to the inferiority of British tanks.

The debate was muddied further by a presentation by Admiral of the Fleet Roger Keyes, who had seconded the motion of no confidence, prompting an MP to comment:

> I am rather confused at the course the Debate is taking. I understood the hon. Member for Kidderminster (Sir J. Wardlaw-Milne) to move a Vote of Censure, on the ground that the Prime Minister had interfered unduly in the direction of the war. The Seconder seems to be seconding because the Prime Minister has not sufficiently interfered in the direction of the war.

Oliver Lyttelton, by then Minister of Production, expounded at length of the numbers of qualities of British tanks and anti-tanks weapons.[36] In response to questions Lyttleton also discussed British air superiority, combined arms and motorized infantry tactics that were being employed.

But as MPs piled criticism on Churchill, throwing up his promises and failures to explain disasters, Member of Parliament for Croyden North Henry Willink turned the debate back to Libya, the details of British artillery, and then unexpectedly, the issue of Alan Cunningham:

> The speech of the Minister of Production was not fairly described by the hon. Member who spoke last. I did not get the Impression at all that my right hon. Friend was saying that everything was very satisfactory. He gave us descriptions of our armament in Libya from time to time. But five or six months ago we heard that on 24th November a general in whom we at that time had great

confidence, General Cunningham, had been replaced, or superseded, as I gathered because he felt that it was wrong to go further with that campaign at the moment.

Willink was questioned about statements in Parliament regarding Cunningham's health and responded:

> It was said that the general was suffering in health, but the reason for his supersession was, I gathered, that he was not pushing on as fast as he should. He was "under the weather" as one might put it. It looks as if a decision not to go further at that point might have been the right decision at that time.

Welsh politician Clement Davies and Liberal Party member hammered the point:

> All I know is that the appointments are under the control of the Prime Minister, under the direct control of the Prime Minister. They could not have been satisfactory. To us who know little about those things General Wavell has been held out as one of the great geniuses, but he was sacked.

> The next one was General Cunningham, and he was hailed as a great leader. A day or two afterwards came the dread news that he was suffering from a break down, although he appeared to be perfectly healthy when he arrived in this country. He was followed by the young General Ritchie. There was great praise again for him, but five days after the event the Prime Minister comes down to the House and tells us that he has been replaced and that General Auchinleck is in command.

The question of Churchill's leadership, and military appointments, dominated much of the remaining debate. Finally, Commander Robert Tatton Bower, a Conservative representing Cleveland, rose in defence of Cunningham:

> One of the things about which I frankly quarrel with the Prime Minister is this extraordinary game of musical chairs in which he indulges when Parliament gets so troublesome that he feels he has to make a change. Once you reach a certain stage in the hierarchy of this country, you never get the sack. People like my friend and colleague Sir Alan Cunningham, and General Ritchie go; they have not quite got to the rank where you are safe. Get into the higher hierarchy and you are all right.

The debate adjourned at 2.40 am. Churchill spoke the next day and the no confidence motion was defeated by an overwhelming margin. The name Alan Cunningham was not mentioned again in the House of Commons until 1946.

The four Members of Parliament who raised the issue of Cunningham were not disinterested parties. Major Richard Stokes was a graduate of the Royal Military Academy and had served with distinction in the Royal Field Artillery during the First World War. His uncle, Sir Wilfred Stokes, had invented the trench mortar that addressed a serious need for short-range weapons suitable for trench warfare. Stokes evidently knew Cunningham but the precise nature of their relationship is unknown.[37]

Sir Henry Urmston Willink had also served with the Royal Field Artillery and was much decorated during the First World War but is best remembered as Minister of Health from 1943 to 1945 and an advocate of the National Health Service. Except for the shared Royal Artillery connection, his relationship with Cunningham is also unknown. Both he and Stokes may have been part of the Royal Artillery network that Cunningham had reached out to upon his return to Britain.

The two other politicians who had raised the Cunningham issue have more attenuated connections. Lt Colonel Sir Thomas Cecil Russell Moore was a retired Royal Army Service Corps officer and, along with Commander Robert Tatton Bower, a member of the prewar Anglo-German Fellowship. Bower was famous for having yelled 'Go back to Poland!' at fellow Member of Parliament Emanuel Shinwell during a 1938 debate, at which point Shinwell crossed the floor and struck Bower in the face.

Why two MPs with prewar fascist sympathies should have spoken up for Cunningham is unclear. Moore was a Scottish MP but from a district far from the Cunningham family's base in Edinburgh. As a naval officer Tatton was close to Roger Keyes and is likely to have retained his service's consternation towards Churchill and affection for Andrew B. Cunningham, but as with Moore, he has no documented connections with Alan Cunningham. Bower however, who by then had returned to active duty, blamed Churchill and the defence establishment for the fall of Singapore.[38]

The debates in the House of Commons suggest that Cunningham had communicated with Royal Artillery officers, sharing with them specifics regarding British tanks and anti-tank artillery which were circulated in some part to counter accusations regarding Cunningham's mental state. But more importantly, Cunningham's supersession had become a political issue, along with inadequate equipment, arrayed to show that Churchill's leadership and the overall direction of the war were inadequate. These particular arguments were not enough to topple Churchill, but they contributed to both Cunningham's rehabilitation and the shaping of the debate over *Crusader* towards questions of inadequate armaments and away from command failures.

The fruits of rehabilitation and the cause of history

Cunningham's rehabilitation was pursued by his reaching out to fellow gunners, in Parliament, but also in a far more consequential venue. Cunningham's future employment was raised in the War Cabinet on 9 March with the novel suggestion that he be appointed 'chairman of a Committee to review the transport establishments of field force units'.[39] But, after being reminded that Auchinleck had 'lost confidence' in Cunningham, the cabinet 'were informed that there was no question of giving Sir A. Cunningham any further operation or field force command. The issue was whether he should be considered for further employment in an administrative role.' The issue was raised again in the War Cabinet in May and the matter was deferred.[40]

But a third meeting on 20 October was entirely different. Present at the meeting was Field Marshal Smuts, who had been approached by Brooke on matter of Cunningham, and the question was suddenly raised from the last to the first item under consideration. After the Secretary of State for War made it clear that Cunningham would only be considered for an administrative position, Smuts spoke in his defence. Smuts recalled Cunningham's 'brilliant campaign' in East Africa and claimed that at the time of his removal from command, Cunningham had not been 'physically fit'.[41] He added that while he 'was all in favour of a strict attitude being adopted towards officers who held high commands and who were proved failures in the field, he felt strongly that in Major-General Cunningham's case it would not be right to take a line which would debar him from further employment'. Churchill replied that in light of Smuts's view, he would withdraw his objections to Cunningham's future employment. The next month Cunningham was appointed Commandant of the Staff College. His exile had last less than a year. Smuts's influence had helped establish Cunningham's role in *Crusader* and, more consequentially, had restored his career thereafter.

It is not possible to say how Cunningham's communications affected perceptions of him within the military. Figures far from the nexus of military and political power like Blewitt, and serving and well-connected officers such as Wemyss, Lund or Haining, were Cunningham partisans but their larger influence on decision-making or perceptions is unclear, despite their likely influence on a few Members of Parliament. The key figure was another gunner, Brooke, at the epicentre of power, who quietly waited until the opportunity arose to put Cunningham forward again. Smuts's intervention was the key.

While he waited Cunningham pursued two other concerns. One was material, the matter of his substantive rank and thus pay and status. He had been promoted to Major General in 1937 but was given the temporary rank of Lieutenant General before *Crusader*, which he relinquished upon his relief. Cunningham pursued this question in letters to the Undersecretary of State in May and June 1942.[42] The Military Secretary to the Secretary of State, General Henry Colville Barclay Wemyss, replied on 26 June to say the matter of his appointment was still 'under active consideration'.[43] But in August Wemyss replied to another letter from Cunningham which had complained that other general including the recently relieved Neil Ritchie 'had been going about as Lt. Generals + I had been ___ immediately upon arrival'. Wemyss assured Cunningham that 'Ritchie's case is in abeyance and the letter about rank has not yet been dispatched, but I saw him to-day (in plain clothes) and I warned him of the position'.[44]

Cunningham pursed the matter of rank even after regaining a command in November 1942. He complained to Wemyss in June 1943 that other Major Generals had been promoted ahead of him: Wemyss replied apologetically, but assured Cunningham that he had discussed the matter with the Secretary of State and that his reappointment was 'our objective'.[45] Finally, on 23 October 1943 Wemyss wrote to inform Cunningham that his promotion to Lieutenant General had been approved, backdated to 23 July.[46]

Cunningham had finally regained his standing, but he was about to fight another equally important battle in the War Office, one over history.

5

The Evidence of Other Voices

For decades popular accounts of *Crusader* and the removal of Alan Cunningham have tended to rely on the same small number of secondary accounts. Overlooked evidence generated by participants on the scene provides a clearer picture of the events, including the condition of Alan Cunningham and the role of Alexander Galloway. But what were the contemporary perspectives of first-hand observers? How did these reflect the perceptions of other officers and how were these incorporated, or not, into historical narratives? Overlooked documents provide additional information regarding the story of *Crusader* and how news of Cunningham's supersession spread through military and political circles.

Tedder to Portal, 9 December 1941

Air Chief Marshal Sir Arthur Tedder, Air Commander-in-Chief of RAF Middle East, had almost been relieved in the weeks prior to *Crusader*. Unofficially, Tedder also served as Air Marshal Portal's eyes and ears in the Middle East, and throughout 1941 and 1942 he wrote his superior frank and frequently severe letters about the situation, particularly regarding the Army's leadership and its shortcomings. As the crisis of *Crusader* unfolded, Tedder went to the front with Auchinleck and observed the situation, and Cunningham, at first hand.

On 4 December Tedder gave Portal his assessment of the command change, which was[1]

> effected in the nick of time – and it was a great relief to us all that we would receive such emphatic support from home. I'm afraid I had felt very uneasy about Alan Cunningham from the beginning. Again and again he struck me as taking counsel of his fears. He seemed obsessed by the counting of heads. He gave me the impression of feeling completely at sea as regards armoured warfare & two or three times remarked to me "I wish I knew what Rommel means to do" – which

struck me as a rather strange outlook for the commander of a superior attacking force. Then when the real battle began he fluctuated between wishful optimism and the depths of pessimism. After a day or two of it "Mary" Coningham got so worried about it that he signaled asking me to come up. Shortly afterwards Cunningham himself asked Auchinleck to go up "since major decisions might be required" i.e. a general retreat. Auchinleck had an immediate tonic effect and since things seemed to be all right again proposed to come back with me the next day. I urged him to stay at least another day since I felt that Cunningham would inevitably relapse. A. stayed and Cunningham did relapse. A. discussed the affair with "Mary" (whom I had told to speak frankly) and with the B.G.S. (Galloway who is levelheaded and sound but felt of course he must be loyal to Cunningham). A. discussed it with me when he got back. He told me he had decided an immediate change in command was needed & I assured him he had my complete support.

"Mary's" comment to me in a note the following day was "the change in command has been made and the whole atmosphere has altered. The position was really becoming most serious and it was beginning to reach down to units."

Tedder's characterization of the events and Cunningham's state was repeated closely in his later book. But Tedder's recording of these impressions to his superior just a week after the events is significant: his judgement regarding Cunningham seems clear. Tedder's use of the term 'relapse' implies a medical condition, but more significant may be his description of Cunningham fluctuating 'between wishful optimism and the depths of pessimism'. This vacillation, whether clinically manic or simply inconsistent, speaks to Cunningham's comportment, which, according to Coningham, had begun to be known at the headquarters level where it undermined confidence in command. Also important is the fact that Auchinleck had discussed the matter privately with Coningham and especially Galloway.

Theron to Smuts, 18 December 1941

Major General Frank Theron was the General Officer, Administration to the Union Defense Force's Middle East Force, appointed by Prime Minister Jan Smuts as liaison to the British Army.[2] On 18 December 1941 – less than a month after Cunningham's supersession – Theron reported on *Crusader* to Smuts on a tour of the battlefield and the status of South African units, with particular emphasis on the destruction of the 5th South African Infantry Brigade. But he also included the following information:[3]

> Sandy Galloway has succeeded Ritchie here as D.C.G.S, and has been promoted Major General: I am sorry to say he and 1st Division did not hit it off. I have had a preliminary talk with him, pointed out their difficulties, and we are dining together soon to discuss matters further when I hope to smooth out misunderstandings which have obviously arisen. He tells me that, when Rommel's diversion column was reported in the rear of our forces, Cunningham almost lost his head and wanted to retire at once, and he had the greatest difficulty in keeping him steady until C.-in-C. arrived, who immediately released Cunningham from his command and put in Neil Ritchie. It is extraordinary that Cunningham should have reacted in this way, and I remember the apprehension by the Ou Baas 5000 miles away, when discussing the object of the raid, he immediately sized it up as a diversion, conceived with the intention of stampeding us. Ritchie is doing extremely well and his calm and balanced judgment and attractively friendly manner have a wholesome effect on the army, and we feel that he is going to be a great success: George Brink likes him and D.P. speaks in terms of the highest praise of his contact with him.

Theron's report to the 'Ou baas' ('old boss', a popular nickname for Smuts) is extremely informative since it confirms that Galloway was a source for negative information regarding Cunningham and that Galloway had a difficult relationship with South African forces, including divisional commander Major General George Brink.

Lyttleton to Margesson, 21 December 1941

Minister of State for the Middle East Oliver Lyttleton had remained in Cairo while Auchinleck and Shearer flew to Advanced Headquarters. On 21 December he wrote to Secretary of State for War David Margesson about the affair:[4]

> I sh[?] two very curious [?]. The first was by far the most [?]. This was on the first Sunday after the battle had begun it would be the 23rd Nov. I had a feeling in by bones at the GHQ conference on the night of the 22nd that something was developing and sure enough on the 23rd about 10:30 we heard [??] the hun recaptured Sidi Rezegh. Well this was nothing much in [?] I went back to my office [?] piano had not more. At about 12 the Auck put his head around my door and said I was going to the Western Desert Cunningham wants me to make a decision. We talked it over but I could only see one [?] course [?] were with the decision must be whether to go on or go back Cunningham's reputation and as well his appearance and [?] all gave me the impression that he was in [?]. Therefore it [???] our losses in tanks and MT were so far the [?] were [???]

or else C had lost his nerve or whatever you like to call it. Either alternative appeared faulty [?]; indeed it would have been an withdrawal situation if I had not known how the Auck was sound as a bell. We exchanged few words about it – it was unnecessary because he said if you are right and that is the decision I was called on to make this is only one answer – to go on. ([?] an the following conversation took place in a rather tense moment at GHQ. The Auch – "Well, Oliver if I may call you in private by your Christian name – if we can't retake Sidi Rezegh well damn it I must be vulgar you can kiss my –." O.L. "Faced by this horrible dilemma I prefer that S.R. should be retaken." This [???])

The Auck came down from the Desert I think it was Tuesday evening that would be Nov 25th. I actually saw Tedder first who said "I am sorry the Auck is coming back" and [???] "Alan is very tired." I said You mean he has lost his grip. Tedder Well yes. When I saw the Auck he said he was [?] by Alan talking about his flanks [?] his rail head. I [??] he had already made up his mind to replace him but was uncertain whether to do it right away or to wait for a few days. I said I though it should be done at once and I could see that it was what he wanted to hear.

It probably knowing of political repercussions [??] so the and [?] that Alan had recovered his poise – of course his personal courage and energy were never in doubt but the moment I came for immediate replacement he said he thought that was his only [?] to do and I am pretty sure that short of opposition from me he would have done it the next day at the latest. He is a proud man.

Lyttleton shows that both Auchinleck and Tedder believed Cunningham was in distress. His exchange with Tedder – 'Alan is very tired. I said You mean he has lost his grip. Tedder said Well yes' – shows also what might be called strategic understatement. This cultural trait, stereotypically British, may here be read as a rhetorical strategy intended to elicit deeper clarification. Lyttleton saw through Tedder's initial obscurity and grasped the problem, at least in a military if not clinical sense. It also raises the question of what and how others throughout this affair were trying to communicate through sometimes vague and usually stolid language, and how understated messages were received.

Another important aspect of Lyttleton's note is that his description tracks almost precisely with that presented decades later in his memoir (see below). Finally, it shows that information about the incident and, in this case by implication, regarding Cunningham's condition, was transmitted to political authorities besides Churchill in London immediately following the affair. Ironically, Margesson's own fate was to be sacked in February 1942 after the fall of Singapore. No one, not even a long-time Tory whip and Churchill ally, was indispensable.

The Miller Report, 1942

Charles Miller was Deputy Adjutant and Quartermaster General of the 8th Army. In a report in his archive probably dating to 1942, on administrative aspects of desert campaigning in 1940–2, Miller noted:[5]

> At the height of the Crusader battle at Sidi Rezzeg + the Tank Brigades milling around the desert north of the wire Army HQ was at Madaleina. The Army Commander called me into his caravan one early morning + told me he though the information such that I ought to consider the possibility of a retreat. Some time later Gen Auchinleck arrived. He saw me alone and asked me what I thought of the situation – I replied that as far as the supply position was concerned if the battle continue for another 48 hours my information was that Rommel's supplied would be 'out' + he would have to withdraw whereas we were able to keep our forces going for another week. He said he agree, said no more + left me. That afternoon Neil Ritchie flew in. The battle continued and a day or so later Rommel was in retreat to behind Aghielah.

Miller's account compresses the chronology of events – Ritchie arrived the day after Auchinleck left 8th Army headquarters – but confirms Eve Curie's 1943 account regarding Auchinleck's assessment of Rommel's logistics. More importantly, Miller confirms that Cunningham was contemplating some sort of withdrawal.

The Cunningham Letter, 1943

Cunningham himself provided one additional clue to *Crusader*. In November 1943 Cunningham, then GOC in Northern Ireland, wrote to his solicitor in Edinburgh and instructed that it be added to a file labelled CRUSADER. It reads:[6]

> A story told by Mrs John Shearer, wife of John Shearer, brigadier Intelligence Cairo during the period I was in command of, and later left, 8th Army.
>
> "Shearer came down to see me at my H.Q. bringing with him some information which would show me "how to win the battle." I refused to look at it. He went back and told Auchinleck who then came down to see me. The later found me "quivering and quaking" and removed me."
>
> This story, libelous in the extreme, has no relation what-ever to fact.
>
> Shearer did not come down to see me until after Auchinleck had left.

Auchinleck did not come down to see me until I myself, [???] tanks were not while to meet the Germans on equal terms, and finding my tank strength was below theirs, felt I should ask him to come down so that I could tell him the true situation. He came at my request. The communiqués and press directions issued by Shearer in Cairo were optimistic far and above what I knew the facts and what I would have authorized. As soon as they came to my notice they formed an additional reason why I wished Auchinleck to come down. Auchinleck came down and spent three days at my H.Q. (Incidentally although he secretly discussed the situation constantly with my B.G. S. and even told him he was going to remove me, he never made any suggestion of this to me.)

After Auchinleck had gone, John Shearer arrived. Auchinleck had made some suggestions that he (Shearer) should stay at my H.Q. It was at the time when Rommels penetration into Egypt had had some success, and as it appeared likely at that time that my H.Q. would have to move back, I told Shearer that I did not want extra people there. He made no suggestion that he had special information.

Shearer has now been proved as what I always knew he was, a wishful thinker. All his intelligence, sometimes from the most doubtful sources, e.g. Rommel chauffeur, was interpreted as what he would like it to appear. This can be confirmed by several commanders who were in the Western Desert before I was.

The story mentioned above was told me Mrs Patsie Lyon – daughter of Lady Hambro. I had it direct from Mrs Lyon within a few days of her hearing it. She can vouch for it in every particular, and indeed was even prepared to go to court and swear to it. I was most reluctant to involve her and hence took no action.

In respect of the suggestion that when Auchinleck came down he found the 8th Army on the defensive, this too has no foundation in fact what-ever. The offensive would through on my plan and was never halted.

My uncertainty lay in the doubt whether we could afford the losses, which I have indicated were great. This was a question I was not in a position to answer myself.

I did not know when this offensive started that the Germans had mounted a 50mm. gun in their Mk III tanks, nor that they had added extra armor. Neither did Willoughby Norrie. Yet War Office (Weeks) told me that they had heard this first from M.E. in October!

If ever this whole situation is to be elucidated, this very illuminating fact should not be forgotten.

The letter represents the last documented time Cunningham responded directly to the question of his mental state during *Crusader*, albeit in the form of addressing rumours. The run-on language of the note, and the tone that alternates between the defensive and the accusatory, if not paranoid, reflects, if nothing else, Cunningham's mental state when retrospectively addressing the question of his condition in November 1941.

It also provides a few additional details. Shearer was at 8th Army Advanced Headquarters with Auchinleck and Tedder, observed Cunningham first hand and with others brought that information back to Cairo.[7] Shearer's wife Ann was one of Auchinleck's private secretaries (at least by 1942) and conceivably had access to observations regarding Cunningham through her husband and Auchinleck. But there is also later evidence that Cunningham had objected to Shearer's intelligence estimates for *Crusader*.[8] How this attitude influenced the 1943 letter, or grew subsequently, is unknown, but Shearer's dismissal in February 1942, precisely on the issue of inaccurate intelligence assessments related to German armour, may have influenced Cunningham's later account.[9] And, confusingly, Cunningham's letter asserted that Shearer had come after Auchinleck's departure in order to offer suggestions. He had in fact come with Auchinleck and may have stayed behind until Ritchie and Smith arrived the next day.

Third, in 1943 Cunningham remained not only stung by his supersession but was increasingly concerned about his legacy and the writing of history. This concern would only grow during 1944 with the appearance of a War Office pamphlet on the campaign. Despite being far from the desert Cunningham continued to collect documents and potential witnesses to make his case. Ironically, the individual he named in the letter, Patricia Hambro, was the widow of an officer killed on 25 November 1941, Lt John Scott Limnel Lyon. Had Cunningham ever called upon 'Lady Patsie', her testimony may not have been what he expected.

Perhaps most significantly, Cunningham's account indicates that rumours regarding his state and the events in the desert were circulating in Cairo shortly after his supersession, giving second-hand confirmation to Theron's account. This is not surprising, given the large numbers of military personnel in Cairo and, as importantly, the complex social setting of headquarters, bases, hotels, clubs and wives. Many accounts show how rumours, innuendoes and accusations circulated freely in Cairo at all levels.[10]

Finally, and most importantly, Cunningham confirms Tedder's account that Galloway had consulted privately with Auchinleck during the latter's visit to 8th Army headquarters. As such, it lends greater weight to Theron's letter to Smuts, in which he stated that Galloway had told him in Cairo shortly after the events that Cunningham had 'almost lost his head'. This would only be implied in Francis de Guingand's 1947 book and fully articulated by Galloway himself only in 1968.

The Galloway accounts, 1968

Alexander Galloway's archive is small but includes important items written during the 1960s that contribute to the discussion of *Crusader*.[11] Most important is a 1968 letter to his former War Office colleague and fellow Cameronian Eric Sixsmith, commenting on a draft chapter from the latter's book *British Generalship in the Twentieth Century*.[12] In it Galloway presents his account of the events of November 1941. It is reproduced here in full:[13]

> Comments on the Draft Chapter on the Western Desert battle CRUSADER – vide Eric Sixsmith book 'Generalship XXth Century (British)
> Comments on your Draft which you sent to me dated 12th Jan. '68
>
> Page 1
>
> 1. I don't think this is fair on Wavell. If his estimate was the same as that of the High Command (Nazi) he should be praised for it. And how on earth was he to know the characteristics of a man (Rommel) whom he had never seen: and who had only recently arrived: and had not so far given any evidence of opportunism other than the fact of his Nationality and such information as there was available concerning his performance in previous World War II Campaigns in Europe? Hindsight should not be so penetrating as to expect a C.-in-C. (let alone a British C.-in-C., in Egypt, at the early stages of a War) to have the vision of the Almighty.
>
> 2. What is a failure? "CRUSADER" was the name given to a Task which became a battle. The Task given to the VIII Army was:–
> (a) To relieve TOBRUK
> (b) To drive Rommel (and his Army of course) out of CYRENAICA.
> (I haven't the map in front of me.)
> This was done. What is a failure? I think you want to be perfectly clear about this and separate this phase of the campaign from what follows afterwards. I have no notes but my memory is not yet gone. On 18th November the advance of CRUSADER started. I think I left VIII Army on or about 14th December. By then both (a) and (b) Tasks had been achieved and more or less cleared up. And Neil Ritchie was beginning to "shoot his mouth off" about Rommel "sticking his neck out" etc. etc.!! We were just beginning to be trans. Atlantic [handwritten]
>
> Page 1 reverse
>
> Having reported to G.H.Q and formed it in September with Charles Miller (13/18 H.) (now my best friend).

Page 2

The battle was won before he arrived. If an Army goes into battle and fulfills both its tasks given it in written directive, is it a victory or a failure?

I have one further matter in this context of CRUSADER to tell you. About the second week of December when it was clear that the Germans/Italians were clearing out, we had one complete (guards) Brigade Group intact and not yet used AT ALL. After working things out with Charles Miller (A.Q.) and the A.O.C., all three of us tried hard to get Ritchie to agree to let this reserve loose toward Benghazi, (in close imitation of O'Connor). The Germans had withdrawn every single gun from Benghazi and packed all they had got to the front. All our information was they were in a really bad way and could not withstand much in the way of an appearance of fresh troops behind them. Mobile, "supplied" and with ammunition and air support. Ritchie refused to do it: against the advice of all three of us, including Conyngham (A.O.C.) who was not in the habit of giving his air support to doubtful frolics. Remember that (I think) Ritchie had previously commanded a Battalion only and had never had to make decisions of this sort: I am certain – forgetting hindsight – that had this happened we would have had an 80% chance of knocking out the Panzer Army for months. We would NOT have caught Rommel. I bear no resentment. But what are Army Commanders there for if not to take such decisions? We stood to loose practically nothing and the prize was twenty times as great as the Italian Comic Opera. Dick O'Connor was superb. But mind you, he did not have to deal with Rommel. I cannot describe to you how hopelessly futile the Italians were in 1940. I/

Page 2 reverse

This of course means that the scales overall were heavily weighted in favour of the Germans. No British formations had fought this kind of battle for hundreds of years. We were just beginning to learn how to do it and what we needed to do it with, besides guts which we had. The more highly complex modern life, including war, becomes, the more must professional experts handle what has to be handled. Which means that those who intend to influence affairs amongst nations must be qualified and prepared to take part – even in going to war. Lesson after lesson after lesson – up to utter sickness – points to the opposite as far as G.B. has been concerns. Politicians render early success in big wars impossible: they start interfering and thus prolong the agony.

Fortunately that is over now for Grand Mother Britain. So why bother to write your book!!

Page 3

I tell you all of this, because the facts of Crusader have been lost in the bright light of Monty's P.R. exercise after he got to Egypt. I have told him so: Often! Lost in the arguments about tanks and leadership and God knows what else. Monty for example laid great comment on the fact that when he got to Alamein he found Army and R.A.F separated etc. etc. I told him that at CRUSADER we had one joint operations and intelligence set-up. Always they worked together. I saw Conyngham every day by walking 150 yards 2 or 3 times a day for 3 months. The Army Commander saw him as often as he wished. I only quote this to assure you that VIII Army was good: and did its stuff against very great odds i.e. senior leadership (i.e. lack of knowledge and "flair" AND EXPERIENCE) and a Prime Minister who still thought he was on a horse at Omdurman. But that is Great Britain at war!! One has to experience it to believe it.

3. Tanks, Guns, Armour, training and actual battle experience. I cannot honestly argue about tanks and armour in that and subsequent battles. As a soldier you will now perfectly well that, experience (4 German campaigns big and little, including one in the desert); confidence in one's tanks and guns; absolute affection for and utter belief in one's leader; count for a great deal amongst soldiers and junior leaders when, before going into battle, they have to clear their mind regarding a possible sentence of death (c.f. Dr. Johnstone). All I can tell you is that the Crusader tank was fast, not well armoured, badly under-gunned, and UN-reliable. That are FACTS. I don't care about who wrote WROTE what e.g./

Page 4

e.g. all I know about Liddal-Hart [sic] is that he made a profit on his books, owned a Rolls-Royce and sent his son to Eton! The Honeys were very light, fast, reliable, really under-gunned and very manoeuverable [sic]. The troops liked them. Troops have to fight battles. And remember that the VIII Army was facing its first battle, as an Army, against all that we knew of Rommel and his Panzers. And remember that the Commander elect of the 30th Corps (which included the Armour, other than Infantry Tanks (13 Corps) was Pope Lt. Gen.: killed the day after his arrival from U.K. to take command. He was THE chosen Commander – a R.T.R. Lt. Gen. who I suppose knew what to do and how to do it. He and Hugh Russell (ex Brigade Commander in 7 Armoured Division under O'Connor) were killed when their aircraft crashed on take-off when they were flying up to VIII Army Headquarters for a vital conference. Willoughby-Norrie took over. He came out with 1 Armoured Division and as the Division were still assembling he was given 30th Corps. I will never know how good he was. He played polo and has been Governor General of New Zealand since the war. When you consider these facts you may wish to use your imagination and think what all this meant to a Commander of a newly formed Army, about to take on the World's greatest Tank Army Commander …….. and remember that the main Infantry part of the 30 Corps was the 1ˢᵗ South African Division which had recently (a matter of weeks) appeared from Somaliland or somewhere. They knew nothing of the desert which is an awesome place to learn to live in: let alone manoeuvre and fight in. And the Division was supplied with M.T. of all sorts and had to train themselves to move <u>AT ALL</u>. <u>THEY KNEW NOTHING</u>. And compared with Australians, N.Z., and Canadians/

Page 5

Canadians they were and are <u>brittle</u>. These factors caused the Auk., under cruel pressure and insulting cables from the Prime Minister, to ask for several more weeks in which to bring this important and crucial Division up to the mark. The result believe it or not was a few days which resulted in our moving out to battle on 18ᵗʰ November instead of about the 15ᵗʰ November. Can you beat that?

I love <u>Auchinleck</u> [hand underlined three times] and admire him more than I can say. If he had had his way, then time would have been taken: the Germans would probably have committed to attacking Tobruk; and the plan would have been much easier and possibly more straight forward. At least the main objective would have been clear. As it was, the VIII Army, an ad hoc formation of experienced and inexperienced formations, without any overall battle experience as such moved out into the blue and gave battle: one of the hardest things to do. In World War I Jellicoe never did it once. And his fleet was enormous and his battle-cruiser leader was not killed on his way to take command of his Squadron at sea – as Dolly Pope was on land, his first morning in the Middle East. Think of these things, c.f. "Out into the pale moonlight rode the six hundred"……..
    Skit: "Forward" cried Drury Lowe,
        "I can't see any foe,"
        "Goodness knows where you'll go"…….
        "Out into the pale moonlight"…….. etc.
        "Whilst 'fellahs' wondered!"
        (You can say that again)

I remember my father reading this out of pictorial, when I was eight (crossed out and 7 handwritten) (S.A. War) [handwritten]

Page 5 reverse

I was in U.K. when Monty went out. I saw him in Reigate before he left, at his request: and told him that the first thing he had to do in my view was to organise his H.Q. so that he could fight a modern battle: and not one on the Somme. Ask him!

<u>One</u> of the reasons why Rommel was defeated was distance from base. Philip Neame and Neil Ritchie were defeated 1000 (?) [crossed out, 500 handwritten] miles from their base, strung out, exhausted and mechanically in need of great care and attention.

I cannot understand why historians do not comment on what Moses would have done. After all he was in a Desert. Why only refer to Wellington, Marshal Saxe, Napoleon and Liddal-Hart [sic]? Does NO ONE yet understand how the British go to war?

Page 6

4. I don't know about 10th Corps. I have referred to 30th Corps which was the formation on 18th November, 1941. That 1st South African Division was present was not of course solely because of its A.T. Guns. Politics entered into the selection of Divisions (Dominion) as indeed it did in all else – both before and after Crusader. Other comments: –

> (i) Churchill from 'X'000 miles away dominated the scene and should not have done: and did not do so under Monty.
> (ii) I have said enough about Italians and R.N. O'Connor. It was spectacular, but quite different: and after the first and second phases, mainly a huge admin. problem.
> (iii) By the time Monty took over, the Army had already halted Rommel, defeated him, and learned what to do and HOW TO DO IT. What is "blood, sweat, and tears" if it isn't learning the hard way. In 1938 & 9 the R.T.R. were accusing the Cavalry of only being able to use polo ponies and sticks. The Cavalry referred to the R.T.R. as garage mechanics. Both trained their Commanders with green and yellow flags 2/6 each, representing Army Groups, etc. !!!

5. <u>The Actual Battle</u> (Crusader)
I don't differ from what you have written. I have said enough to show you that although Charles Miller and I and VIII Army Headquarters Staff and Corps Staff organized the Army, planned its assembly and movement to suit the plan and delivered it correctly, and with "Surprise" at the appointed hour, many were apprehensive of what would happen when we/

Page 6 reverse

I flew up in a Lysander + R.V.? (?) with him in the forward desert. We knew that we had to hang on: resume the action, with more weight on 13 Corps + get on with it. Nothing else. Quite simple really!! [handwritten]

Page 7

we advanced into the blue – a queer sort of initiative if you eliminate the Tobruk element. No one was certain as to how the 30th Corps part of it would work out – a new Commander (Norrie) just out – a change of plan – and the 1ˢᵗ South African Division, by golly – no wonder we were uncertain. As to my part in it i.e. in the crisis or whatever you want to call it. I have a lot of sympathy for Cunningham (who after all was not his brother). He didn't really know the VIII Army except the South African Division. They didn't know him. Charles Miller and I had never heard of him! Etc. etc. I don't think he had any real knowledge of the high command of Armour, separate from or together with Infantry formations. He knew artillery, being a gunner. But even so, he didn't seem to support the conviction that the battle, even in the desert, should not get beyond the switching support of ALL the main Artillery. Anyhow he was sick i.e. he wasn't <u>NOT</u> sick. We didn't know that of course.

<u>Also</u> since communications play a great part in life (and death), be it known that the new VIII Army had as its Signal Unit South African signals and some others – Yes. I (think) can't remember. <u>Enthusiastic amateurs</u>. (Great Britain goes to war). There was only time to get them harnessed up so to speak and <u>none</u> to get them really acclimatised. Enthusiasm cannot replace every one of the other necessities i.e. campaign experience. Yet what could we do? I cannot get out of my mind:–

"Out into the moonlight rode the 600." etc.
Comment:– There has to be a first time.
As to the real crisis i.e. that of Commander and his orders, it wasn't all that difficult, 'though very awkward. I knew what Godwin-Austen –Comd 13 Corps thought and felt because I had seen him – (see comment sideline). I knew pretty/

Page 7 reverse

Tedders book is incorrect. The A.O.C. did <u>NOT</u> contact the Army. I did – Conyngham may of course have spoken to Tedder. That was agreed between us.

Page 8

Pretty well what was going on in 30th Corps, Norrie had nothing to do as the things had got somewhat beyond him – his facilities for <u>exercising</u> his command. The fight was divisionalized. i.e. "a soldiers battle almost." That was the critical time really. You can imagine it! But the main thing was clear. We couldn't move except locally, sideways, upwards, forwards but <u>NOT</u> backwards. We could only remain and feel that things would sort themselves out as indeed they did: and do our best to help by keeping the F.M.C.'s working and helping to R.V. various Brigades and formations as they came onto the scene: or re-appeared.

Therefore, when Cunningham said "Lets get outa here" (U.S.A.) it was only necessary to say: not only is this wrong and not the answer, but simply isn't possible. At the moment no such orders would or could take effect. (Terrific!!) It was then that I consulted A.O.C. and he agreed to help by alerting Air C.-in-C. (Tedder) of what I was going to do. I cannot, strangely enough

<u>now</u> remember whether or not I told Cunningham what I was going to do. I think I must have obtained his permission. I would have done it in any case. The rest you know. <u>Except</u>: that when Auk. arrived, he, Cunningham and I held our meeting in <u>my</u> caravan (i.e. a three ton lorry in these days). I was the only one present in the whole Army – while the two of them had it out. The Auk. then re-wrote his directions in pen and ink and read it out to Cunningham. Cunningham then went back to his own caravan and I was left with the Auk. He took me out of the caravan and walked about holding my arm and said "Now, if this doesn't work I will do something about it. You must, repeat <u>MUST</u> let me know at once." He then said (to comfort me I think) that never would he forget what I had had to do: and done. We then discussed (very/

Page 8 reverse

You mustn't laugh! [penciled line and arrow] read M's letter.

Page 9

(very shortly) what to do it something had to be done. He asked about who locally should do it. I said no-one in front of Army H.Q. because of the battle going on and their ESSENTIAL presence, e.g. Godwin, Harding, etc. He then mentioned Ritchie: Would I serve under him, "Yes, of course." "Would I [double underlined by hand] do it" I would if ordered. But if that had to be (and I was in the overall picture as much as anyone living and more that Rommel it appears!) then I would only say yes to his (Auk's) question if someone from U.K. were cabled for at once. So then he said that if anyone came from locally (Egypt) it would be Neil and that would only be for a week or two. He accepted the advice re getting someone from Europe. He never took it. [handwritten]

    I can never forget this: <u>or the Auk</u>. It is or should be one of the smaller corner stones in our history. No one has ever asked me about it. You can put these actual pages in the Regd. Museum if you wish. All I that I have told you is true. Why should I embellish it? The Auk. knows it all. And some of the performance is already in print.

    What is loyalty?
    May I suggest that the two questions:–
    1. "What is failure?"
    2. 'What is loyalty?'

Can give you much food for thought. <u>Much</u> more important for our future generations including Prime Ministers, Angels and Ministers of Grace than stating that some armoured Brigade was sent to the wrong place and fell over a precipice, 27 years ago.
    There/

Page 9 reverse

Leave it to the Oil Companies!

Page 10

There is no point in discussing historical happenings of long ago in the context to the Middle East any more than commenting on the decisions regarding Honours and Awards in the Congo by Mobutu. But some things are ageless. And when the present tyrrany [sic] is over past, why then the future young will read your book and may be helped by learning something from it. But NOT, my dear Eric, from the movements and orders true or false, to some fighting unit in a desert.

So far is it all removed now, that one is tempted to say:–

What the hell! But that's not right either.

"Know thine enemy" is another one. In the desert that didn't only apply to Rommel. It applied in a way to political interference from U.K. …….

and sometimes to one's own self.

I left the desert after Tobruk was relieved and we were kicking the German Panzer Army OUT. I was at G.H.Q. for a time and in April flew to U.S.A. to fix various supply questions for the Western Desert Army – another story. BUT [double underlined by hand] I know nothing of what happened after about January/February, 1942 and was not there in the sense that I cannot comment on your account which is doubtless fair enough.

Never please think that because I emphasize that Dick O'Connor had a completely different problem, his performance was not perfect. You should have seen him. Supreme control coupled with modesty and self elimination except as regards his presences always at the place that mattered, made the Saga of 1940 in the desert.

The VIII Army Crusader Headquarters picture was scarsely [sic] that.

A.G.

Page 11

P.S. GREECE

Be careful about this. Jumbo Wilson [F.M. Sir Henry Wilson, I was his Chief of Staff.] was grand. We never had a hope. If we had had a Panzer Division and 5000 aircraft we would have had to come out of Greece, An entire national army packed it up, poor things, and we had to retreat and get out or go in the bag. That is simple enough. Jumbo was in complete control all the time, except the Germans who were in even greater control.

I was last out of Gallipoli (except for the R.N.R. Sub. Lt.) from Cape Helles at 0400 hrs. 9th January 1916. AND last up the side of a Cruiser (following dear old Bernard Freyberg) when we left Greece – World War II – date forgotten.

> I may yet write a book – "Campaigners Grave and Gay II"??
>
> A.G.
>
> NOTE: The figure '8' on the Desert Medal can only be worn by those who were there from 23rd October – onwards. At Chequers I asked Winston WHY? He said, "You must ask General Montgomery." When I asked Monty afterwards, he said: the Prime Minister did it. Ask him. We advised the Monarch!! c.f. the House of Commons – Question Time!

Galloway's account confirms and amplifies those that had appeared over the prior two decades, specifically de Guingand, Connell and Tedder and, more pointedly, Cunningham's 1943 account to his solicitor. Cunningham did indeed have something like a breakdown; Galloway had indeed committed insubordination by contacting Auchinleck and preventing a withdrawal; and he had conferred privately with Auchinleck about the possibility of taking command. While precise details remain difficult to reconstruct, Galloway confirms the narrative of a Cunningham breakdown and not Cunningham's own, which became that of the British Official History, Auchinleck's 'loss of confidence'.

It is not known whether Galloway and Cunningham ever had contact after *Crusader*. Some interaction might have been expected when Galloway was at the War Office as Director of Staff Duties or even after the war when both were political soldiers (Galloway in Malaya and Austria, Cunningham in Palestine). Both provided comments during the writing of the Official History in the early 1950s but neither wrote a memoir or commented publicly on *Crusader* or the Desert War (with small and specific exceptions in Galloway's case). But while Galloway appears to have put the matter almost entirely aside after 1941, the same cannot be said for Cunningham.

The Ritchie interview, 1984

Cunningham was relieved on 26 November 1941 by Neil Ritchie, who arrived at the 8th Army's Advanced Headquarters with Arthur Smith. Ritchie's testimony must therefore be regarded as being from a participant in the drama. In an interview recorded in 1984 with his nephew Alastair, Ritchie describes the supersession in this way:[14]

> Q- When you took over from Cunningham Auchinleck didn't dismiss Cunningham personally
>
> A- He didn't no, he dismissed him by letter, which letter was taken up and handed over to Cunningham by Arthur Smith. You see we went up to the

The Evidence of Other Voices

Western Desert to the headquarters of the 8th army and when I say we this consisted of Arthur Smith and myself. Auchinleck had intended, I don't know at least I think I told you this before, Auchinleck had intended that I should go up by myself and walk and say to Cunningham look here you go away I'm taking over from you but Arthur Smith said look that's a pretty sick thing to ask Neil to do that after all he is junior to Cunningham and the rest of it and so he decided to come up with me Arthur did and I think that is where he was such a help because I would have found it quite an impossible situation but Arthur came up and he delivered the knockout blow to Cunningham

Q- And did Cunningham take it badly

A- Yes

Q- He didn't realize he was sick

A- He didn't realize he was sick no, he took it very badly, and he never got over it at all

A- Mind you he was he was very sick there's no doubt about that his nerves had completely gone

Q- Would his chief of staff really would be running the thing, his BGS

A- Well, I think so, well, Sandy, I think so because Sandy was an absolute rock, splendid fellow.

Ritchie's comments were made when he was eighty-seven years old but have obvious value. He had observed Cunningham at the height of the *Crusader* battle and with Smith had administered the final blow to Cunningham's command of the 8th Army. The framing of the questions to Ritchie regarding whether Cunningham 'realized he was sick' echoes Arthur Smith and later history writing. But the fact that Ritchie – who was also to be superseded by Auchinleck – never wrote a memoir or commented on the Desert War in any way until long after the debates over history were concluded (in contrast with de Guingand or Tedder) – gives his statement particular gravity.

The question of Cunningham's mental state

Contemporary accounts and Cunningham handwriting evidence suggest he was under enormous strain by 25 November. The medical report, orchestrated by Andrew B. Cunningham, cannot be taken at face value due to Dr Small's conflict of interest with the Cunningham family. Galloway's comments to Sixsmith and the Ritchie interview, although presented with the benefit of hindsight, were from two participants who had been closest to the affair. Other senior officers had observed Cunningham's reaction to the stress of *Crusader* and regarded it a threat to the operation's success.

There are later data that suggest that Cunningham was prone to stress. During the research and writing of the South African Official History the lead South African historian, John A.I. Agar-Hamilton, sent British historian Basil H. Liddell Hart a draft chapter on *Crusader*. Liddell Hart's notes on the manuscript (dated 6 August 1954) included the comment that 'Cunningham's firmness in a crisis had been doubted even during his period as an A.A. division commander at home during the first part of the war. (It might be worth referring to Pile.)'[15]

Liddell-Hart went even further to Brigadier Harry B. Latham, head of the Historical Section at the Cabinet Office saying, 'Tim Pile expressed the same view to me when Alan Cunningham was appointed shortly before "Crusader." Cunningham had been one of his A.A. divisional commanders, and even in that relatively easy position he left doubts about his steadiness under strain. I understood at the time that Alan Brooke was his chief backer.'[16] Unfortunately, there is no information in Frederick Alfred Pile's documents, including his uniquely voluminous correspondence with Liddell Hart, which clarify the comments regarding Cunningham.

Another letter from Agar-Hamilton, this time to Latham, also implied Cunningham did not react well to stress:[17]

> I know that Cunningham was nervy and testy in East Africa, and the evidence of a South African Liaison Officer is that 'he got ants' during the opening moves of Crusader. He had been bundled off by 13th Corps H.Q. when the flap began, and I have a sort of feeling that the Auk's impassivity in time of danger was the sort of thing which would drive a highly-strung commander to near breaking-point –perhaps 'off his rocker'.

This letter, however, does not appear in Latham's file of official correspondence, which was heavily sanitized.

One final piece of indirect evidence from long after the fact has a bearing on the general question of Cunningham's health in 1941, from the memoir of James Marshall-Cornwall, a brilliant linguist, gunner, and fellow subaltern of Cunningham's in a Royal Horse Artillery brigade in Edinburgh in 1907. By 1941, after a fascinating and diverse career, Marshall-Cornwall was made General Officer in Command British Troops in Egypt, an establishment that had assumed administrative functions in the rear of the theatre. In August Smuts had brought Cunningham to Cairo to meet Auchinleck regarding command of the 8th Army and he had stayed with Marshall-Cornwall:[18]

> Cunningham was an old friend of mine. He was three weeks older than me, and we had served as fellow- subalterns in the same field artillery brigade between 1907 and 1910. When he arrived in Cairo he stayed with me for three days while we found a suitable lodging for him. As we finished dinner on the first evening he suddenly collapsed, his head falling on the table in front of him. With the help of my two ADCs we got him to bed after undressing him. When I turned his light out he was fast asleep. The next morning he was perfectly normal again. His collapse was doubtless due to the mental and physical strain of his East African campaign.

Marshall-Cornwall's memoir was published in 1984 when he was ninety-seven years old, but by his own account he was tremendously active until that time. There is no reason to doubt his description of Cunningham's dinnertime 'neurasthenic' episode, only to assess its significance. Cunningham's active involvement in the East African campaign had lasted from October 1940 through May 1941. By the time Cunningham met Marshall-Cornwall, he had not seen combat for at least two months. That he should have been suddenly overcome by fatigue is perhaps understandable, but the timing was inauspicious both for him and his host, and suggests a susceptibility to stress and overwork that could manifest in unfortunate ways.

Given the available evidence, we may conclude that Cunningham was sufficiently rattled by the events of *Crusader* to exhibit behaviour or demeanour sufficient for the Auchinleck to lose confidence (and to be obvious to Galloway and Tedder). Whether this loss of 'phlegm' – the external projection of imperturbability in Lord Moran's words – constituted a clinical breakdown in the modern sense, or even according to the standards of British military psychiatry in the early Second World War, cannot be determined. But the episode would have appeared out of character and inappropriate to the situation, particularly given the behavioural parameters of Cunningham's class and command responsibilities. This manifestation of 'exhaustion', which to key observers and readers of reports would have seemed very much like the 'shell shock' they had all witnessed during the First World War, was disqualifying in an army commander.

What seems likely is that Cunningham had been promoted beyond his level of competence, had overworked himself, had exhibited signs of physical strain and had stopped smoking, was confronted by shocking battlefield reverses, and had almost been killed in his plane as the battlefield situation literally collapsed around him. The result, in contrast with his earlier breezy overconfidence, was a 'collapse-like' state of nervous indecision and irritability that, at the very least, did not project the focus and determination required to lead the 8th Army, and which stood out not simply in the context of his command position but in terms of his professional and social class. His position of command did not permit him to be returned to the battlefield after a short rest. But, like many soldiers removed from the line, Cunningham quickly recovered and was able to regain focus, which he directed at the questions of his reputation and the writing of history.

6

History and Memory in an Era of Commemoration and Forgetting

Writing wartime history in postwar Britain

The world in which the history of Operation *Crusader* and the Desert War was written was suddenly different from that in which they were fought. The end of the war brought the fall of Churchill and the wartime political coalition and the swift and unexpected rise of the Labour Party to power along with its version of state socialism. There was rapid demobilization of the military, which was not nearly fast enough for the millions of soldiers who were languishing for months, sometimes years, overseas. Within the military the crisis of returning soldiers from the Far East was even enough for the Adjutant General, Richard O'Connor, to resign in protest in September 1947.[1] Demobilization was also followed by a crisis of social reintegration, as soldiers who had been overseas sought to reestablish their lives in a society that was as underwhelmed by the sacrifice of soldiers as it overwhelmed by the perception of its own wartime sacrifices.[2]

The end of the war economy also quickly brought massive housing and employment crises, the creation of the National Health Service, and the nationalization of many public services and industries. The sudden end of Lend-Lease forced the Anglo-American Loan of 1946 that prompted a currency convertibility crisis the next year. All of this fed the continuation – indeed, deepening – of rationing and widespread fears of a return to the Depression, something all too familiar to most Britons. It was a new world but with frighteningly familiar overtones and negative possibilities.[3]

To compound matters there was chaotic decolonization. At the end of the war there had been hopes for orderly transitions to self-rule; instead, there was massive bloodshed. One result was rapid abandonment of colonies. Hundreds of thousands of British soldiers were caught between Hindus and Muslims in India, and between Jews and Muslims in Palestine; within three years they would all be withdrawn. But while the Empire and its aftermath remained a preoccupation for segments of the Establishment, like the war itself, the middle and lower classes appear to have been happy to put distance between themselves and the Empire they had helped sustain militarily for centuries.

The American ascension to global prominence was equally palpable, with its domination of both the global military balance and within new multilateral political and economic arrangements. So, too, was the fading of the self-image of the British Empire, its putative glories, often real opportunities and still crushing responsibilities. This brought old and new resentments, the need to understand recent history as a means of creating a viable immediate future, in an island nation that was suddenly much smaller.[4]

The British Army had a new place in postwar British society. Before the war it had been an institution of career officers, drawn from the upper and middle classes, subject to painfully slow promotions and, for those without other means, borderline impoverishment,[5] and lower-class soldiers, often from the ranks of the truly downtrodden. But the war had touched society at all levels and millions had served and sacrificed. The postwar army quickly returned to its previous state as an underfunded bastion for officers drawn from the upper classes.[6] But demobilized soldiers and their families no longer had the same attitudes towards public institutions and the concept of authority, tied up in the class system and tempered by a myriad of social and educational experiences.

Deference was no longer the rule: wartime experiences had eroded the overt structures of the class system both at home and abroad. Bombs on Britain had made no class distinctions, and what had mattered on the battlefield had not been class or background but grit and competence, attributes too often lacking in commanders. Wartime memoirs would begin to reflect these realities, narratives in which the perspectives of commanders or the upper classes (or their inherent wisdom, goodness and competence) would not be the exclusive ones.[7]

Relations between the Labour government and the army also deteriorated with successive crises over demobilization and decolonization, growing Cold War and military personnel needs, and budget crises that forced consolidation and the decommissioning of entire regiments. There were even Labour proposals for shop steward-like positions to mediate between commanders and enlisted personnel.[8] To the extent it can be measured, the Labour government tended to believe that senior army commanders supported the Conservatives, while commanders in turn believed that Labour politicians were 'putting class interests before the national interest'.[9] These tensions continued well into the 1960s.

Substantive social changes in British society, however, would be long in coming, and there would be a nostalgic or reactionary reversion in parts of

British postwar culture to traditional class deference until decisive new voices emerged during the later 1950s.[10] But Official History, written by representatives of the Establishment with an eye towards issues of strategy and command, the planning and execution of the war by the perforce class situated military and civilian elites, against a subtext of individual and institutional reputations, was inevitably class based. In a New Britain where class had a different meaning, it was also inevitable that Official History would be relegated to a different place as audiences and interests diverged. The contradiction was that Official History was a state-directed enterprise, albeit a very minor one, at a time when the British state was dramatically expanding its reach with imposition of socialism, the nationalization of industries, creation of the National Health Service, and with the 'nationalization of culture' and the arts through state subsidies.[11]

This points to the larger question, how to reconcile the leftward shift in the social and economic life of postwar Britain with the conservative direction of the nation's mythos, above all the 'myth of the Blitz', the images of a timeless and unified England, and the attendant notions of a strong consensus about national identity founded in stoicism, humour and tolerance. As Angus Calder noted, 1940 was the point of origin for this positive consensus, but the disastrous years of 1941 and 1942 saw it undone by successive calamity and cynicism.[12]

But rather than being a reactionary backlash, it may be posited that conservative culture during the postwar period, particularly during the mid- to late 1950s, which focused on the Blitz, Dunkirk[13] and the 'finest hour', was generated 'unconsciously' as a means to reintegrate a society undergoing rapid and uncertain transformation. Histories and memories of the war were duly situated in terms of heroism and sacrifice, tinged with appropriate but not excessive criticism. Unhappy periods such as 1941 and 1942, mostly bereft of victories and comforts and replete with disasters abroad and unpleasantness at home, were elided.

In turn, this issue of the opposite trajectories of postwar politics and culture raises the question about how to situate history and memory against the thesis of British 'decline'. The issue here is not the 'reality' of measurable postwar political or economic decline, brought about by decadent elites dedicated to amateurism over technocracy, a public school system which neglected science and technology for the Classics and games, class conflicts that impeded the creation of efficient and internationally competitive industries, or other aspects of British society, but rather the *perception* of decline and its subsequent impact on history writing of the war. Arguably, the existence of a 'declinist' school of thought, which burgeoned in the 1960s and 1970s, is evidence for such *perceptions*, at least among segments of the elite from both sides of the political spectrum, whether as a lament or cause for celebration.[14]

The issue of British 'decline' may be succinctly described as winning the war while losing the peace and losing the plot. Again, this debate cannot be resolved here; arguments have been made for and against the thesis. The manner in which Britain divested itself of its two most troublesome responsibilities, India and Palestine, may be regarded as either the necessarily messy business of cutting irredeemable Gordion Knots, with results achieved in the best manners possible, or catastrophic failures of will brought about by incompetence and duplicity that spilled oceans of blood.[15]

But within the problem of 'decline' is the matter of situating wartime activities, such as grand strategy, industrial production, technological innovation, and the design and execution of military operations such as *Crusader*. Special note should thus be made of Correlli Barnett's books, including *The Audit of War, The Collapse of British Power* and *The Lost Peace: British Dreams, British Realities, 1945–1950*, which saw a military historian with deep cultural interests turn to questions of economic and national history. The decline thesis as articulated by Barnett flows directly out of his revisionist military history of the Desert War, at whose centre was the problem of Operation *Crusader* and his technological, economic and cultural explanations for operational failure, command lapses and for Cunningham's supersession.[16] Barnett's same arguments regarding how the 'unfortunate Cunningham had picked up the bill for twenty years of military decadence'[17] were in later years vastly expanded into a sweeping portrait of British society from the nineteenth century onwards. Within this the failures of 1941 and 1942 were pivotal to both the military and the economy, but also to the postwar period, which in Barnett's view saw another more generalized failure to capitalize on whatever advances made from 1942 to 1945.

Regardless of the state of British industry in the years after the war, the army itself was in especially dire straits. The government's budget crises of the postwar era were real, and the traditional British pattern reasserted itself. Military budgets were massively slashed even as more than a million men remained under arms in what would be, by the 1950s, an increasingly hollow conscript force.

Britain's overextended strategic situation did not encourage measured assessments of wartime history. Tenuous agreements with Egypt, Jordan and Iraq were the foundation of Britain's strategy 'east of Suez' as the Cold War began, but the imperial remnants in Africa and the Far East that these bases were meant to cement were also crumbling. Hundreds of thousands of troops would be deployed overseas well into the 1960s, policing the ever-shrinking slices of empire and fighting Communist insurgencies and 'national liberation movements', from Malaya to Kenya to Aden, and standing guard on the borders of the Iron Curtain, far-flung global responsibilities which diminished rapidly after the Suez Crisis of 1956.

Defence of the very concrete Empire gave way to defence of ill-defined interests, the assertion of British great power pretensions and a slew of small, ugly wars. The twin realities of a mass British force on the Continent, hopelessly outgunned by the Soviet Union and increasingly dependent on the doomsday resort of nuclear weapons but otherwise underequipped and quiescent, and the grinding brutality of small-scale counter-insurgency operations in Cyprus, Kenya, and elsewhere, increased distance between society and the military still further. The place of history writing in this world is difficult to define, especially as a consumer society was gradually re-established at home.

Finally, there was the Empire and the Commonwealth. With the former beginning to dissolve, the latter's political and economic importance to Britain continued to rise, at least in aspirational terms. Barnett described at length how Britain used Commonwealth defence obligations as a rationale for oversized military expenditures; at the same time those countries made it clear they would contribute little to any future conflict in which Britain was involved.[18] But the war had created much additional baggage for Commonwealth nations, themselves engaged in coming to grips with the war and creating a new future. History and memory in Australia, New Zealand, Canada and South Africa followed unique paths[19] but were united by a few common threads, not least the need to understand the sacrifices of the war and lingering resentment at treatment by British commanders.

Memories of the Desert War had to be fitted into these and other contexts. In a larger sense, two irreconcilable imperatives vied for emotional and practical resources, the need to forget the war and move forward, while at the same time honouring the sacrifices made by soldiers and society as a whole. In this, concepts of national identity and Britishness were also being reformulated, including by the British Nationality Act of 1948 that gave citizenship to residents of the Commonwealth. After an epoch of colossal bloodshed, what did it mean to be British? How would the war, in all of its parts, serve to redefine British character and society, and to contribute to a sense of national identity and cohesion? History writing is rarely generated with such explicit goals in mind but implicitly feeds such debates.

History and memory would be generated through journalism, historical writing and technical military analyses, personal memoirs of leaders and followers, and through literature and film. But it would also come through commemorative activities such as veterans associations, battlefield pilgrimages, the consecration of cemeteries and monuments, the seemingly mundane conventions of naming sons and streets, and the celebrations of leaders, which, as time went on, increasingly took the form of funerals and obituaries. Three of these elements and their interplay are discussed here, namely Official History, journalists and memoirs.

The three sides of war history

Official History, journalism and participant accounts are notionally separate, but in reality they were not fixed categories in either social or intellectual terms. Then, as now, journalists were given privileged access, accounts by participants were regarded as having semi-official character and other participants behind the scenes helped shape the histories without attribution.

The supreme case in point remains Churchill's version, the magisterial six volumes of *The Second World War*, produced from 1948 to 1953 by a 'syndicate' of assistants (including two retired generals, Hastings Ismay and Henry Pownall, who referred to Churchill privately as 'Master'), the assistance of two Cabinet Office officials, and with unique access to documents – including his own papers which should have been deposited with the government – that were off-limits to others.[20] Though hardly official, except in a formal Churchillian sense of being written with singular authority and sweep, the final product was the result of a dialectical process between the author and the government that put forward a narrative acceptable to both. For obvious reasons, and in the temporary absence of other narratives with stature or style, Churchill's volumes assumed a quasi-official, or perhaps better, canonical, status.

Churchill's depiction of Operation *Crusader* in his 1950 *The Grand Alliance* comprised an entire chapter and the problem of Cunningham's supersession ran over several pages. Praising Auchinleck, Churchill published several of their cables; most critically, Auchinleck's 25 November message describing Cunningham as having 'begun to think defensively' as well as his 1948 despatch saying Cunningham had been 'unduly influenced' by Rommel's counterthreat. Churchill concluded on a characteristic note, at once magnanimous and disingenuous, saying, 'Here I shall leave this incident, so painful to the gallant officer concerned, to his brother the Naval Commander-in-Chief, and to General Auchinleck, who was a personal friend of both.'[21] Churchill's praise of Auchinleck during *Crusader*, however, was largely the result of pressure from Ismay and Pownall, who repeatedly pointed out to the 'Master' that he had publically stated his confidence in the Auk prior to and during the operation.[22]

Unlike Churchill, voted out in 1945 but returned to office from 1951 to 1955, Montgomery remained on active duty with the British Army and NATO until his retirement in 1958. But Montgomery had also retained documents that were official government property and this became a problem for the Cabinet Office and the official history project as early as 1949. Unlike Churchill's papers, their legal status was not ambiguous, but the status of the holder precluded easy solutions. After several overtures Montgomery informed the Cabinet Office in 1953 'that he had not the slightest intention of allowing any of the historians to see these documents' since 'many of the documents in his possession would be quite likely to start another world war, and he thought that it would be quite improper for the historians to see them'.[23]

The saga of these documents played out for close to a decade, giving Montgomery the opportunity to shape official history. But Montgomery also actively shaped history from the very moment the war ended. Elevated to the peerage in 1946, the newly christened 'Montgomery of Alamein' had already inadvertently discovered the political power of narratives when in October 1945 a lecture of on wartime strategy in Europe misrepresented certain facts and caused a minor conflict with American forces.[24]

The conflict over memoirs would enmesh Allied Commander Dwight Eisenhower, particularly after the publication of his aide Harry Butcher's *My Three Years with Eisenhower*, one of the first and most intimate memoirs published after the war.[25] It then expanded exponentially with the publication of Eisenhower's own memoir *Crusade in Europe* in 1948, which criticized Brooke and Montgomery, reigniting a feud with the latter that lasted until Eisenhower's death more than 20 years later.[26] This was followed by another feud with General Omar Bradley regarding his 1951 memoir.[27]

The Desert War was also quickly drawn into the conflicts over memoirs. Montgomery's book *El Alamein to the River Sangro*[28] was published in 1946 by the British Army and purported to be the official 8th Army narrative from the summer of 1942 onwards. The account criticized and occasionally misrepresented Auchinleck's strategy, tactics and his defensive preparations and implied that withdrawal from Egypt was a real possibility rather than a contingency.[29] But as Montgomery put it to the War Office, it was also intended to 'counter the spate of "books and articles containing much indiscrete matter and misinformed criticism"',[30] that is to say, to grasp the problem of shaping history. These same criticisms, slightly blunted, also found their way into Montgomery's 1958 memoir.

Britain's most famous soldier had also commissioned his first biography from one of the most famous war correspondents and Desert War chronicler, Alan Moorehead. The biography was framed as an exploration of how 'The minor soldier who had spent half a century inside the narrow walls of a regular army becomes overnight an inspirational leader, a household word among millions, a public figure approaching the war-time popularity of Churchill in Britain and Roosevelt in America.'[31] Was his victory at Alamein the product of 'merely good luck and a certain amount of native cunning' or 'was there some mystical experience in the desert?'

The book represented the culmination of Moorehead's interpretative journalism, a capstone to his three books on the Desert War[32] and one on the European campaign.[33] The biography's depiction of Montgomery was unusually sensitive and not completely flattering: Montgomery's ascetic and relentlessly single-minded personality was especially well described. But the concept of a new, successful and heroic era beginning in 1942 with the appointment of Montgomery was inescapable, as were misrepresentations regarding the alleged inadequacies of Auchinleck's organization and command. Serialized in the *Daily Express,* the book was a keystone to the Montgomery hagiography.[34]

Complementing these books, and bringing popular focus back to the question of *Crusader* for the first time in several years, was the publication in 1947 of *Operation Victory*[35] by Frederick de Guingand, former chief of staff to Montgomery. de Guingand's memoir was not the first but it stands out in several ways. Capitalizing on Montgomery's fame and his own literary abilities, de Guingand's is a portrait of command, as he put it of, the 'war's leading personalities', a commentary on the war and its direction, told from a point of view close to Britain's most popular general.[36] There would be many other memoirs and analyses in the years to come from figures of responsibility but de Guingand's sense of freshness and immediacy gave it particular resonance.

But de Guingand's memoir is also the only one from a senior officer whose tenure in Egypt spanned the Wavell, Auchinleck and Montgomery commands. From that perspective alone it is valuable. While identifying himself overall as Montgomery's man (and indeed, Moorehead credits de Guingand as an advisor to his biography of Montgomery), he was also sympathetic to Wavell and Auchinleck and their very different challenges. His description of *Crusader,* from the perspective of a member of the Joint Planning Staff, and future Director of Military Intelligence, in Cairo, is especially important:[37]

After about nine days' fighting our losses had been so heavy – our tanks being no match for the enemy anti-aircraft guns and tanks- that doubts arose in the Army Commander's mind as to the advisability of pursuing the original plan at such a cost. General Auchinleck decided to fly up to Eighth Army Headquarters to study the situation. I understand that he arrived at a moment when orders had actually been issued for the move of the Headquarters back into Egypt. Galloway, the B.G.S., deserves great credit for his part at this juncture. He was convinced that such a move back of the Army Headquarters would most certainly mean the end of the offensive. He therefore played for time until the Commander-in-Chief arrived. Some caravans and tents were taking an exceptionally long time to get packed up! It is, I'm sure, not betraying a confidence when I say that when asked his opinion of the situation by Auchinleck he advised strongly in favour of the continuance of the offensive in its original form. Galloway had seen far worse situation when holding the appointment as B.G.S. to General Wilson in Greece. It was then that the Commander-in-Chief showed great courage and leadership. He decided to make a change in command, and to drive the Army forward in spite of what they had suffered. Our Intelligence showed that the enemy's situation was anything but good. This must have been a bitter blow to Cunningham. He had done magnificently in East Africa, but the strain of the campaign had told on his health, and he was not allowed a day's rest between his hold and new commands. At the opening of the battle he was not fit, and unless a commander is so at moments like this he is at a grave disadvantage.

The source of de Guingand's information is not clear, but the odd statement regarding 'betraying a confidence' implies that the account came from Galloway himself or another officer who had been at the Advanced Headquarters. de Guingand addressed this event again in 1964 but his initial narrative, emphasizing the basic soundness of the *Crusader* plan (in contrast with a more ambitious but logistically problematic alternative), command failures brought about in part by Cunningham's health and Galloway's critical 'playing for time', were highly influential.

In contrast, another form of Official History appeared in early 1948 with the publication of Auchinleck's despatch in the *London Gazette* on military operations in the Middle East, covering the period from 1 November 1941 until 15 August 1942.[38] Assembled in the aftermath of the battle[39] by Captain R.M.C. Kittoe, a Territorial officer, and Colonel R.G. Thurburn, a Cameronian, and written in late 1942 for Auchinleck by an unnamed Indian Army officer who was later killed in action, the despatch presents the closest thing to Auchinleck's own politically shaped account of *Crusader* and subsequent battles.

Auchinleck's strategic perspective was laconically described in the introduction to the report, 'Of the numerous problems of the Middle East Command two ranked high above all others: to destroy the enemy in North Africa and to secure the northern flank.'[40] These were interrelated and the failure in one would have brought about the collapse in the other. The introduction described *Crusader* succinctly:

> In November, there were sufficient troops already in the Middle East and enough reinforcements promised, to allow me to conduct an offensive in the west and yet be able to stave off a possible threat from the north. The scope of the proposed offensive was ambitious, but it could be contemplated without running undue risks elsewhere, provided that the destruction of most of the enemy forces was effected in Eastern Cyrenaica. Above all, it was essential that there should be no delay.

Hidden in this anodyne statement were the myriad political pressures exerted by Churchill and his allies, Auchinleck's *Ultra* intelligence and much more. Still, 'the offensive was a success, more costly, and less complete than I had hoped. Nevertheless, of the enemy forces in Cyrenaica over two-thirds were destroyed'.

Readers who proceeded beyond this first page were then provided with an only slightly less laconic version of the background to *Crusader*, 'With the approval of His Majesty's Government, I laid my plans and made my preparations not only to defeat the enemy forces in the field, but also to occupy the whole of Libya.'[41] Auchinleck took full responsibility for all aspects of his command but made it clear throughout in an understated manner that he operated in a political context where negotiation and persuasion were necessary. At the same time, Auchinleck also telegraphed a key lesson:[42]

> As far as training was concerned, we had much to learn. In November, 1941, a British Army for the first time took the field against the Germans with a superiority in numbers, for the first time we possessed an imposing array of tanks, for the first time the Army enjoyed full air support in a major offensive against the Germans. All commanders and troops had to learn to use these unaccustomed benefits. An adequate system for controlling air support had been devised, liaison was close, and headquarters of land and air forces formed one camp; but many improvements were possible. Our experience with tanks was less happy: there was much that there was no time to learn and much that could be learned only in action. To learn to handle tanks cost us dear, particularly when we found that ours were no match for the German tanks and that our own anti-tank guns were greatly inferior to the German.

The despatch was, at its core, an explanation of a series of failures, perhaps necessary and unavoidable ones.

Auchinleck's description and analysis of how *Crusader* broke down on 21 December were also spare. But his comments regarding the 5th South African Infantry Brigade's 'inexperience in handling the very large number of vehicles with which it took the field' and the 'grossly exaggerated' reports of German tank losses were stinging.[43] So too were descriptions of the South African unit's destruction, and the 1st South African Infantry Brigade's inability to come to the aid of the New Zealand Brigade, which was 'comparatively inexperienced' as well as outgunned.

The picture was of inexperienced and outgunned troops, unable to handle equipment they had or communicate effectively, and unable to exploit the narrow victory when it eventually came. Overstretched supply lines, overconfident intelligence assessments, and equally overconfident assessments of Italian forces and equipment, particularly when buttressed by Germans, rounded out Auchinleck's understated but frank analysis. From a command and control perspective only close cooperation with the RAF and Royal Navy was genuinely praiseworthy. And having stabilized the front and learned vital lessons, at the beginning of 1942, a substantial portion of Auchinleck's forces and reinforcements was diverted to the Far East and to the defence of the Northern Front. The German offensive of 23 January soon followed, and the British were pushed back to the Gazala line.

Regarding the core failure of *Crusader*, in which he himself was also implicated, Auchinleck stated:[44]

> This shifting of the balance of strength between the opposing armoured forces produced a most critical situation and led General Cunningham to represent to me that a continuation of our offensive might result in the annihilation of our tank force, and so endanger the safety of Egypt. I visited General Cunningham at his advanced headquarters on the 23rd November and told him to continue to press the offensive against the enemy. He loyally gave effect to these orders; but on my return to Cairo on the 25th, I most reluctantly decided that I must relieve him of his command, as I had come to the conclusion, after long, and anxious consideration, that he was unduly influenced by the threat of an enemy counterstroke against his communications. I therefore replaced him on the 26th November by Major-General N. M. Ritchie.

The phrase 'unduly influenced by the threat of an enemy counterstroke against his communications' was wholly new and its meaning was mostly ambiguous. Was it a question of a tactical or interpretive disagreement or something more?

What is clear, however, is that Auchinleck chose not to mention anything about Cunningham's mental or medical condition. But his rationale cannot be discerned. Was he protecting Cunningham, himself, or the critical and the British alliance with Smuts and South Africa?

The impact of Auchinleck's Despatch was significant, less with respect to *Crusader* and Cunningham than the surrender of Tobruk.[45] The despatch had been submitted to the War Office in 1943 but since their publication had been suspended that year the final version did not appear until 1948. By then the surrounding politics had dramatically changed, particularly with regard to South Africa.

The surrender of the Tobruk garrison, commanded by South African Major General Hendrik Klopper, on 21 June 1942 had been a titanic shock to Churchill himself, who above all had been responsible for pressing his commanders to occupy the site for no discernible military advantage. Excoriated in the press, Parliament, and in public opinion, and with a confidence vote suddenly looming, Tobruk precipitated an immense political crisis for Churchill.[46] The prospect of Churchill being replaced by Sir Stafford Cripps was raised, and the issue of Cunningham's relief was briefly resuscitated in Parliamentary debate as a bludgeon against Churchill. Eventually the process led to the relief of Auchinleck and the appointment of Montgomery to head the 8th Army.

But in South Africa, whose troops had been lost by a decision taken by a South African general, the affair also had immediate political ramifications. Not only had 13,000 South African troops been captured, almost the entirety of the 2nd South African Division, but the convening of a British military court of enquiry in Cairo raised the prospect of a South African general being found responsible for their unnecessary captivity. The surrender of Tobruk also came only six months after the destruction of the 5th South African Infantry Brigade during Operation *Crusader*. The political impact was immediate: John Agar-Hamilton, the South African historian, related 'the old joke in the Eighth Army that whenever S.A. forces had had casualties Smuts flew up to see how many "votes" he had lost'.[47]

These twin blows had raised questions in all parts of the Commonwealth about British strategy and leadership. Throughout the summer of 1942 Smuts's domestic political opponents had used Tobruk as a bludgeon amidst growing rumours regarding Klopper's decision and competence.[48] After much bad publicity and frantic efforts at press censorship, the court of enquiry was held in secret and its results kept private. Klopper, who had been captured, could not be questioned. Smuts, and the South African contribution to the British war effort, survived the political turmoil.[49]

But the longer-term ramifications of Tobruk re-emerged with Auchinleck's despatch.[50] The draft had been read by the Dominions Office, which warned that its personnel lacked the technical competence to offer comments, as well as by various commanders. In the middle of 1945, however, the draft was sent to South Africa for comments. Klopper himself had escaped from his German captors in 1943 and had made his way back to South Africa whereupon he was appointed commander of the army's staff college. But upon reading Auchinleck's despatch he produced a furious defence that cast blame on 'chaos' and on the failure of British forces to counterattack.

A slow-moving exchange ensued between the South Africans, the War Office – which called for a shortened version – and Auchinleck, who was reluctant to make changes. By later 1946 another version had been produced, which was also unacceptable to the South Africans, who feared Auchinleck's despatch was incomplete, possibly erroneous and could cause 'public controversy'. Klopper, aided by the South African Official Historians with access to the classified Court of Enquiry, produced further objections. This use of classified documents produced objections from the British, as it had with Auchinleck's initial drafts.

As the matter dragged into 1947, with both sides floating proposals about emendations and the possible inclusion of comments from Klopper as a counterbalance, the involvement of a British military representative with the South African Chief of the General Staff, Pierre Van Ryneveld, only made matters worse. But a second meeting with South African historian John Agar-Hamilton changed the British representative's mind, who then petitioned his superiors to request Auchinleck make almost two dozen changes. Pressured by the War Office with the implied threat to relations with South Africa, Auchinleck agreed. Still, when the despatch appeared, Klopper was incensed at the Auchinleck's statement that the garrison commander had been given permission to withdraw, insisting that no such order had been received. Klopper demanded that Smuts either exonerate him or accept his resignation. But Smuts declined to become involved and the matter receded quickly.

The imperial politics surrounding Official Histories were still, in the late 1940s at least, raw. In the case of South Africa the question of Tobruk and to a lesser extent *Crusader* had direct implications for Smuts, whose support for Britain during the war had been unpopular with Afrikaaners, along with his comparatively moderate views on racial segregation during the 1940s. For these and many other reasons, the 1948 elections saw his defeat and the rise of the National Party, and with it the imposition of Apartheid.[51]

The South African relationship to Tobruk and *Crusader* is extreme but instructive. It was under the Apartheid regime that the South African Official History of the Second World War was written by the Union War Histories Section. But only the books on Tobruk and *Crusader* were eventually published, along with one on South Africa's naval war. The rest of the section's extensive studies were never published before it was shut down in 1961. This history has been closely studied by a new generation of South African military historians interested in both tactical and historiographic insights.[52]

In the longer term Official History everywhere had to triangulate not only against various official accounts (and their complex political backgrounds) but also against other competing unofficial accounts which were far more compelling, such as poet Keith Douglas's 1946 introspective memoir *Alamein to Zem Zem*, which unsparingly recounted the confusion of battle in crystalline prose and granular detail, driver Robert John Crawford's view of the Desert War from below in *I Was an Eighth Army Soldier*,[53] tank commander Robert Crisp's 1959 memoir *Brazen Chariots*,[54] at once breezy and gritty, and Spike Milligan's seven-volume memoir of his experiences during the war and its aftermath, kaleidoscopic, surreal and tragic.[55] Which shaped history and memory more?

The problem of Official History

Scholars have discussed the creation of Official Histories but few have focused on its goals and impacts, or on the position of the Desert War as a whole in the process of history writing. Official historical writing about *Crusader*, however, began while the war was still raging. These included a series of brochures and reports, some book length, the primary goals of which were to determine lessons to be learned from the campaign, establish a baseline of facts for rudimentary historical understanding, and to lift morale.[56]

After the war British commanders produced despatches, in effect the official report on regions and commands, which were published in the *London Gazette*. These provided seemingly authoritative after action reports, albeit from individual commanders' perspectives, which were also accessible to the public. Despatches, as well as other evidence such as unit histories, historical brochures and preliminary syntheses called narratives, created a foundation for the Official Histories of the 1950s. No fewer than four enormous volumes, British, South African, Australian and New Zealand, have *Crusader* at their core. Unravelling their interrelationships is at one level as simple as reading their acknowledgements, in which each credits the other for access to documents and for comments. But behind this is a web of interests only partially expressed, or preserved, in private correspondence between the historians, battle participants and other commentators, including their bureaucratic minders.

The British Official History project effectively began in July 1941 when the Sub-Committee for the Control of Official Histories approved an outline plan for series of volumes on military,[57] diplomatic, civil[58] and medical history, along with an Advisory Committee of historians and 'narrators' who would produce drafts. The scope and scale of the proposed volumes were much debated over the next few years, and the problem of finding qualified writers was especially vexing. Serving or retired officers were preferred for their familiarity with operations and documents, but often their research and writing skills were lacking. A meeting in Washington, DC in early 1948 attended by American, British, Canadian, Australian and New Zealand historians was also key to establishing the groundwork for cooperation between various national projects with regard to sharing of documents and draft narratives.[59]

Certain mechanics of the British Official History are well understood.[60] As Keith Hancock, editor of the civil history project, put it:[61]

> As might be expected, tension arose from time to time between historians and administrators as successive volumes approached publication. This tension was resolved creatively. It was essential that the historians should seek frank and forthright comment upon their advanced drafts from experienced administrators; it was equally essential that the administrators should not press their criticisms to the point of putting into question each historian's right and duty to make his own interpretations and judgements. To reconcile these two requirements the following drill was worked out. The Secretary to the Cabinet circulated the final draft of each history to the departments that had been most closely concerned with the problems discussed by the historian. He invited them to return their comments to the editor. The editor, after examining the comments with the author of the book, wrote to the department to thank them for their helpfulness and to enumerate the criticisms and suggestions which he and his colleague had found unacceptable. Sometimes a meeting ensued, with the author and editor on one side of the table and departmental officials on the other. The object of the meeting was not to achieve diplomatic compromise, but upon every issue to get as close as possible to the historical truth. Sometimes the author and editor would find themselves obliged to pursue further historical researches. The final decision was theirs, except when a genuine issue of security arose. As to that, the editor had a clear policy. He was prepared to withhold a volume from publication on real grounds of surety; he was not prepared to emasculate it.

But the question of what constituted security was a problem. The rules as a whole included severe limitations on citation of Cabinet minutes, quoting individual Cabinet officers and other officials, particularly with regard to debates and disagreements, and obvious limitations regarding access to and citation of classified materials. 'Annexes' or versions with full citation of classified materials were therefore produced for departmental use.

The complete ban on mention of *Ultra* intercepts had a greater impact on the writing of diplomatic and strategic history than on military history, although in some cases, such as the Battle of the Atlantic, the tactical use of those data was vital. In terms of the Desert War as a whole, the omission of *Ultra* intercepts made the strategic decisions by Cunningham, Auchinleck and then Montgomery often appear fortuitous or intuitive rather than well-informed. The ban had an even greater impact on Churchill's accounts and on the official narratives of Grand Strategy.[62]

But the concept of security had broader political connotations as well. As J.R.M. Butler, editor of the military series, put it, 'The Government are not bound to publish matter which they consider contrary to the public interest.'[63] In the absence of clear guidelines, however, defining the public interest was a matter of interpretation for historians and their masters, made long after the events in question. The limitations on characterizing Cabinet debates and on official quotations were more political than security oriented, designed to retroactively defend the political decision-making process.

In 1970 it was still possible for the eminent historian Geoffrey Elton to confidently state:[64]

> For the historian, however, everything pales before the serried ranks of the so-called Official History, the *History of the Second World War* commissioned by the government, organized by the cabinet, but controlled by independent professional historians and mainly written by professional historians who enjoyed the advantage of personal experience. It is perfectly plain that if there was pressure of any sort it was very small, and everything except really deep secrets was made accessible. The very fact that the volumes are often extremely critical of the war-time leadership inspires confidence.

While there has been relatively little direct scholarship regarding the inner workings of British Official Histories of the Second World War, Elton's assertion can hardly be sustained. The biography of Keith Hancock, chief of the civil series, provides the most detail regarding the internal politics of that project and the Cabinet Office.[65] Historian Noble Frankland's description of his early years on the staff of the Air Ministry's history project is also valuable for its perspectives on military sensitivities, and those of former military personnel.[66] The handful of accounts by other participants, especially Michael Howard,[67] touch on certain issues and concerns, especially notable in the histories of intelligence work and strategic planning, where secrecy and politics, respectively, were paramount. In general, however, the personalities of historians and their supervising bureaucrats are nearly absent.

But, also contrary to Elton's confident portrayal of the process and results, at its very inception Official History was a contentious issue among the British historical profession. A 1948 essay by the preeminent diplomatic historian Herbert Butterfield, 'Official History: Its Pitfalls and Criteria', described the problem that the government had created for the profession.[68] In it he expressed the ideal of 'an independent science of history, not hostile to the government but standing over against it-a science which will seek to present the cause of historical truth as distinct from the things which might be promulgated from motives *raison d'état* or for the sake of a public advantage or in order to cover the imprudences of politicians or government servants'.[69]

Butterfield expressed suspicion, if not contempt, for the very relationship of government to history: 'I must say that I do not personally believe that there is a government in Europe which wants the public to know all the truth'[70] and went on to offer warnings regarding the redaction and even the hiding of documents from historians by governments and 'officialdom'.

Finally, he lamented the effect of the war on the historical profession in Britain, including '"independent" academic historians, controlled by the Official Secrets Act, even amenable to instructions, and not authorized to tell all the truth they know'.[71] Who Butterfield had in mind is not clear, but Basil H. Liddell Hart – who had long blurred the categories of journalist, historian and government advisor – comes to mind. Butterfield, with many colleagues, was also strongly opposed to accepting research done for official histories as qualifications for Cambridge degrees, on the grounds that working for governments inevitably compromised the independence of scholars.[72]

This attitude lay somewhere between petty small mindedness and overwrought protection of the historical profession and its histories yet unwritten, affected several scholars involved with the enterprise, most notably Noble Frankland.[73] Engaged, after a four-year search, to write a history of strategic bombing, Frankland, a former RAF navigator, described an especially convoluted process wherein he would write two-thirds of each manuscript and a senior colleague Sir Charles Webster would write the rest. The draft would then be read by the Chief Military Historian, J.R.M. Butler, Regius Professor of Modern History at Cambridge, and his committee of advisors, and then the Air Ministry, War Office, Admiralty, Foreign Ministry and Commonwealth Relations Office (formerly the Dominions Office), and finally by the Cabinet Office and its head, Norman Brook. These factions 'did not have the power to alter or suppress them … If they wished to do that, they had to resort to complex tactical methods of obstruction'.[74]

Indeed, there were many such obstructions. Sir Arthur Harris, the former head of Bomber Command, illustrated these methods by simultaneously speaking freely with Webster and excoriating him as a communist to former colleagues. Lord Portal declined to read the book, other senior officers like Tedder were helpful and positive and Richard Peirse threatened legal action for libel. And at the instigation of Harris, former Permanent Under Secretary of State for Air Sir Maurice Dean attempted to quash the entire publication until Norman Brook dismissed his objections. In doing so, however, Brook involved then Prime Minister Harold Macmillan. Fortunately, 'Brook also soothed the Prime Minister with the thought that official histories "do not normally attract much public attention."'[75]

Many such controversies and personalities are likely to have surrounded and penetrated the creation of Official Histories. But it is also one of the many ironies of the twentieth century that while the Second World War was, for Britain especially, the 'People's War', the writing of its Official History was largely arrogated by the Establishment and its bureaucrats. Britain's underlying class structures endured through the war even though the war itself had temporarily created a democratic army where most of the ranks were based on merit. But the army's command structures, and more importantly, controlling institutions such as the War Office and Cabinet Office, were largely untouched by either the army's wartime meritocratic evolution or the class 'revolution' that was being ushered in by the Labour Party's electoral victory in the summer of 1945. Amidst the endless operational detail there is an underlying tone of Whiggishness in much Official History, a sensibility that suggests an underlying inevitability in the course of events and the inherent wisdom of British participants.

Official History writing was the product of middle-class academic and military professionals subservient to the political class that still dominated the government bureaucracies with deeply held norms and beliefs. The political class was accustomed to seeing itself as the indispensable caretaker of Britain's long-term self-interests through a ministerial system run by permanent civil servants who had enormous leeway to exercise power quietly. Shaping history was hardly a primary concern, particularly in an era long before Freedom of

Information Acts and mandatory declassification timetables. But the amount of time and energy devoted to these issues demonstrates it was taken seriously.

British historians, official and otherwise, also had to take into account the narratives of allies and the concerns for ongoing alliances. This is to say, politics of the past and the present shaped historical narratives being written for the future. Commonwealth politics in particular shaped accounts of the Desert War, and it is precisely in South Africa and New Zealand that the most historiographic work has been done.[76] The competence of Commonwealth commanders and the bravery of the soldiers were delicate matters for the British, and in return, the competence of British commanders, from Churchill on down, was a burning issue for Commonwealth historians. South African and New Zealand historians felt an obligation to the troops who had been lost in *Crusader* and other operations, to find explanations for national sacrifice. The loss of men and the failures of British commanders were still raw issues being spoken about in the press and in parliaments. The past exerted an unsubtle call to shape the future.

The competing sources of Official History

The British Army and the War Office began producing historical documents about *Crusader* not long after the battle itself. The first pamphlet to discuss *Crusader* was *They Sought Out Rommel: A Diary of the Libyan Campaign, from November 16th to December 31st, 1941*, published in June 1942 in the series *The Army at War*.[77] It is described as 'a diary, kept by a Public Relations Officer whose job it was to conduct a party of newspaper correspondents into battle'. The author is named only indirectly, in an introductory quotation from a war correspondent on the overleaf; 'and that our little party of war correspondents was able to see what watching civilization so hungrily desired to read was largely due to the zeal, foresight, courage and energy of our conducting officer, Captain Sean Fielding of the Green Howards, the writer of this diary'.

The author of the pamphlet was no ordinary 'conducting officer'. Captain (later Colonel) Sean Fielding was a former journalist with the *Daily Mail* who went on to create the military magazine *The Soldier*, become controller of Army Newspaper Services at the War Office and later to edit the literary journal *The Tatler*, the news magazine *Time and Tide*, and the tabloid *Daily Express*. He was both an experienced journalist and a stylish writer, who would also write the scripts for the 1943 documentary film *Desert Victory* and the 1958 feature *Desert Patrol*.

Assigned to escort journalists Sam Brewer of the *Chicago Times*, Matthew Halton of the *Toronto Star*, and Alaric Jacob of Reuters, Fielding's brochure was brief but vivid, describing Cunningham on the eve of battle as a 'hoarse-voiced cherub of a man'. The party's initial goal was 30 Corps headquarters, but their truck's radiator sprang a leak and 'nearly reduced me to tears by using precious water as if it were a hungry Russian eating caviar at a wedding feast'.[78]

Wandering about the battlefield they encountered a variety of combat scenes including tank and infantry battles and crashing aircraft. The overconfidence was palpable: 'It is the British fighting the Germans, at last on something like equal terms, and we are hammering the living hell out of them.'[79] But by the morning of 24 November, writing at 7th Armoured Division Advanced Headquarters, things began to look 'a trifle sticky' and by mid-day Fielding and his charges were being shelled. The next night Fielding noted: 'This has been a horrible 36 hrs.'[80] He recorded a chaotic evacuation of the area under fire, a 'seething mass of our transport', which mostly sped past the correspondents leaving their small convoy virtually alone. Following tracks they eventually rejoined the army and crossed back into Egypt. After much peril, including relating a fear on 28 November that 'at the moment the people here seem to think we might get wiped up',[81] the tide turned. Fielding did not mention Cunningham until 4 December when he records meeting Ritchie, 'who has taken General Cunningham's place'.[82]

Fielding's narrative of the first half of the offensive is not critical of the army but his descriptions can hardly be described as flattering. He did not, however, discuss the Cunningham supersession in any way, but merely noted it days after the fact. Some 50,000 copies were sold,[83] but this figure pales beside the hundreds of thousands of pamphlets sold that discussed other campaigns. Some, like *Combined Operations – The Official Story of the Commandos*, were also sold in the United States as part of the Book of the Month Club.[84] The impact of Fielding's pamphlet is difficult to assess but it appears to have been of greater interest to later historians than to the contemporary reading public. Though thoroughly journalistic in tone, since it was issued by the War Office it must be regarded as official 'proto-history'.

The follow-up pamphlet in 1943, *The Battle for Egypt*,[85] elided the Cunningham supersession and the fall of Tobruk. It treated Auchinleck's 1942 defence of Egypt respectfully but did not deify the new commanders, Montgomery and Alexander. Instead, it highlighted the courage and prowess of the army and air force. The lavishly illustrated pamphlet was less anecdotal, and much less stylish, than *They Sought Out Rommel* and must be regarded as simple propaganda.

'The Eighth Army'

The same cannot be said of the next pamphlet *The Eighth Army, September 1941 to January 1943*.[86] The pamphlet is solely a summary of 8th Army operations and barely mentions the war under Wavell. But it operates, uniquely, on several levels. The photos and captions uniformly cheered the fighting spirit and courage of the troops themselves while a portion of the narrative did the same, celebrating the feats and bravery of soldiers and units. But the narrative was much more detailed and analytical, examining the strategy and conduct of battle. And it was here that nascent historical writing in both the descriptive and analytical senses began to bear down on Alan Cunningham.

With considerable understatement the text described how 'on the evening of the 23rd, therefore, the battle had reached a critical and far from encouraging phase'.[87] It then presented several long paragraphs describing how both British tactics and equipment were not yet adequate: infantry without sufficient numbers of powerful anti-tank weapons; severely under-gunned tanks; and implicitly, poor communications and intelligence regarding the strength of British forces. But the command factor was not neglected:[88]

> These serious considerations were very present to the mind of General Cunningham, the Commander of the Eighth Army. He had won a tremendous and well-merited reputation for drive and daring in the Abyssinian campaign when he had commanded the Army in its startling rush from the Juba to Addis Ababa, and his appointment to command the Eighth Army had been particularly welcome to the South Africans. By a curious coincidence his brother was in command of the Fleet, and the command of the air Forces was called Coningham, so that a Low cartoon at the beginning of the battle showing a van labeled "Cunningham, Cunningham and Coningham – Removal Contractors" was a near summary of Allied hopes. General Cunningham was certainly not a man to cry halt without good reason. He had tried resolutely to carry out General Auchinleck's plan of campaign. But he had now reached the conclusion that it could not be done, that the operation should be abandoned, and all troops withdrawn for re-grouping.

> Nothing is more fatal than to entrust the conduct of a battle to a commander who does not think he can win it. Lee might have won at Gettysburg if he had replaced Longstreet after the latter had declared that Cemetery Ridge could not be carried. In the circumstances, General Auchinleck, after a personal visit to advanced H.Q., decided to entrust the command of the Eighth Army to his own Deputy Chief of Staff, Major-General Ritchie, who had taken part in all the

original planning and was intimately acquainted with his views and processes of thought.

> The continuation of the battle, if there as still the slightest chance of military success, was dictated by every other consideration The whole of the Middle East had been keyed up to expect a resolute trial of strength. The troops had started the battle convinced that at long last they were to fight the enemy on more or less equal terms. Malta's supplies at this hour were low, and the possession of the Cyrenaican airfields, from which cover could be given to convoys, was an essential objective, apart from anything more ambitious. The political and military consequences of recoil would have been appalling. The event proved that General Auchinleck was right in thinking that victory could still be won, and afforded an interesting example of how the personality of a commander can still permeate a modern army.

It is unknown who wrote these passages or the brochure as a whole, but the writer had both considerable literary and military skills. One indication is that praise of Cunningham was tempered by an allusion to the American Civil War that would have been lost on the average reader. Another is that Auchinleck's decision to replace Cunningham was contextualized by comments regarding both the morale of the 8th Army and the broader Mediterranean strategic situation. The writer is thus unlikely to have been a moonlighting war correspondent like Sean Fielding but rather a military professional, either serving or retired.[89] Finally, and significantly, the narrative did not mention Cunningham's medical or mental states; there is no insinuation of 'breakdown' but rather the implication of Cunningham's 'loss of initiative' that resulted in Auchinleck's 'loss of confidence'.

Even this was too much for Cunningham. In his own copy of the pamphlet he highlighted four items from the fateful page: that he had been welcomed by the South Africans, that he had tried to carry out Auchinleck's plan, that he had concluded the 'operation should be abandoned' and the phrase 'how the personality of a commander can still permeate a modern army'.[90]

Cunningham's reaction to the pamphlet was predictable and furious: on 31 March 1944 he wrote to John Noble Kennedy, Assistant Chief of the Imperial General Staff, to complain. Although Cunningham's note is not preserved, Kennedy's response on 3 April indicates their shared upset; 'We were furious about that 8th Army booklet – it was never referred to any responsible person on our side the house and we have made a row about it – unfortunately too late for June. It is so hard to keep an eye on all the bloody fools!'[91]

A month later Cunningham went to see General Henry Colville Barclay Wemyss, Military Secretary to the Secretary of State for War, in order to be assured that 'no further publication would issue which had not any way had the benefit of considering my point of view'.[92] Wemyss replied to Cunningham with just such an assurance:[93]

> On the question of the evidence that you have that certainly ought to be available for the official history, I have discussed the matter with General Kennedy. He would be glad if you would send him copies of any documents you wish to send and he will ensure that the branch which is preparing data for the histories will have them properly filed and the existing documents so annotated that there is no question of your point of view being overlooked.

Cunningham did not pass up the opportunity. Less than a week later he wrote to Wemyss and included a copy of his December 1941 report to Brooke, noting, 'As I have said I thought that the above would be sufficient record for war time purposes, but have been sadly disillusioned by the publication of the 8th Army pamphlet.' He went on to complain that, from his perspective, it appeared that his report had not been consulted by the pamphlet's writer, which he believe defied his 'original request that they should be kept for study'.[94]

Yet another month later, after discussing the matter with Kennedy and Brooke, Wemyss replied Cunningham that 'Colonel Robertson, who is in charge of the section preparing material for the history, should have access to your letters to the C.I.G.S. and General Auchinleck, which the C.I.G.S. has in his safe, and prepare a statement, which, if the C.I.G.S. approves, will go into the records on which the historians are now working'.[95] He went on to assure Cunningham that Robertson was 'the right man to make the appropriate abstracts'.

It is remarkable that on the very eve of the Allied invasion of Europe, the highest levels of British command should be addressing matters of historical interest, however cursorily. But Cunningham continued to press certain points. In June he wrote yet again to Wemyss asking whether proofs of the official history would be sent to commanders for comments.[96] This would not occur for another decade. And puzzlingly, Cunningham noted: 'I mention this matter, because the 8th Army booklet gives a garbled version of the actual plan for the battles of November, '41. I never issued any written orders, so I imagine the only person who can give a correct version of this plan is myself, I have of course a number of documents bearing on it.'

The significance of this statement is difficult to assess. On the one hand, it is not possible for a major military operation to be planned and launched without a slew of documents, including orders. On the other, the postwar historical narrative of the operation made clear that these orders consisted of only initial tactical objectives and the broad strategic goal of pushing Axis forces out of Cyrenaica and relieving Tobruk: 'It was Lieutenant-General Cunningham's wish to dispense with detailed operational orders: changes in circumstances, in particular in enemy dispositions, would entail frequent amendments to orders; any plan should, he considered, be elastic.'[97] The wisdom of this decision notwithstanding, in 1944 Cunningham was positioning himself as the pivot for writing the history of *Crusader* and to shape the problematic question of planning.

Kennedy reassured Cunningham that he would indeed have the opportunity to review the draft history and asked for Cunningham's planning documents and details regarding verbal orders.[98] But Cunningham had the last word and ended the exchange on a typically unctuous note:[99]

> I am sure you will appreciate that I would not have thought of bringing this matter up at this time had it not been for the publication of the 8th Army booklet, regarding which it seemed to me the only action could take was to get an assurance that I would be given the opportunity of presenting my own story for consideration before anything else was written under official aegis. That assurance has now been given me, and I am quite happy about the future, when I will know that anyway my side of the case has been studied, and when I will be in a position, or my executors will be, to counter anything said with which I disagree. Actually I hate the thought of the whole business, silence in my view is indeed golden, but one seems to get forced into these situations willy nilly. I might be excused perhaps for thinking the 8th Army booklet was a dastardly stab in the back.

At last Cunningham revealed the true extent of his feelings regarding the pamphlet and perhaps by extension his supersession, a 'dastardly stab in the back'. And, by chance, through the pamphlet's publication, he was able to complain loudly enough in order to position himself such that his narrative – the core of which he had given to Brooke in 1941 – would be at least considered when the Official History was written. Draft chapters would not reach Cunningham until 1955. But his narrative, which had hitherto resided in the CIGS's safe, would become the core of the War Office's version of *Crusader* and the supersession, and then the Cabinet Office Historical Section's.

CAB 106/655

Some measure of the importance assigned the Cunningham supersession was reflected by the fact that in 1942 the CIGS, Alan Brooke, opened a Top Secret file on the affair, containing copies of Cunningham's report on *Crusader* and his correspondence with Auchinleck. In 1944 officers led by Colonel Robertson in the Military Operations (MO 1) branch of the War Office responsible for Despatches studied the file and produced their own summary that was appended. The file, still classified Top Secret, was then forwarded in 1949 to Brigadier Harry B. Latham of the Cabinet Offices Historical Section for use in the Official History.[100] The file would grow over the next few years with the sporadic addition of correspondence with Commonwealth historians.

Cunningham himself prompted the 1944 re-examination, Robertson's report noted, and alleged that the pamphlet *The Eighth Army* had[101]

> given a wrong impression of these circumstances; presumably he refers in particular to the passages on page 21 commencing: "General Cunningham was certainly not a man to cry halt without good reason. He had tried resolutely to carry out General Auchinleck's plan of campaign. But he now reached the conclusion that it could not be done, that the operation should be abandoned and all troops withdrawn for re-grouping." He has asked that the Official Historians should be given, in due course, his story of the events so that it can be given due weight when the official history is given.

The report forthrightly noted, 'The matters which appear to be in dispute are (1) Gen. Auchinleck's reasons for superseding Gen. Cunningham. (2) The justification of this supersession. (3) Gen. Cunningham's state of health at the time.' It added: 'The original material on which it is based is in the C.I.G.S. confidential file P/74/17 and (for medical history) in Gen. Cunningham's personal file P/74/16.'

The analysis proceeded on Cunningham's terms. With his tank forces dramatically reduced, 'Cunningham felt he should lay all the facts before General Auchinleck so that he could decide whether the attack was to continue or not and he accordingly asked him to come to his headquarters'. There is no mention of Galloway's meeting with the Corps commanders or a 'flap' at 8th Army Advanced Headquarters. More significantly, there is no correspondence in the file from Arthur Smith, only with Auchinleck himself who had focused on the question of Cunningham's strategic judgement, not mental health, in his communications with both Cunningham and London.

After reviewing the letters exchanged the report concluded Auchinleck had removed Cunningham 'because he had begun to have fears of the effect of enemy attacks on his lines of communication and rear areas' and that 'he had not formed the opinion that General Cunningham was unable to carry on because of the state of his health'.

The report also concluded that

> General Auchinleck's opinion of General Cunningham's state of mind was based on close contact with him for two to three days at his Headquarters and it is quite clear that it was absolutely genuine. He was most reluctant to make the change in Command. General Auchinleck states that his opinion was shared by several senior officers; there is no direct evidence in support of this statement but it is hardly conceivable that General Auchinleck would have made it if it were not in fact true.

In fact, as letters from Smith and Tedder show, many senior officers shared Auchinleck's opinion and even anticipated it. But the fact that no documentary evidence to this effect was contained in the file made the point easy to elide.

Finally, on the medical issue, the report noted: 'There is no record available of the result of the medical examination which took place on arrival at hospital.' But on the basis of Dr Small's specialist report and Cunningham's own exculpatory description, it concluded that 'when General Cunningham went into hospital on 26th November, 1941, neither he nor General Auchinleck believed he was ill' and that 'there can be no doubt that he was a very tired man but it is doubtful if he could be described as "sick" in the ordinary sense of the word'.[102] But Small's report, as shown above, cannot be considered conclusive, given his connections with the Cunningham family, and must be contrasted with the results of the medical board that graded Cunningham 'D' upon his return to England in December 1941.

The Military Operations branch analysis proceeded on the basis on the selected documents Cunningham himself provided and this had the intended result. Cunningham was effectively 'exonerated' before the war even ended. The file and its conclusions then became the foundation of the Official History of *Crusader*. Once transferred to the Cabinet Office Historical Section it sat until it became the topic of reanalysis and lively debate among British and South African historians.

Before that, however, another copy of the file that remained with the CIGS was to take a very different path, one that tracks with the larger political issues surrounding Cunningham's supersession. Bernard Montgomery obtained a copy of the file after he became CIGS in June 1946.[103] His August 1946 letter to George H. Hall, Secretary of State for the Colonies, strenuously opposing Cunningham's appointment as High Commissioner in Palestine – many months after he had taken up the position – speaks only of Cunningham's supersession during

Crusader and his being 'quite unable to make up his mind what to do'.[104] Beyond this one datum, however, the impact of Montgomery's objections belongs to the later period of Cunningham's career and the last years of the British Mandate for Palestine.

The history of failure and the Crusader narrative between three countries

Understanding *Crusader* was not simply a British concern but an issue that hit especially hard in South Africa and New Zealand. Writing official history was not a formal joint effort but ran in parallel, sharing certain concerns and the circumstances of continually diminishing resources and interest. It also brought participants in each country closer as individuals, strengthening informal class ties between men with common military and intellectual backgrounds, many of whom knew each other well, facing confronted similar historical and political problems.

Addressing British-led failures during the early war years was a common thread in each country. Four episodes from 1941 and 1942 stood out as objects of historical and political concern: the failed Greek expedition, the losses incurred during Operation *Crusader*, the fall of Singapore and the fall of Tobruk. Each cast doubt on British political judgement, and on military commanders, who regularly appeared to be callous incompetents more than ready to sacrifice Commonwealth lives.

The fall of Greece in early 1941 was the preface to the disasters that followed. But while the decision to commit British and Commonwealth forces has been much discussed, the subsequent historiography has not. In general, there has long been a consensus that Greece was a politically driven fiasco that diverted resources at the expense of exploiting the British advantage and the potential for driving the Axis out of North Africa. More recently, the late Robin Higham argued that the operation was actually a feint orchestrated by Wavell to nominally fulfil unrealistic political commitments to the Greeks and divert German forces away from a potential thrust into the Middle East through Turkey. Most fundamentally, however, the operation was intended to distract Churchill from promoting more dangerous schemes. In Highham's view, the Greek operation was carefully designed to deploy a minimal force with the inevitability of withdrawal always in mind.[105]

This grand strategic interpretation makes a great deal of sense but, as Higham pointed out, cannot be confirmed without access to Wavell's diary, which is still held by the family. Regardless, Commonwealth historians after the war saw mostly political folly and military failure. The Australian Official History offered a tactfully divided opinion, recognizing the political need to come to Greece's aid while ruefully detailing the military inadequacy of the effort and the hopeless condition of the Greek government and military.[106] The New Zealand Official History was far more critical, offering a detailed analysis of not only the operation itself but the various justifications and comments offered by British commanders and politicians after the fact.[107]

The fall of Tobruk and the effect of Auchinleck's despatch on British relations with South Africa and the shaping of historical narratives have been discussed above. The surrender of Singapore in February 1942 and its British-led garrison of over 100,000 men was an even greater calamity and is emblematic of the fall of a dramatically underprepared and overwhelmed British Empire across all of Southeast Asia. As a result, it has been debated repeatedly from many perspectives including long-term British diplomatic and naval strategy, military preparedness and logistics, diplomacy, and the centrality of Churchill in decision-making. The historiographic saga of Singapore had far greater implications than that surrounding Tobruk or even Greece and involved the incompetence and neglect of British planners and commanders, above all Churchill, accusations of desertion and disloyalty against Australian and Indian troops, British and Japanese racism against one another and local populations, and horrendous Japanese war crimes.[108] It was the antithesis of a 'clean war' fought 'without hate'.

The historical and historiographic literature on Singapore is vast but a few comments are in order. Historian Cat Wilson has recently argued that Churchill's relative neglect of the Far East and Singapore in his monumental history served a twin purpose to deflect attention from the lack of any serious British strategy in the region save the unarticulated hope that the United States would shoulder the primary burden in the event of war with Japan, and the ex post facto touting of the US–UK 'special relationship'.[109] Hack and Blackburn also make the point that while there was a geopolitical context, or even exculpatory rationale, to British strategic decisions, including Churchill's own, the balance of historical writing on the question is resolutely negative, particularly in Australia.[110] The same authors have also detailed the ways in which history writing has been complicated by national and ethnic myth-making and commemoration. This began from the very moment of the Japanese victory, the 'liberation' of Singapore from British imperialists, and continues through today as various communities of Singapore and Malaya come to grips with their own histories during the war, a process that relates directly to contemporary culture and politics.[111]

The problem of *Crusader* was more subtle and throughout the 1950s Official Historians debated among themselves 'who won' the battle, a question in which individual successes and failures of men, machines and tactics were intrinsic. From an historical point of view the questions were at one level technical regarding the training of units, their equipment and readiness, and about specific command decisions. At another level the questions were strategic, including the allocation of resources to various theatres and to the Soviet Union, the wisdom of the Greek campaign and the concerns regarding a northern front. From a historiographic point of view the failure of *Crusader* stood below Greece and certainly Singapore, and as a prelude to Tobruk, but raised many of the same questions about the leadership of the war from Churchill on down to field commanders.

The mother and daughter nations approached Official History in different ways and with different emphases. Each also had long and difficult experiences with producing their histories of the First World War; the last volume of the British history of the Great War appeared in 1948 and was worked on continually throughout the second conflict.[112] Whatever the lessons learned, however, were only partially internalized; the final volume of the British history of the Second World War appeared in 1988.

Finding the personnel to undertake these projects was a serious problem. Professor J.R.M. Butler, the British editor in chief, described the problem as a choice between[113]

> academic historians with no professional knowledge of military affairs and Service officers with no experience of historical method. Of the first class, most of the younger historians had been engaged in war work, whether military or in Whitehall, and were eager to return to their universities, while the Service officers whom a temporary job as a historian was like to attract were senior men, retired or on the point of retirement, whose professional knowledge might not be up-to-date and who might find historical research demanding.

Another problem that arose quickly was the discouraging policy of prohibiting narrators from submitting their products to universities as dissertations, a policy that, as Herbert Butterfield indicated, was also supported by the universities. Nonetheless, teams were assembled and out of the immense mass of documentation narrations began to appear.

One further restriction deserves highlighting: 'The principle being observed that no-one should be employed to write the history of operations in which he had himself played a major and responsible role.'[114] This sensible policy, however, extended only to British narrators; it did not apply to supervisory personnel or to members of other nations' teams of historians.

Creating the received versions of Crusader

Three countries, three versions of *Crusader* and of Cunningham's supersession: The British version was anodyne and stalwart:[115]

> On 25th November General Auchinleck flew back to Cairo and that evening took a decision on a matter which had been occupying his mind. He had been satisfied with General Cunningham's conduct of the battle and with the steps taken to carry out the instructions that he had himself given after he had come forward at General Cunningham's request. He had nevertheless formed the opinion that Cunningham was thinking in terms of defence rather than of offence and he (Auchinleck) had therefore lost confidence in the Army Commander's ability to press to the bitter end the offensive he had been ordered to continue. The decision to remove General Cunningham from his command was an extremely painful one to take, but General Auchinleck was convinced that it was right. ... General Cunningham, though he could not bring himself to agree with the Commander-in-Chief's reasons, took the heavy and unexpected blow with complete loyalty and selflessness.

In contrast, the South African version was allusive:[116]

> The long flight back to Cairo gave the Commander-in-Chief ample time for turning over in his mind the events of the last three days, particularly the 'alarm' of that morning, and for meditation on the grave misgivings which the Air Force Commanders, Tedder and Coningham, had expressed regarding the Eighth Army Command. He arrived in Cairo convinced that General Cunningham's anxiety was not of the kind which would respond readily to encouragement and exhortations, and he went at once to interview Mr. Oliver Lyttelton, Minister of State, and local representative of the British War Cabinet.

After informing Churchill, Auchinleck wrote the fateful letter to Cunningham: 'The reason he gave was once more that the Army Commander was beginning to "think defensively," and was no longer able to press the offensive to the bitter end.' Ritchie and Smith were sent on their mission. Cunningham was superseded and Churchill himself reported to the Parliament "'a few days later" that "General Cunningham ... has since been reported by medical authorities to be suffering from serious overstrain and has been granted sick leave.'"

The New Zealand version was bitter and contrarian:[117]

> In his various statements on the subject Auchinleck gives three reasons for dismissing the Army Commander: defensive thinking due to heavy tank losses, undue concern about Rommel's dash to the frontier, and lack of confidence in his ability 'to carry out my intentions'. With his calm presence and firm insistence that Crusader must continue, Auchinleck had achieved his purpose regarding the first and Cunningham obeyed him 'loyally', though there was in fact every justification for 'defensive thinking' by the evening of the 23rd. On the second score, both Auchinleck and Cunningham greatly under-estimated the scope and power of Rommel's move, which was on the face of it highly dangerous. The third point was an afterthought. Auchinleck talked things over with Tedder, who was more than once critical of his Army colleagues, and when he got back to Cairo in the afternoon of the 25th he consulted the Minister of State, Oliver Lyttelton ... But it was a grave and dangerous step to take and in the long run Eighth Army paid dearly for it, while in the short term it made little difference to the desert fighting.

The Australian version, told largely from the perspective of forces penned up in Tobruk, added a sarcastic note: 'Never to be dismayed by misfortune was the theme of Auchinleck's substitution of Ritchie for Cunningham, which precept seemed to epitomise Ritchie's ill-starred exercise of command in the ensuing seven months.'[118]

Approaching this far-flung and slow-moving enterprise is another historiographic challenge. Doing so in an economical fashion also requires reducing the enquiry to three core features, Cunningham's mental state, Galloway's role and the men behind the histories. All three primary versions, as well as that of Australia, rotated the same key pieces of the puzzle but yielded different results. The process was social enterprise revolving around a limited number of individuals in several countries. How were the issues analysed and debated, and by whom?

The key questions surrounding the Cunningham supersession were already evident in wartime accounts and were raised in the pamphlets and then narratives produced by various national teams. All teams were fundamentally dependent on access to British documents and limited in their assessments of strategy and decision-making by the absence of *Ultra* information.

But the command issues had been given precise focus by Francis de Guingand's 1947 memoir that cited Galloway as the force behind the scene who prevented the crumbling Cunningham from abandoning the battle. The historiographic conundrum was thus a question of evidence, operational documents against personal accounts, verifiable orders against individual quotations, one man's word against another's. The dialectic would go on until the early 1960s.

In Britain, Lt Colonel George R. Johnston had compiled the British *Crusader* narratives from both operational documents such as unit diaries and signals and from preliminary narrations prepared by the War Office.[119] After working on the various Desert War campaigns since 1943, Johnston completed his narratives (and extensive notebooks) in 1948,[120] while Brigadier George F. Ellenberger completed his narratives on the later parts of the operation from 1948 to 1952. Neither had participated in *Crusader* but both had published articles in military journals during the 1930s and had an interest in military history. Ellenberger, of the King's Own Yorkshire Light Infantry, had no apparent regimental connections to any of the *Crusader* principals, while Johnston was an officer in the Royal Field Artillery. According to his superior, Brigadier Harry B. Latham, Johnston was 'never a fit man' and was 'in a very queer state when he compiled this narrative', and was discharged shortly thereafter.[121]

Johnston's narrative simply quoted Auchinleck's despatch that stated that Cunningham had been 'unduly influenced by the threat of an enemy counter-stroke'.[122] In general, his narrative – the first draft of which was literally pieced together out of strips of paper pasted into an album from various sources – is a minimally fleshed-out account comprised of countless elements. The second draft merely added words to make full sentences. Johnston, by design or default, perceived all the trees but struggled with the forest, which was added by the volume's actual author, Major General I.S.O. Playfair of the Historical Section.

In contrast, Ellenberger's narrative of the latter phases of *Crusader* was framed with analytical statements and was constructed with more of a synthesis in mind. His portions may be said to have some flashes of 'literary' value, a quality almost wholly lacking in Johnston's dry and detailed recitation. Even so, upon reviewing a draft of the entire history in 1956 Sir Ian Jacob quietly suggested: 'There should be more of the human thought and feeling brought out in the account particularly at some of the moments of crisis and interest.'[123] Jacob's call for 'a little personal colour' would go unmet.

The flap

But Ellenberger and Johnston were not the only British narrators writing about *Crusader*. The 1948 Royal Air Force narrative had included a description of planes being hastily redeployed eastwards on 24 November 1941 as a result of the German thrust, and of the generalized chaos that prevailed as British forces fled eastwards. This much was well known. But one influential footnote in the narrative quoted Wing Commander James R. Gordon-Finlayson, Senior Operations Officer assigned to the 8th Army Advanced Headquarters who, 'less restrainedly', declared '30th Corps lost control of the situation and there ensued a most interesting period, which as a study of panics, chaotics and gyrotics is probably unsurpassed in military history'.[124] This statement was then quoted in the 1953 official RAF history but was prefaced by the statement: 'The whole headquarters was thrown into confusion and was unable to exercise effective command.'[125] With the 30 Corps context relegated to the background, the RAF history thus interpreted Gordon-Finlayson's general observation as specifically referring to the situation at Advanced Headquarters.

Another source, a 1952 memoir by New Zealander Brigadier George Clifton, who had seen the rout for himself further to the west, claimed that he arrived at the headquarters just as a report of twenty German tanks was received 'and the resultant flap was a balm to my injured feelings'.[126] *Crusader* participant Major Michael Carver, in an early analytical piece, also claimed that there was a reported threat, which caused one British force to be diverted and another to be held in reserve before 'Army H.Q. called down again'.[127]

The 'flap at headquarters' and the Carver and Clifton statements thus became objects of contention for Commonwealth historians. The British Official History took the story of the 30 Corps headquarters being routed and noted: 'Acted on by rumour a stream of this sort tends to swell and gain speed. This one was no exception. Some lorries had never traveled so fast. To use the current slang, there was a good deal of "flap."'[128]

November 24 was indeed chaotic but aside from Clifton there is a record neither of a 'flap' nor of any threat to the 8th Army headquarters. Operational documents include an unconfirmed report from the RAF of twenty-five tanks and other armoured vehicles in the Maddalena-Sidi Omar area on the early afternoon of 25 November.[129] The South African historians depicted Cunningham as having responded to this supposed threat by insisting that Auchinleck depart immediately. But Auchinleck's famous 'attack and pursue' message was not entered into the war diary until two and a half hours later,[130] suggesting either that Auchinleck was not under pressure.

To compound the confusion, various accounts including Johnston's narrative, Auchinleck's despatch, the published British history and Connell's biography of Auchinleck do not mention the incident at all, whereas the South African history and Correlli Barnett do. Was the 'flap' a single incident, dated to the 24th or the 25th, or a period of extended confusion that began on the 24th or even earlier? That such a turning point could not be agreed upon points to the problems of evidence and rumours, which played upon the historians a decade after the events in question.[131]

Galloway in the eyes of historians

The 'flap' was only one ambiguous element debated by Commonwealth historians. Most substantive of all were Cunningham's condition and Galloway's actions. The British and New Zealanders looked harshly on both but chose to protect Cunningham, while the South Africans took a more ambiguous view. The reasons were in part a function of professional outlook; the South Africans were trained historians first and military officers second, inclined to use all the evidence at their disposal equally, while the British and New Zealanders were above all military officers and under the close watch of the Cabinet Office. Another reason was that the British and New Zealand officers responsible for the histories had been participants in *Crusader*.

The British treatment of Cunningham has been described above. Galloway, however, is not mentioned in the published book, not in relation to the planning of the campaign, the Corps commanders meeting or the summoning of Auchinleck to Advanced Headquarters. This appears to be a deliberate and telling omission. By design the book does not have any critical apparatus of notes on sources, which could credit observations and insights to individuals. The underlying narratives credit various sources, including Auchinleck's despatch and de Guingand's book and thus neatly avoided addressing attributing critical comments to junior officers or analysing command problems in depth.

But the British team had consulted and in turn debated Galloway extensively with regard to two specific issues, the Corps commanders' meeting on 23 November and the Cunningham supersession.

When approached initially in 1950, Galloway stated that his goal at the conference was to 'get a picture with which to convince the Army Cmnd that all was not lost'.[132] And indeed, this had the intended effect, 'always convinced that we never had any alternative to going on with the battle, we all did what we could, each in his own way, to convince the Army Cmnd that to fight it out was not only in accordance with our very clear instructions, but also obvious'. As for Cunningham, he was, 'I regret to say, the opposite of Rommel.'

Brigadier Harry B. Latham, Head of the Cabinet Office Historical Section, expressed thanks 'a thousand times' to Galloway but his follow-up letter a week later pressed on exactly the same points. Galloway returned the letter with handwritten comments in the margins on Latham's summary. Regarding the Corps commanders' meeting that broached withdrawal, he added, 'There was not much "discussion."'[133] Furthermore, on the matter of orders for a withdrawal, which Latham noted could not be found, Galloway added: 'You may take it from me that they were, very definitely. Furthermore I was in spite of my somewhat procrastinate qualities, instructed to prepare an official plan. I did not do so.'

Two other items deserve note. Latham noted that his office possessed the Cunningham supersession file (CAB 106/655), 'deposited with me by the War Office at the request of General Cunningham and presumably agreed by General Auchinleck'. Galloway circled the word 'presumably' and commented 'I do not know. I would not accept that unless the "agreement" of Auchinleck is included in the summary. I can if you wish come to your office to check on whether the summary is factually correct.' There is no indication that Galloway ever visited Latham, and so Cunnngham's version was accepted as authoritative.

Another was Latham's closing comment that 'it must have been a very awkward and unpleasant time for you and I am most grateful for all you have told me'. Galloway circled the words 'for all' and commented, 'It had its moments.' This brief phlegmatic aside may have been symbolic of the differences between him and Cunningham.

Galloway's comments complemented those of Godwin-Austen, who had described the conference and Galloway's statement that Cunningham's concerns were 'so serious indeed that there was a question as to whether would be wise to continue the battle'. 'I was horrified' at the idea of a withdrawal, stated Godwin-Austen.[134] Latham added in a note to New Zealand historian and *Crusader* participant Howard Kippenberger: 'I remember hearing at the time that it was Godwin Austen who stopped the rot, and that the words he used to Galloway were to the effect that "if you call of this offensive now it will be the greatest disaster the British Army has suffered for centuries."'[135] Galloway's testimony that the Corps commander meeting was a meeting of like minds in which his own galvanizing role could not be disguised by his own understatement.

But throughout 1953 Galloway expanded his comments on the South African draft narrative, which Latham then shared with South African historian John Agar-Hamilton. The correspondence runs to many pages but several comments deserve highlighting, in part because they were unexpectedly sympathetic towards Cunningham and because they foreshadowed Correlli Barnett's revisionist critique of the British Army, for which Galloway was a key source.

Galloway recalled, 'The really grueling thoughts and arguments which assailed poor Alan Cunningham as to how best bring about the battle within his terms of reference,' a battle whose scale would be 'so much greater than before'.[136] He repeatedly emphasized how 'Crusader was a valuable mile stone on the road to the high achievement of the Allies' in which 'mistakes were made all around', but that any optimism was of 'a very sober sort'.[137] The 'exceptionally difficult circumstances of "putting to sea" and bringing the enemy to a battle', a 'headquarters which bore some resemblance to a previous war' in which Cunningham 'very quickly got out of touch with the incredibly confused situations which followed one another in quick and gloomy succession', were made worse by politics, the 'relentless pressure came from W.S.C.', including to utilize the untrained South Africans which a 'more ruthless and less partial Commander' would have resisted.[138]

Galloway's comments became more pointed as the year went on. He even stepped in to defend Cunningham against South African criticism, after a fashion. 'Of course Cunningham was useless, or perhaps one should say, unfitted for the task. But what a task!'[139] In parallel he offered candid thoughts on one of the 8th Army's most pointed critics, Bernard Freyberg, 'I get a bit fed up with Freiberg [sic]. Brave yes: after that you've had it. He was expert at always knowing better and wanting to do someone elses job: but when he got on he was always fussing about N.Z. Govt. He was a man who need to be kept to quite simple things involving a Div plan max incl A-B and C-D bravery etc., etc.' [Emphasis in the original]. And he frankly characterized the relief of Tobruk as 'incidental'.

The comments on Cunningham and Freyberg were not forwarded to Agar-Hamilton, but a transcript of his handwritten comments in the margins of the South African draft was, including the line 'C lost his nerve completely, but not on 20 Nov'.[140] Regarding Ritchie, Galloway noted: 'The moment Ritchie appeared in the desert it was clear that he was the answer in one sense and not in the other. He re-enlivened our spirits; but it soon became evident that he lacked the experience and "know-how" of High Command.'[141]

By July Galloway had become even more frank. The meeting in his caravan with Auchinleck and Cunningham 'was of course depressing, since C. made it clear that the battle was lost and laid much emphasis upon the necessity of getting out of the area and back to somewhere where it would be possible to save Egypt'.[142] But, in a famous comment that was included in the final South African version, 'A. was at his best. He informed C. quite emphatically that it was not his business to consider Egypt's safety, but to get on with the battle … It was his "finest hour" so far as my experience goes'. But he also introduced a final ambiguous observation: 'Theoretically (in retrospect) it might have been better to execute a limited withdrawal, nevertheless in the circumstances at the time, A. acted as only a true Commander could and should.'

Latham, and much later I.S.O. Playfair, would follow up with Galloway on a third issue, an abortive plan late in *Crusader* to send a brigade against Benghazi and thus to cut off Rommel. Holding no grudge against Ritchie, who by then had taken command, Galloway added: 'War fighting is like marriage. Clearly everyone wishes to make a success, but as things develop & scenes change, differences arise.'[143]

But Galloway's responses to Latham became in turn a topic of intense discussion between the latter and Agar-Hamilton and eventually their superiors in the Cabinet Office. To understand why Galloway's remarks were so controversial requires a closer look at the men behind the Official History.

Behind the Official History

While Major General I.S.O. Playfair was the lead author of the British Official History volumes dealing with the desert war, he drew heavily on Johnston and Ellenberger's narratives. A Royal Engineer with an eclectic career and no background in history or writing, it is unclear how Playfair became involved in the project. Called 'Bungy' by his military associates, his contribution is difficult to perceive, except inasmuch as he was responsible for soliciting comments on drafts.

But above Playfair was another more important figure, Brigadier Henry B. Latham. From his position as head of the Army Historical Section in the Cabinet Office Historical Section he occupied a central position; yet, like most of those involved in the Official History he is little known.

Latham's animosity towards Alexander Galloway is barely disguised in his correspondence with counterparts, although one attempt was made to do precisely that. On 1 December 1955 he wrote Agar-Hamilton to discuss the Cunningham affair yet again. He reviewed evidence that Agar-Hamilton had used to 'discredit' Cunningham, including the quotes from de Guingand, Clifton and Galloway, but at the bottom of the page, he added: 'I hope you will forgive me if I make some further comments on the authors I have listed above. I only do so to show you that some of the things they have said want verification before being repeated.'[144] The following page, however, begins with 'Now! I have let my hair down to try and help you but don't forget this letter is for your "Eyes Only."' And Latham added a hand-written note, 'In view of the remarks on Galloway – perhaps you'd better burn this!'

This is precisely what Agar-Hamilton appears to have done. The page with Latham's uncompromising comments on Galloway was expunged from the file. Not only was the letter sanitized in Agar-Hamilton's official files, it was not included in Latham's own voluminous files in Britain.

Latham's family could not explain his apparent animus towards Galloway but a closer look at his career might.[145] Latham was a gunner who had served in the desert with the 2nd Armoured Division, including periods in command, until it was disbanded in early 1941. He then became the chief artillery officer for 13 Corps and held the position through *Crusader*. He was apparently relieved in May or June 1942 and returned to Britain, remaining in the army until his retirement in early 1946.[146] Like many other officers Latham had written short pieces for military journals and in 1945 wrote the history of the 49th (West Riding) Division. By 1949 these efforts had brought him to the Cabinet Office Historical Section.

But unlike other personnel involved in the British Official History project, and in contravention of the convention that historians should not write about operations in which they had participated, Latham had been directly involved with *Crusader*. As head of artillery Latham would have been in direct contact with Galloway during the planning phases and during the battle itself. Lt Colonel Johnston mentioned Latham frequently in many of his letters to fellow officers requesting interviews or information, often noting that Latham had pinpointed an officer at a particular place during a campaign, and he interviewed Latham himself several times about various campaigns.[147]

Although he was neither an author nor an editor, Latham was responsible for shaping the Official Histories at many levels. He oversaw the narrators, was interviewed by them and conducted interviews for them, corresponded with foreign historians and with outsiders such as Liddell Hart. Finally, he commented on the multiple drafts and participated in the meetings of the Advisory Committee. His comments on the many *Crusader* drafts were long, detailed and often irritated, both with the text and the conduct of the battle. In the long and recursive process of the Official Histories, Latham was present at every step.

Throughout, Latham assessed Cunningham's shock at the 8th Army's losses in the context of his own experiences and therefore regarded both his summoning of Auchinleck and even the proposal to withdraw as correct. As for Cunningham, 'If he lost his head so did Rommel and the battle was saved by Godwin Austen and XIII Corps which eventually smashed up the Panzers.'[148]

As late as 1956 Latham commented that it was the 'plan which was the basis for all our troubles' and that the 'trouble was that Cunningham and most of the Eighth Army staff were quite inexperienced in armoured warfare in the desert'.[149] And by 1958 Latham was anonymously reviewing Official History volumes for the *Royal United Service Institute Journal*, stating certain authors were selecting facts in a manner that was 'unfair to the intelligence of the reader', an accusation that caused consternation with James Butler, the series editor.[150]

There is also evidence that Latham had indirect contact with Cunningham after *Crusader* through James Blewitt. In January 1942 Blewitt wrote to Cunningham that in January 1942, after leaving Cunningham's side, he had been reassigned to an artillery unit and had reported to 13 Corps headquarters, where he met Latham.[151] The particular unit Blewitt was joining, however, was being rotated to the rear so he requested to be assigned to the frontlines.

But another more direct reason for Latham's animosity is found in a letter to *Crusader* participant and Official History writer, New Zealander Howard Kippenberger. Latham described visiting Belhamed shortly after the *Crusader* battle and reconstructing the scene from the perspective of the defenceless New Zealanders, who on 1 December 1941 put up a stout defence in the face of German armour. 'Something has happened here quite out of the ordinary', Latham commented, in a tone more elegiac than angry.[152] But the New Zealand positions were cut in half and hundreds of troops were forced to surrender lest they be slaughtered. The divisional headquarters had almost been lost and one entire battalion was destroyed.

Latham's disapproval of Galloway thus stemmed from his dislike of the original *Crusader* plan, the inept conduct of the battle and his apparent belief that Cunningham was correct in wanting to withdraw, command failures made real by the terrible fate met by South African and New Zealand units. Galloway's two acts of insubordination, rallying the Corps commanders and meeting with Auckinleck behind Cunningham's back, were both disloyal and thwarted what should have been the proper command decisions.

But other teams saw matters differently. The intent and structure of the New Zealand Official History were far different from that of Britain. A War History Branch had been created in 1945 and Major General Howard Kippenberger, a lawyer and student of military history, was appointed as head. But Kippenberger had also been an active participant in New Zealand's war, commanding a battalion in Greece and Crete, a brigade in North Africa during *Crusader*, where he had been wounded and put out of action, and finally the 2nd New Zealand Division in Italy, where he was severely wounded by a mine, losing both feet.

During *Crusader* he had been commander of 20 Battalion, which in part thanks to his own errors had been badly mauled in fighting at Belhamed, south of Tobruk. Not only had he been injured in the fighting, but he was temporarily taken prisoner by the Germans before escaping. Kippenberger was also an early memoirist, whose book *Infantry Brigadier* was notable for its down-to-earth tone, graphic depictions of battle, self-criticism and bitterness towards British commanders.[153]

Kippenberger approached his role as a historian not simply as a participant but as a chastened commander. This may have helped shape his unique articulation of the Official History as something 'which will meet the needs and expectations of the people of New Zealand, including returned and home servicemen, workers in the war industries and members of the general public, and which will at the same time establish in countries overseas the facts of New Zealand's war effort.'[154] And indeed, the New Zealand Official History is unique in its focus not only on strategy and operations but on the experiences of individual soldiers of all ranks.[155] The usual Commonwealth narrator structure was even supplemented by data from questionnaires circulated to retired servicemen's organizations and at reunions.[156]

Kippenberger's own view of *Crusader* was bluntly expressed in his 1949 memoir:

> It has been said that at the Somme in 1916 British tactical doctrines reached their lowest depths, and it seemed to me that Libya '41, or the Winter Battle, or Auchinleck's Offensive, or 'Crusader', as it was variously called, was fought with an equally total disregard of what one had understood to be the principles of war – with two exceptions. Surprise was achieved and thrown away, but there certainly was economy of force, a nicely calculated or perhaps unavoidable minimum for every operation, and there was a most obstinate maintenance of the objective.[157]

With his prejudices already published, Kippenberger led the New Zealanders in a dialogue with their counterparts, including John Agar-Hamilton of South Africa.

New Zealand commander Bernard Freyberg, too, was not enthusiastic about Galloway. In comments on a draft he reported that at the *Crusader* planning conference he had 'listened in cynically' and rejected the proposal that his forces 'go out into the blue against unbeaten armoured formations unless I had tanks under my immediate command. I had had differences of opinion with Brigadier Galloway in Greece, and I had no confidence in his judgment'.[158] Freyberg was so opposed to the plan that he eventually contacted Cunningham, commenting, 'I have always been upon most friendly terms with the Army Commander, for whom I had great regard.' Freyberg was unhappy with many aspects of the Official History and complained bitterly but was unable to reshape it.

The wounded Kippenberger had watched the battle from a distance, including the destruction of the battalion that he had once commanded,[159] while Walter Murphy, the future New Zealand historian of *Crusader*, was a wounded prisoner of the Germans not far away. The same day a British armoured unit commanded by Brigadier Alec Gatehouse could have rescued New Zealand units fighting at nearby Sidi Rezeg but Gatehouse simply refused to engage the Germans. The day was almost as traumatic for the New Zealand Division as a few days before had been for the South Africans. Senior New Zealand commanders, who like Freyberg had disliked the plan for *Crusader*, held Gatehouse in particular contempt, along with South African general Dan Pienaar.[160] Overall the New Zealanders had lost some 2000 prisoners of war, including several brigadiers and other high-ranking officers. Both Kippenberger and Freyberg would go on to serve with Galloway in Italy at the even more traumatic battle of Monte Cassino.

Using the British narrative and the South African draft chapters, the New Zealanders quickly focused on the problematic medical explanation for Cunningham's supersession. Both Kippenberger and Murphy commented to Agar-Hamilton that Ellenberger's draft narrative had dismissed Cunningham's mental health in favour of a medical explanation, with Kippenberger going so far as to complain that

> unless you have information as to Cunningham's health which we do not possess I think you are on weak ground in suggesting, in fact saying, that he cracked up personally before his supersession. Ellenberger, evidently using documents or information not cited, definitely says that Auchinleck did not realize at the time that Cunningham was ill. No matter what the doctor's report said subsequently, that statement and Norrie's evidence (he saw Cunningham after the Auk's departure) seem to me decisive support for the view that the Despatch does give the real reasons for his actions. If his real reason was that he saw Cunningham was ill he was both cruel and untruthful in his Despatch.[161]

But Latham's objections were construed as interference regarding the account of Cunningham's supersession. Agar-Hamilton complained to Murphy of 'correspondence with the Cabinet Office people, who suggest politely and charmingly that there is no need to rub in the facts of Cunningham's dismissal'.[162]

Latham's objections were articulated precisely to Kippenberger in January 1956.[163] First was the use of de Guingand's account as evidence of a 'flap' at the Advanced Headquarters and plans to withdraw, neither of which could be confirmed from official documents. Most of all, Latham was incensed by quoting de Guingand's comments regarding Galloway 'playing for time', 'a travesty of the truth and undiluted Cairo gossip. If repeated in an official publication the reader will assume that it has been verified whatever comment is made on it. It decries Cunningham and shows Galloway in a most unenviable light as the Staff Officer disloyal to his own immediate boss'.

Latham provided a point-by-point rebuttal of de Guingand but could not articulate the 'real' reason for Cunningham's dismissal. Remarkably, he turned instead to Cunningham himself, who 'came in to talk over this very point with Playfair and his comment was that he would have acted in the same way as Auchinleck did if faced with the same situation'. But the same day that Latham wrote to Kippenberger, he wrote also to Agar-Hamilton, and then once and for all dumped the matter of the South Africans in the lap of his superior, Andrew B. Acheson.

Unlike the British project, the South African Official History had two professional historians at the helm. The primary force behind the South African narrative was a now-forgotten historian, Leonard Charles Frederick Turner.[164] Born in South Africa of English parents, Turner was a graduate student at the University of Witwatersrand when war broke out and seems to have served in a South African unit during the East Africa campaign. After time at the Staff College in Haifa he spent the remainder of the war as a staff officer in Kenya. Turner joined the South African history project in 1946 and co-authored three volumes, including two on the Desert War. A man of liberal convictions, he rankled under the National government and in 1956 emigrated to Australia where he taught at several universities including the Royal Military College.

Although he was a professional historian whose 'tendency toward dogmatic judgement'[165] often rankled his counterparts,[166] Turner was not a fully disinterested party. He had served indirectly under Cunningham in East Africa and through the Haifa Staff College was acquainted directly or indirectly with the iconoclastic Eric Dorman-Smith. The small size of the South African officer corps also suggests he was personally acquainted with many participants in *Crusader*. After the war Turner was also directly acquainted with another *Crusader* participant, German General Frederick von Mellenthin, a staff officer in the Afrika Corps and later a divisional tank commander in Europe, who had emigrated to South Africa after his release from an Allied prisoner of war camp in 1947. In 1956 Turner edited von Mellenthin's influential *Panzer Battles*,[167] which was simultaneously a tendentious celebration of German armour prowess and a memoir of personal exculpation.

Unlike Turner, the editor of the South African Official History, John A.I. Agar-Hamilton, had no direct war experience under British commands but was also a professional historian and later an Anglican minister. Born in Egypt to Scottish parents, raised and educated in South Africa except for a brief period at Keble College, Oxford (where he was for a time a schoolmate of the future British Official History overseer, Andrew B. Acheson), Agar-Hamilton returned to South Africa to what would become a productive but fraught period as a professor. As an English speaker and a liberal in an increasingly repressive Afrikaner environment, Agar-Hamilton was hounded by students and colleagues alike at the University of Pretoria for his refusal to conform to the *voortrekker* narrative. When offered the opportunity in 1940 to join the South African military as a records officer, he eagerly accepted and ultimately spent almost two decades as a military historian. Along the way he became an ordained Anglican minister.[168]

Unlike his counterparts, Agar-Hamilton was continually looking at the larger contexts to explain Auchinleck, Cunningham and Galloway. His early experience as a historian in an environment of conformity and repression had also made him sensitive to received wisdom and easy answers.

Agar-Hamilton's attitude towards Cunningham and Galloway was thus different from his counterparts. As he put it to Latham,

> I was interested, however, to find that General Galloway confirms that Cunningham "lost his nerve completely" at a later date. We shall certainly not put it so bluntly, and I have always maintained, and Turner agrees, that Cunningham was perfectly justified, on the evidence before him, in calling off Crusader. I am equally certain, that had he not been overruled by the Auk he would have lost everything as far as the Nile, probably the Suez Canal, and very likely beyond. But that his decision was both justifiable and justified I would not deny. Cunningham's decision was 'correct' but Auchinleck showed that touch of insight which makes the 'competent' commander into the man of war.[169]

But, to Latham's continual protests about the South African draft citing Galloway and de Guingand, Agar-Hamilton responded repeatedly that he was doing so in order not to endorse their accounts but to discredit them. This technique left Latham at a loss and increasingly frustrated.

With Agar-Hamilton on one side, and Latham and Kippenberger on the other, and with all sides pressured to downplay the medical evidence, the matter was at an impasse. By March 1956 Kippenberger commented to Latham that 'whatever the rights and wrongs I am satisfied that it is none of our business and do not intend to let my author get worked up on the matter'.[170]

But Cunningham himself was also given one more chance to shape the British narrative. In response to a request from I.S.O. Playfair for comments on an early draft, Cunningham wrote a long note recalling he had only been given one plan, as opposed to several options, reviewing again the relative weakness of British tanks and weapons, and, repeating his summoning Auchinleck to the front.[171] But he urged Playfair not only to cite his motives as the diminishing number of operation tanks but 'most optimistic reports' from Middle East intelligence headquarters. Finally, Cunningham was adamant that he had 'never mentioned adopting a defensive attitude or even breaking off the battle. It was in my mind to find out how important it was for the offensive to be continued. I never even considered how to switch to defense. These are facts. It is try to say therefore that I wished the C in C's advice on the continuation of the offensive, but that was all'.

This description does not accord with the original memorandum of the 23 November 1941 meeting between Auchinleck, Cunningham and Galloway which Cunningham himself had deposited with the War Office. Over the course of 15 years Cunnngham's perception of his own position had become less tied to documentary evidence. But in the end the South Africans acknowledged Cunningham's 'overstrain', while the New Zealanders made the issue into a theoretical, wondering (following Liddell-Hart) 'if Rommel did in fact intend by the sudden move of his whole armoured force to the frontier area to shatter the nerve of the opposing commander and cause him to withdraw into Egypt',[172] without articulating a medical much less psychological problem. But the British stuck to 'loss of confidence'. By and large, Cunningham's narrative had held.

Above and behind Official History

Andrew B. Acheson, The Hidden Hand

An even more obscure figure behind the Official Histories was Andrew B. Acheson. A decorated First World War veteran of the Machine Gun Corps, Acheson entered the Colonial Office in 1920, was made private secretary to the Permanent Under-Secretary in 1923 and then rose to Assistant Secretary by 1942. In 1948 Acheson became Assistant Secretary of the Cabinet Office, a position that included the role of secretary of the Cabinet Advisory Committee on Official Histories.

As a consummate Establishment functionary, Acheson was accustomed to dealing with sensitive and diverse issues. In his long career at the Colonial Office he handled controversies on many continents, as head of the Pacific and Mediterranean Department and then of the General and Defense Department. At the Cabinet Office Acheson handled many administrative aspects of the Official History project, including budgets, personnel and relationships with other national teams. He also chaired the meetings of the Advisory Panel for the Official Military Histories of the War, at which the heads of the military historical sections met along with representatives of the services and Churchill, including Ian Jacob.

Some of Acheson's remit was granular and mundane; in one letter to the National Health Service he advocated for one of his employees be issued eyeglasses because of the nature of her work with documents.[173] At another level he dealt with very large questions, such as the disposition of Churchill's papers and the return of captured documents to Germany.[174] Throughout he could be relied upon to represent the Establishment's interests. When those interests impinged on Churchill's or on questions of the 'higher direction of the war', Acheson referred the matter to his superior, Sir Norman Brook, Secretary of the Cabinet.

Noble Frankland's autobiography describes repeated encounters with Acheson, mostly unpleasant, during the course of his work as co-author of a history of the RAF's strategic bombing campaign. These included Acheson's lack of concern over Frankland's pay and status as an employee of the Official History project, efforts to prevent him from travelling to the United States to examine records, forbidding him from giving public talks about his work and declining to intervene when Frankland's work was plagiarized by another historian.[175] Though numerous authors, official and otherwise, offered him thanks in their prefaces, Frankland's mentions of Acheson suggest a rigid and unsympathetic personality. His political leanings are obscure, but may be reflected in a rare expression in which he described 'American policies on Suez and almost everything else are impractical, unrealistic and ineffective'.[176]

Formally, Acheson was not an editor. But as the person to whom requests for access to documents had to be made, and since sensitive matters regularly arose within the various parts of the Official History project, such as sharing drafts with government departments and with other national teams of historians, and finally as the person to whom comments on drafts were addressed, Acheson was continually drawn into editorial matters. These included the writing of the Official History of Northern Ireland, which repeatedly touched on sensitive questions of Irish loyalties,[177] the treatment of Middle Eastern issues in Commonwealth histories, such as the Abdin Palace incident of 1942, which almost forced the abdication of King Farouk of Egypt, and the politically sensitive problems of Tobruk and Singapore. Operation *Crusader* was another such issue.

On 26 January 1956, after years of corresponding with Agar-Hamilton and with the New Zealand and South African drafts being finalized, the frustrated Latham finally put the matter of Galloway into the hands of Acheson. 'The trouble with these overseas authors is that they are not satisfied with the fact of Cunningham's dismissal and want to read more into it than exists. They are annoyed because so far Cunningham is the only interested party who has said "nowt."'[178] Moreover, 'they are too ready to blame the Commander concerned for the failure of their own forces in any particular operation', and while a fair assessment of Cunningham was necessary, the use of quotes risked turning 'gossip' into 'fact'.

Once again Latham made his case. The de Guingand quote 'not only serves to discredit Cunningham but in addition shows General Galloway in a most unenviable light as the Staff Officer disloyal to his immediate chief'. But in doing so Latham quoted extensively from Agar-Hamilton's many letters, allowing him to make his case for using de Guingand, Galloway and Carver judiciously about circumstances and 'atmosphere', but not events. Latham argued they were not 'sources', Agar-Hamilton argued the opposite, while both agreed that the facts of Cunningham's supersession were not in dispute.

True to his task, Acheson dutifully took the matter up with Agar-Hamilton, giving 'not my official view (officially all I can say is that there is nothing in your draft to the publication of which we could raise official objections), but my personal impressions'.[179] He continued his disarming tone by stating that he was not a professional historian and had no particular qualifications for expressing an opinion except as a general reader. Acheson raised no objections to the South African picture of Cunningham's 'irresolution' but only to quotes from Galloway and de Guingand related to Cunningham's state of mind. Galloway 'is very much an interested witness, and the quotations suggest that he is mainly concerned after the event to protect his own reputation'. As to the argument that the quotes should be included to express something of atmosphere of the times, and having overseen the production of numerous bland volumes completely bereft of human interest or colour, Acheson added: 'Neither as regards atmosphere nor as regards accuracy does Galloway appear to me as a reliable witness.'

After years of correspondence with Latham on the issues, in letters that had become shorter and shorter, Agar-Hamilton was moved to respond to Acheson in many pages. 'Personally, I was inclined to rate Galloway's character pretty low, but Turner, who has followed the documents much more closely than I, is inclined to award him a rough courage, and, after his experience of Wilson in Greece, some idea of how a general should behave in a crisis. He was not a good chief of staff, but was capable of initiative when he saw things going dangerously wrong.'[180]

With Acheson's intervention Agar-Hamilton reviewed yet again the material from Galloway and pared it down further, much to the relief of Latham, who commented: 'In my letter to you dated 1 December 1955 I have already said more than I should about Galloway.'[181]

Ultimately what distinguished the South African historians from their counterparts was the willingness to use all categories of evidence, to consider contradictory positions and to understatedly construct arguments they believed would lead readers to subtle conclusions. As Acheson put it in his final missive to Agar-Hamilton, 'Your feeling, as I understand you, is that you must, on important points, take account in your history of all available evidence. If some of it is, in your opinion, inconclusive, you feel at liberty to indicate as much in your text,'[182] a position that Acheson believed weakened the argument. Fairness to 'poor Cunningham' was a paramount concern. But their delicacy was being overtaken by events. And by the time the final South African publication was transmitted to the Cabinet Office Historical Section in late 1957, Acheson had retired because of ill health. He died in 1959 at the age of 64.[183]

Basil Liddell Hart, The Official Unofficial Historian

Britain's most famous military analyst Sir Basil Liddell Hart was a public commentator, advisor to the British and Commonwealth historians, and sometime adjudicator of legal disputes between aggrieved historical figures. Among others his long-time friends within the military Frederick Pile, and especially Eric Dorman-Smith, kept him abreast of military developments and bombarded him with ideas. From 1942 onwards, Dorman-Smith had shaped Liddell Hart's thinking regarding the Desert War, and they would continue to correspond on the matter until the former's death in 1969.

Liddell Hart was acquainted with all the participants in *Crusader*, but there is no direct correspondence with either Cunningham or Galloway in his vast files. During the middle of the war, however, Liddell Hart communicated with then Director of Staff Duties Alexander Galloway through Frederick Pile. In May 1942, Pile had passed on a memorandum detailing his conversation with Galloway regarding the general execution of the Desert War and the future structure of the army.[184] In 1943 Pile responded to Liddell Hart's unusual request for an assessment of Montgomery by saying he would first ask Galloway.[185]

Liddell Hart's files also contain many discussions related to *Crusader*, initiated by himself as well as others. In 1951, during the first round of conflict over Churchill's history, Liddell Hart had contacted Auchinleck who responded: 'I find it difficult to give a complete answer to your letter of the 21st about Cunningham, but I will try to answer your queries as best I can. You will realize that there was no hard and fast decision between the various stages of the action I took in relieving C.'[186] And for close to a decade Liddell Hart's comments on the draft South African, British and New Zealand *Crusader* narratives had been solicited, putting him at the centre of a network of participants and commentators. With Playfair's permission Liddell Hart had even passed the British draft on *Crusader* to Establishment nemesis Dorman-Smith for review.[187] But comments from this 'Unknown Correspondent' were read and dismissed.

A typical Liddell Hart comment was a long analysis of Rommel's counter-offensive during *Crusader*, which attempted to reconstruct Rommel's strategy and thinking without the benefit of primary documents such as war diaries and signals.[188] This necessitated an even longer analysis by Kippenberger and Murphy on Liddell Hart's 'fantasy' using documents, including German war diaries.[189] Throughout 1954 a slew of letters from Liddell Hart to Playfair refocused discussion among all the historians about the relative power of German and British weapons. One impetus for this came from Liddell Hart's own publication of Rommel's account, as well as use of German officers as consultants. The effect was to shift focus onto hardware but at the same time to downplay command problems, much as Cunningham himself had attempted. For all his commentary, however, Official Historians held Liddell Hart in low regard. Even Latham commented to Kippenberger on Liddell Hart's 'glorification of Rommel' in his analysis of *Crusader* as well as his unreliable translation of Rommel's papers from German into English.[190]

Other writers and historians dutifully pursued a connection with Liddell Hart, in part because he was a singular source of information. For example, Liddell Hart had provided David Belchem, formerly GSO 1 (Staff Duties) for the 8th Army, with a copy of the draft South African narrative. Belchem's resulting comments closely mirrored those he would later publish. Liddell Hart also provided a copy of the draft to Charles Broad, an armour officer who had retired in 1942 as General Officer Commanding-in-Chief of the Eastern Army in India.[191] Much later Liddell Hart provided copies of this correspondence and comments to military historian Ronald Lewin.

Writers also sought Liddell Hart's approval in order to transmit their own views more widely. Colonel Michael Carver, formerly operations officer for 30 Corps, began a long dialogue with Liddell Hart in 1953 on *Crusader* and the Desert War (after concluding a similar exchange with Agar-Hamilton and Turner which culminated in Carver's receipt of the draft South African narrative).[192] Carver, who had attended the critical meeting as Willoughby Norrie's representative at which Galloway had rallied Corps commanders against Cunningham's proposed withdrawal, had risen rapidly, commanding an armoured brigade from Normandy to the end of the war. He remained in the army, retiring with the rank of Field Marshal in 1976.

A prolific writer, Carver wrote no less than four accounts of *Crusader* over the course of forty years, beginning in 1949,[193] each changing slightly as he rose to his final rank. While he was not on the scene at 8th Army Advanced Headquarters, he was well connected with those who were. In 1953 he stated to Liddell Hart: 'Although the Army Commander panicked, no other senior commander did.'[194] But by 1986 – motivated in part by a desire to respond to 1960s era revisionists – he characterized Cunningham merely as 'depressed', while in 1989 he refrained from describing Cunningham's mental state and spoke only of his suggestion that the 'offensive should be temporarily abandoned'.[195] Most of his correspondence with Liddell Hart, however, focused on operational issues and questions of British and German armour and anti-tank weapons.

Why was Liddell Hart involved at all? Part of the answer was simply longstanding habit on the part of the British military and the military history community. There were few figures with whom Liddell Hart was not acquainted and few issues related to military history and strategy on which he was not consulted, or into which he did not inject himself. But there was another reason for Liddell Hart's involvement. With his journalistic career during the war in decline, overshadowed by correspondents in the field, and his ability to influence policy dramatically reduced, he had needed a new approach. As the war ended he quickly found it only kilometres from his home, in a prisoner of war camp that held German officers.[196] Interviewing them provided important insights on German strategy and tactics, which Liddell Hart quickly put to use:

a book on German generals appeared in 1948,[197] and during the early 1950s he prepared Rommel's diary for publication, as well as a history of the Royal Tank Regiment.[198]

Liddell Hart was the leading individual bringing German voices into the discussion about *Crusader* and the Desert War as a whole. His efforts to analyse, humanize and ultimately expiate German generals had an obvious Cold War context where German rehabilitation as an ally against the Soviet Union required making distinctions between the Wehrmacht and the SS, between generals who were Nazis and those who were not, and between the barbarities of the Eastern Front and the allegedly chivalrous conduct of war in the Desert. Critics and biographers have pointed out the extent to which Liddell Hart was motivated not only by a genuine curiosity in personalities from the 'other side of the hill' but also by an effort to rebuild his own reputation and relevance, including the claim that his own early views on tank warfare had inspired successful *blitzkrieg* tactics. It is also clear that the German generals successfully manipulated Liddell Hart to clear themselves.[199]

One effect of Liddell Hart's book on German generals, along with Desmond Young's 1950 biography of Rommel,[200] and Liddell Hart's 1953 publication of *The Rommel Papers*,[201] was to expand the image of the Desert War as a 'civilized' and chivalrous conflict, separate from other theatres of war, hard fought but free of war crimes and brutalized civilians.[202] This was far from the truth, in terms of German or Italian behaviour, much less the character of German officers, Rommel included. Another result was to recreate a cult of Rommel, elevating him as both a tactical genius and a chivalrous 'German' rather than a Nazi soldier. In doing so, Liddell Hart and Young effectively reversed the policy established in the field by Auchinleck, in which commanders were instructed to tell their troops that 'Rommel though a tough opponent was not supernatural in his attributes' or a 'wizard'.[203] Finally, the Rommel myth constructed an odd symmetry with the Montgomery myth, another strategic genius who stepped in to salvage the situation from the travails of predecessors. Both these tendencies, to see Rommel as a military genius, and to pair him with Montgomery, continue today, often as a form of symmetrical mythologizing in the name of demythologizing.[204]

Despite his own lengthy consideration of the matter, Liddell Hart helped shift the focus of the *Crusader* narrative away in official and unofficial histories from British command problems and towards its materiel inadequacies and exceptional adversary. For whatever reasons, Cunningham barely figures in his published works.

To the end of Official History

The process of Official History involved accumulating operational documents such as diaries which narrators then created narratives, linear recitations of events, onto which analytical comments were then added. Comments from participants were then solicited and the manuscripts rewritten. The process was predictably bureaucratic and intensely time consuming. Simply reconciling various sources to establish the sequence of events was slow, requiring specialist knowledge, such as the ability to understand military documentation.

Classified material was off-limits, and rules for citing Cabinet debates and individuals' statements were equally strict. Various Cabinet departments had to be consulted along with individual overseers. Consulting participants and fellow historians was also slow, as letters and documents made their way through the mail to different countries. Various individuals who were not formally part of the process were privately consulted for information and comments. At the other end of the production process, circulating drafts for comment could take years, as a limited number of copies also made their way through the mail and were eventually returned.

The results, very large books, were read by few but consulted by many, and represented a denatured, consensus public view. The British Official History was an Establishment enterprise, intended to be an authoritative account of the war from the top-down perspectives of strategy, orders of battle, command and operations (as well as the nuts and bolts of 'specialties' such as production, logistics and medicine), rather than a multi-level 'people's' account as in the New Zealand history, or a truly analytical product as in South Africa. The bravery and sacrifice of the individual soldier were never diminished but it was rarely highlighted, except by New Zealanders. And though cognizant of Alan Cunningham's problematic mental state, and Alexander Galloway's insubordinate actions, the Official Histories took pains to push these issues to the background.

The private versions of *Crusader* and the Cunningham supersession, WO 106/5826 and CAB 106/655, were key to it all. But this too would end. The files were created by the CIGS, Alan Brooke, and contained Top Secret documents by and about Alan Cunningham and his supersession. The reanalysis of the original documents, above all Cunningham's accounts, was transferred to the Cabinet Office Historical Section and provided the core for the Official History and the included portions of the debates between Latham and Agar-Hamilton. Their correspondence focused in on the critical issues of Cunningham's decisions and Galloway's actions. The file even played a covert role in Field Marshal Montgomery's unsuccessful attempt to undermine Alan Cunningham as High Commissioner to Palestine.

Its aftermath, however, was not nearly so fraught as its early decades, but it was telling of how the army command and the larger Establishment had moved on from wartime issues. On 26 September 1958 Permanent Undersecretary of the War Office Edward Playfair wrote to his relative Major General I.S.O. Playfair at the Cabinet Office Historical Section, enclosing a copy of the Cunningham supersession file.

> Gerald Templer, on leaving his office as C.I.G.S., has been doing an energetic turn out of the C.I.G.S.'s safe. Among the things in it he found the attached envelope which I think it is simplest to send to you exactly as it stands. I have removed one of the two copies of the report alleged to be in the envelope for the sake of record – at least until this correspondence is over. The enclosure in the envelope and the one which I have kept are both carbons. There is no trace now of the original. We do not know whether Field Marshal Alanbrooke ever sent it to you, nor do we know who abstracted one of the three original copies, presumably some time between 1st May 1945 and the 12 December 1946. None of these points are very important at this late date, but at least it is worth sending the thing to you in case you have not already got it.[205]

Three days later Brigadier C.J.C. Molony responded to Playfair:

> Thank you very much for sending over the papers dealing with the removal of General Cunningham from his command in 1941. It was very kind of you to do so. We had in fact seen a copy of these papers, but it was some little time ago. It may well have been this copy. I return it, with again my thanks.[206]

Molony's polite note is slightly obscure, particularly the meaning of 'some little time ago'. The original CIGS letters went missing and what remained in the CIGS's safe in 1958 could only have been WO 106/5826, slowly denuded of its original three copies. The first missing copy resided in Montgomery's files and would end up in his collection at the Imperial War Museum. But, as Playfair noted, 'None of these points are very important at this late date.' In effect, this was the Establishment's last word on the incident. The once burning issue of Cunningham and *Crusader*, which had flared throughout the 1940s and 1950s, had burnt out even before the publication of the British Official History in 1960.

It was inevitable that the world changed more rapidly than the Official History. The first volume on the Middle East and Mediterranean conflict appeared in

1954, the final one in 1988. Volumes in the parallel Civil Series, written by professional historians or other scholars, appeared much more quickly. But as the 1960s dawned, the era of Official History and Establishment concern regarding the narratives of the Desert War was over and an era of intense revisionism was about to begin. The personal narratives of old men and their younger adversaries came into conflict, and the government and increasingly British society stood aside. But journalists had already set the stage for a shrunken perception of the Desert War.

7

Crusader and the Desert War in the Public Eye

Remembering what to forget

Churchill's famous speech in November 1942 about the 'end of the beginning' came after Alamein. That beginning phase of the war was, however, remembered selectively; arguably, more was forgotten than remembered. After the fall of France, Britain may have been willing to fight alone, and then alongside Russia and the United States. But the circumstances of the war, at home and overseas, were increasingly unhappy, grim conditions that implicitly shaped later memories as well as histories. It was a period seemingly destined to be forgotten.

After the heroic stand against the Blitz from September 1940 through May 1941 the circumstances of war for the British people shifted for the worse. On the one hand, the German invasion of Russia in June launched a titanic struggle whose vast dimensions dwarfed those of Britain, in terms of geography, populations and sheer slaughter. This relieved the burden of Britain standing alone (Lend-Lease notwithstanding) but cast its heroism in a different light. But on the other hand, Russia's sudden material needs began another drain on British wartime production that was just beginning to become organized after a chaotic beginning. Russian needs, as well as those of British forces, put ever-higher labour demands on British industry and were accompanied by growing exhortations for Britain to open a second front. What some referred to as Churchill's private war in the Mediterranean did not qualify. The international and domestic political dimensions of coalition warfare exerted new strains on British society.

In response to growing production needs, the British economy was overhauled once again; there was a shift from voluntary sacrifices to compulsory ones, and to increasingly organized central planning. Railroads and ports, along with their owners and labour forces, had been in a chaotic state in 1940 and early 1941, but new initiatives brought these gradually under control, agreements short of nationalization but which advanced the cause of labour. Registration of men and women for assignment to wartime industries was also introduced, and the maximum ages were progressively increased. Countless workers, firms and industries all found themselves on various essential lists, subject to government controls. But along with the military and Civil Defense, the sheer numbers of bodies required to mobilize Britain to total war was staggering. The military needs in particular required manpower be withdrawn from industry: age limits for workers were continually raised again and by the end of 1941 the conscription of women into the military was necessary. Though in a sense popular with women, who now could do their part alongside men, it was a radical shift for society.

But despite the growing workforce and levels of production, shortages bit deeper and deeper, driving dramatic price inflation and, in early 1941, the introduction of rationing for food, clothing and other goods. At the same time the Battle of the Atlantic took an ever-greater toll on shipping, imports and lives, reaching horrific levels in the first half of 1942. While rising taxes were apparently not an overwhelming social concern, the loss of housing from the blitz and rising food prices were. Evacuations from urban areas to the countryside exacerbated the problems. In 1941 another 300,000 children and mothers were evacuated, bringing to the total to some 3000,000 persons displaced.[1]

Anger against perceived and real inefficiencies, profiteering and waste were also growing, which drove political discontent. The no-confidence vote of May 1941 had been a warning sign, although Churchill received overwhelming support. Another warning sign was the need to reorganize the Cabinet at the end of that year. The confidence vote of January 1942 had a similar result, despite Britain's reverses and dire straits. But the by-elections of early 1942 saw large and unexpected gains by Labour, a signal of discontent not only with the Conservatives but with Churchill himself. The military reverses of 1942 – the loss of Malaya, Burma, Singapore and the Dutch East Indies, Japanese raids on the Bay of Bengal, and finally Tobruk – exacerbated the domestic political problem, which reached a peak in the famous debates of July 1942 and another no-confidence motion.

Britain in 1941 and 1942 was thus neither a happy nor a confident place. The entry of the Soviet Union and then the United States may have changed the course of the war, but in the short term it did not materially improve the lives or perhaps even the moods of Britons at home and on the battlefields. Indeed, these worsened. Journalists, tasked with explaining the war to the home front and the reverse, and explaining both to the rest of the English-speaking world, captured the mood. Their picture was not good, and the war in the Middle East figured prominently.

Journalists and the first draft of history

In his memoir of the Burma Campaign, George MacDonald Fraser, formerly a private in The Border Regiment, reminded readers that 'by rights each official work should have a companion volume in which the lowliest actor gives his version (like Sydenham Poyntz for the Thirty Years' War or Rifleman Harris in the Peninsula); it would at least give posterity a sense of perspective'.[2] For the Second World War, ample numbers of memoirs began to appear immediately. Truly corrective accounts would not emerge until later, but journalism began this work. In doing so, they compounded the negative impression of an already grim 1941 and 1942.

Perhaps more than any other group, journalists were the first to intellectually break down the barriers between the British populace and the history of the Desert War. Their books were a useful corrective to the overly optimistic propaganda from official sources, the emergent Official Histories of pamphlets and then the bulky, unreadable Official Histories themselves, and to some extent their own reporting from theatres of war.

A resurgence of interest in war correspondents has brought their work into better focus, and correspondents working in Egypt in 1941 are no exception.[3] A stream of books, memoirs and analyses of correspondents illustrated their contributions and travails, their problematic relations with the British military, censors and their own newspapers. The problem of their objectivity, which looms as a contemporary intellectual or academic concern, is not easily addressed, except to say that as liberal Westerners they supported the British war effort, if not always its strategy or leadership.

But if their newspaper descriptions at the time were overtly patriotic, overly optimistic or grossly inaccurate, their writers cannot be understood as parrots or Pollyannas. Their reporting was shaped by the information available to them at the time, including their own observations and official statements, and also – as they admitted – by military censorship designed to limit the release of both operational information and negative assessments of the British military.

The general tone of newspaper coverage at the time is succinctly captured by the headline of war correspondent Christopher Buckley's front-page story in the *Daily Telegraph and Morning Post* for 24 November 1941, 'A Modern Blenheim in the Desert.'[4] A commentary published the same day by 'A Student of War' sang that the 'Libyan campaign has opened so brilliantly that all our thoughts tend to be concentrated upon the shifting quadrilateral Tobruk-Sollum-Sidi Omar-Bir el Gubi. Here it is that a large enemy force of tanks and infantry have been outmanoeuvred and are now being outfought'.[5] The author situated the *Crusader* battle, at that moment turning disastrously against the British, in vast terms of the entire European conflict and predicted a successful outcome might even have the effect of keeping Japan out of the war.

Such exaggerations and misapprehensions are common in war journalism, but the realities, once they were learned, were stinging, especially for the journalists themselves. For this reason, rather than catalogue their predictable errors of fact and interpretation made at the time, it is more useful to review the many books war journalists published shortly after the events. A survey of books published from 1942 through the end of the war shows that – in contrast to their newspaper reporting – journalists uniformly saw Operation *Crusader* as a mediocre outing by the military. Comparing them often creates a *Rashomon* effect, where multiple viewers present varying accounts of the same events, highlighting both similarities and differences. These accounts provide a fuller picture of press perceptions that shaped public attitudes and memories, an early and negative narrative that would be amplified after the war by memoirs.

Several journalists – notably Alan Moorehead, Alexander Clifford, Matthew Halton, Richard Busvine, Christopher Buckley, Eve Curie and possibly Chester Wilmot – were at 8th Army Advanced Headquarters during some portion of the *Crusader* operation but none supplied a first-hand account of Auchinleck's visit or Cunningham's relief. Journalist Sean Fielding, serving as military conducting officer for colleagues, also provided an important account of the battle in his pamphlet *They Sought out Rommel: A Diary of the Libyan Campaign, from November 16th to December 31st, 1941*, published in June 1942. Though frank and insightful, as well as popular, it cannot compare with journalistic accounts that would appear from 1942 onwards.

Alan Moorehead and Alexander Clifford were among the best-known and most prolific journalists working in Egypt. Both filed stories continually from the desert but each also wrote multiple books that summarized their observations and judgements. Moorehead's books *Mediterranean Front*, *A Year of Battle* and *The End in Africa*, later published together in a single volume called *African Trilogy*, covered the years of command by Wavell, Auchinleck and Montgomery, respectively, giving him a scope and comparative perspective most war correspondents lacked.

Moorehead's accounts also stand out for their arresting balance of penetrating descriptions of places and people and introspection, rare literary gifts that give polish and depth to his cynicism regarding the absurdity and waste of war. His critical stance towards British authorities, however, must be tempered by the realization that he was also perhaps the war correspondent with the best personal connections to the establishment, by virtue of his wife's role as secretary to Auchinleck and later as Montgomery's biographer.

Moorehead, an Australian expatriate who had travelled widely across Europe and who had already covered the Spanish Civil War, has been studied several times,[6] but several things stand out in his interpretation of *Crusader*. One telling fact is that his 1943 book *Don't Blame the Generals* was retitled *A Year of Battle* before his three volumes were republished together. Another is his assessment of the state of British morale and strategic thinking in August 1941: 'There was something through this quiet time something definitely and deeply wrong with the mental attitude of British forces in the Middle East.'[7] In spite, or because, of Eden's 'optimism and confidence' and Lyttleton's 'appalling dull' and 'bland and evasive' press conferences, 'everyone looked forward to the coming winter campaigns with enthusiasm and dangerously brimming hope'.[8]

Another of Moorehead's penetrating observations is that this was the period of 'a widening political and emotional gulf between the soldiers of the Middle East and the people of England. We had never been bombed in our homes. The men here never knew the long weariness of working day in, day out, in a factory'.[9] Simple necessities such as adequate food, transportation and heating were not lacking in Egypt, yet were so dear in Britain. And at the same time, the desert was 'clear, straight warfare', 'the essential grimness of total war could not be experienced here for this was not total war. The women and children were not involved'.

Paradoxically, then, Moorehead argued that soldiers perceived the desert war less viscerally than the people of England, for whom 'in a certain sense Benghazi was almost as real to them as London. It was the symbol of the success of the weapons they had made and the calibre of the men they had sent out as their champions. They saw the fate and worth of England in the desert'.[10]

Moorehead believed the divide between Britons at home and in Egypt was wider still. British soldiers in the Middle East, 'almost an all-British sphere, full of all-British ways of thinking and some of them a little behind the times', were cut off from the 'increasingly left-wing movement among the soldiers and workers of England'. While it was difficult for men 'reared in the Public-School-University-City-Regular Army atmosphere to adjust themselves suddenly to the idea that they were fighting side by side with Communists', the labour conditions of the 1930s reduced the 'mental upheaval' for the average soldier. The 'seeds of admiration for the Reds' spread and helped hopes in the ranks run 'dangerously high'.[11]

The results of this confluence were clear:[12]

> The optimism of the Cairo spokesmen was no accident, nor were reverses in the field. They flowed logically and arithmetically from the sort of system we were busy erecting in Egypt through this August. No one man was to blame. The false and easy optimism was spread because we misjudged the temper of the people in England; reverses occurred because we misjudged the enemy. We had not then, nor as far as I can see, have we yet learned the simple equations-understate your early successes so that your later successes will appear the greater and later failures will seem the less. And-never underrate your enemy whether you win or lose.

Moorehead's description of the contingent relationship between events in Britain and the desert was unique but was written with the benefit of hindsight, and how he reached his broad conclusions about Britain is unclear. But his emphasis on military overconfidence and on seeing Britain and the desert as a temporarily united entity or continuum is important for understanding the longer-term impact of *Crusader* and the Desert War on British memory. Failure, mutual incomprehension and the inevitable dialectic between optimism and disappointment were to be the drivers of divorce. Moorehead was more negative still about the mediocre quality of Egyptian rule over Egypt in the early twentieth century, about the baleful effects of Egypt's social classes and profiteering on the country's development.

Readers would not fail to understand Moorehead's ambivalent and conflicted take on matters, even as they would be flattered by his presumption that they 'saw the fate and worth of England in the desert'. This ambiguity extended to his assessments of command personnel.

Retrospect also coloured his description of Auchinleck, who to that point 'had been something of a mystery' and whose 'record did not promise genius'.[13] Although Auchinleck's career had, in Moorehead's view, followed a conventional path, the man[14]

> who stepped out of his aircraft one hot morning in June 1941 to take command in Cairo was, of course, utterly different from his reputation ... or, rather, different from what everyone expected him to be. But when people had got over their surprise at finding him so different, and Auchinleck had taken his

two defeats in the desert, it was again fashionable to point to his prosaic career and say, "He lacked new ideas, drive, initiative." Both views-the early reaction in his favour and the subsequent tendency to regard him as just another regular soldier-were hopelessly mistimed and misinformed. This book is no defense of General Auchinleck. But it is an attempt to describe his two campaigns in the desert and explain how they went wrong under the direction of this vigorous and intelligent mind.

Moorehead was thus aware that conventional wisdom was unfair even as he usefully charted it and proposes deeper explanations. One key is Auchinleck himself:[15]

> There is a strange contradiction in nearly everything about Auchinleck, and this in the end is probably the reason why success was always snatched away from him just at the moment when it seemed secure. He had extraordinary charm and gentleness in conversation, and could be utterly ruthless. Half a dozen times he sacked some of his closest associates who failed-sacked them overnight so that one day they were in charge of a sector of the battle in the desert and the next on their way to England and retirement. In each case he maintained a bigoted loyalty to these men until they had made their major mistake, and you might argue from this that he was no chooser of men.

This is the public origin of the idea that Auchinleck was a poor picker of men, one that would be repeated many times in later years, indeed, until the present.

But Alan Brooke had already recorded the idea privately by in his diary on 30 January 1942.[16] This raises two possibilities that the perception of Auchinleck was shared across a broad swath of the military and the media and that these two communities had not only shared but cultivated the idea. Moorehead's assessment that there were a 'half a dozen' sackings refers to Cunningham and Ritchie, 7th Armoured Division commander Frank Messervy, relieved in June 1942, along with 13 Corps commander Godwin-Austen, who had resigned in January 1942 after Ritchie had countermanded an order. As for 'bigoted loyalty', this appears to refer to fellow Indian Army officer Messervy and perhaps Eric Dorman-Smith, who was sacked in August 1942 along with Auchinleck himself, although Moorehead concedes that it 'is only fair to say here that Auchinleck had an amazing run of bad luck with generals' killed, captured or injured. 'This total of nearly twenty commanders goes beyond mere coincidence or the normal fortunes of war ... it meant that Auchinleck simply did not have the men to lead his troops in the desert.'[17]

Moorehead was the first to comment on Auchinleck's other contrasts, his personal warmth and lack of a public persona, his relishing of command and willingness to delegate responsibility, in which he 'kept believing that his commanders in the field possessed the same foresight and rapidity of decision as he did',[18] an assessment echoed much later by Correlli Barnett.

In contrast, Cunningham was a much less interesting person. 'He was a blue-eyed, ruddy-complexioned man with a soft voice, and he smiled a good deal. He looked more like a successful businessman than a general even when he said to us, I am going to attack the day after to-morrow … everything depends on how the battle goes.'[19] And with this underwhelming introduction, and the 'one irresistible thought that filled my mind was that within thirty-six hours all these placid, sleeping men were going to rise up and start killing each other', Moorehead went off to battle.

Moorehead's battle was a microcosm of the army's, filled with confusion, misinformation and violence. With the armour hopelessly divided and outgunned and cut off from headquarters, the scene filled with scenes of personal courage but fortune did not favour British forces. The German breakthrough was and was not a surprise, and with shells suddenly falling on them, Moorehead and his colleagues joined the mad rush eastwards:[20]

> All day for nine hours we ran. It was a contagion of bewilderment and fear and ignorance. Rumor spread at every halt, no man had orders. Everyone had some theory and no one any plan beyond the frantic desire to reach his unit … I came to understand something of the meaning of panic in this long nervous drive. It was the unknown we were running away from, the unknown in ourselves and in the enemy … Had someone been there in authority to say "Stand here. Do this and that" – the half our fear would have vanished.

With the command failures self-evident, Moorehead and his party found themselves at Cunningham's Advanced Headquarters, where it became apparent that the situation, though utterly confused, was not as dire as had been thought. But while 'Cunningham had little hesitation in pointing out that the wisest course was to retire his army out of Libya to re-group,' 'at this moment Auchinleck exhibited a touch of brilliance and moral courage that was the high-water mark of his career. He flew to the desert and opposed a final and absolute "no" to the proposal for retreat.'[21] In the midst of the chaos Auchinleck reorganized the forces and stiffened the army's resolve. Finally, 'returning to Cairo Auchinleck drove to his house on Gezira and late at night wrote the letter to Cunningham which removed him from command. There was no time to consult Churchill or the War Cabinet. Auchinleck himself had to take the decision to depose the man he had sent for so hopefully only a few months before.'[22]

Cunningham was never mentioned again and Moorehead returned to Cairo shortly thereafter for a brief rest. But the portrait he painted of the British conduct in the desert, and his ambivalence about the highest levels of command, was indelibly fixed in readers' minds.

In contrast to Moorehead, penetrating and mordant, Alexander Clifford was a more positive individual with a keen eye for detail. His book *Crusader* was published in 1942[23] and a revised version covering the entirety of the North African war, *Three Against Rommel*, was published in 1943.[24] The description of Operation *Crusader* in the latter book was almost precisely the same, although there were subtle revisions, particularly in the framing of the operation.

Like the best war correspondents Clifford was at once a travel writer, anthropologist, psychologist, political analyst and memoirist. And like all correspondents he observed how alien the desert was and took for granted his ability to travel, relatively unimpeded, from Tehran to Cairo. His first impression of Auchinleck was positive but diffident, 'certainly a fine figure of a man – tall, very well set up, brown, not-very-tidy hair, and extremely striking light-blue eyes', but[25]

> as to ability, we didn't know much ... It became fashionable to say that he was a talented general but not a genius, that he was certainly a good Corps commander or Army Commander, but had yet to prove himself a Commander-in-Chief. That was probably true – in any case, it was as much as anyone could say at the time. But he inspired confidence, his decisions were clear-cut and firm, and he was immediately liked and trusted by those who worked with an under him.

Cunningham, 'hero of the capture of Addis-Ababa',[26] was known only for the East Africa campaign and for having a famous brother. Though 'ruddy-faced, blue-eyed, outspoken', Clifford had little to say about him until two days before the battle when he and other correspondents were summoned to a meeting, where 'we sat round a bare trestle table and drunk whiskies and sodas while he told us what was going to happen.'[27] 'He said would start with superiority in the air, almost certain superiority in tanks, slight inferiority in man-power. He was absolutely confident of success, and though the Italian morale would collapse quicker than ever as soon as the Germans cracked.'

Clifford's reaction was the same as that of his fellow correspondents: 'Most of us felt that the official optimism was being pitched just a little too high. I think newspapermen instinctively distrust optimism.'[28] Clifford's understatement was matched by his colleagues' negativity.

The precisely calibrated launch of the operation quickly disintegrated into confusion for Clifford and his party, who blundered about the desert looking for a headquarters unit without luck. Clifford's initial descriptions unfolded on two levels: battle scenes related in an impersonal manner, with few indications regarding what he actually saw, interspersed with scenes of life in the desert. The cold, dust and cooking have an immediacy that the battles do not, at least until the two worlds collided as Clifford's party was dive bombed and he witnessed the 'grim, frozen look' on the German pilot's face before the plane crashes.[29] Another collision occurred as German forces began their rout, prompting Clifford to comment to his colleague, 'I think this is the real thing.'[30]

The flight to Egypt was a case of 'sheep', the British support forces comprised of unarmoured vehicles, being 'stampeded'. At night Clifford learned from a tank officer just how badly British armour compared to that of the Germans, calculating that this gave the Germans an eighty-second advantage as the two sides would join battle.[31] And upon reaching 8th Army Advanced Headquarters, he found 'the confusion was indescribable ... The operational maps now looked like surrealist masterpieces'[32] as the forces shifted back and forth.

Marie Curie's appearance at headquarters caused a minor sensation, and Clifford felt compelled to note that while she was 'the only woman for something like three hundred miles in any direction. She discovered the disadvantage of his when Major Churchill had to drive her four miles out into an empty patch of desert and discreetly wait with his back turned'.[33] This would be one of many commentaries by war correspondents regarding Curie's bodily functions. But the situation was unstable, and the 'evening before we arrived the whole Headquarters had been warned to get ready to leave at half an hour's notice'.[34] This observation drew directly from his diary, only there Clifford also noted that Churchill had to drive Curie three miles into the desert.

At this point, however, the chronology of Clifford's movement becomes difficult to reconstruct. It appears that he spent several days at Advanced Headquarters, visiting RAF units on 26 November and then, along with Moorehead and Randolph Churchill, set off to find the 7th Armoured Division the next day. Neither his book nor diary gives any indication that he knew that Auchinleck had come to the Advanced Headquarters, although in a discussion of RAF operations he noted that 'Tedder flew back and forth between Cairo and the desert, conferring, planning, organizing, correcting mistakes, foreseeing difficulties', without noting the date.[35] It appears the entire supersession had occurred under the nose of experienced war correspondents, who only found out when they left and then returned to the 7 Armoured Division on the night of 27 November.

Clifford's description of the supersession was the longest and most detailed provided by any correspondent, amplifying greatly the few sentences in his diary:[36]

> The news was so extraordinary that I didn't believe it. We argued about it until we went to sleep and next day we drove back to Army Battle Headquarters to see what we could find out. There were rumours, but no one knew anything definite. Whatever the truth, it was being kept a dead secret.
>
> What had, in fact, happened was this: on November 22 General Auchinleck had come up to the desert. For three days he had worked beside General Cunningham. On the 24th there had come the great enemy break-through down to the border. What happened inside G.H.Q. that day is a story which will have to wait till after the war. But things must have looked pretty black.

Here Clifford published for the first time the text of Auchinleck's 'attack and pursue' instruction. But it was to no avail:

> Next morning, flying back to Cairo, Auchinleck thought the thing over very carefully. On his arrival he held a series of conferences. And the same day he wrote a letter to Cunningham relieving him of his command, and appointed Major-General Ritchie to command the Eighth Army with the rank of Lieutenant-General. Cunningham flew secretly to Alexandria to stay with his brother, the Admiral, and then went into a nursing-home. But before he went he repeated his opinion that the Eighth Army should withdraw from Libya and drew attention to the consequences that might ensue if it did not.

Clifford's account confused the chronology of Auchinleck's visit along with details such as Cunningham's subsequent movements, but he grasped both the necessity of Cunningham's relief and the strategic implications. Still, despite the fighting words, the larger impression of *Crusader* left with the reader was not positive.

Journalists less known that Moorehead and Clifford had interesting and influential comments regarding *Crusader* and their work also show a narrative arc from 1942 to 1945. Little remembered today, novelist and playwright James Lansdale Hodson was an editor for the northern edition of the *Daily Mail* and a prolific war correspondent for the Kemsley Group, which included the *Sunday Times,* eventually writing seven books chronicling his travels.[37] His October

1942 *War in the Sun,* based on his diary rather than dispatches, included an account of Operation *Crusader*.

Hodson was in the group of journalists who met Cunningham in his command bunker prior to the offensive.[38]

> Cunningham shook hands with all of us – over twenty all told. He then leaned his back against the wooden side of the room and talked. He is a florid man – white mustache, blue eyes, rather short. Put him in civilian clothes and he'd look like a country doctor. He's a bachelor and has always lived on his pay – said to be one of our few generals who never went to Staff College.

To this slightly underwhelming description, Hodson added important details: 'He had no plan except to go into Libya and take up positions – then von Rommel would have to act and on Rommel's actions our own would depend. (This did not strike me as genius, but I may be wrong.) He added: "I am not trying to fox you – there is no plan beyond that."'[39] Cunningham's remarkable comment, unquoted by other correspondents, obviously backfired. What was intended as a bold statement regarding an imaginative tactic, however questionable, behind which logically stood a 'plan' in the sense of immense logistical preparations, was uniformly received as credulous or worse.[40]

Hodson's own view was made through a quote from an unnamed source: 'Later, one of our chief Intelligence officers said to me': 'If the enemy had gone back, withdrawn, six weeks ago, we should have been done.' His opinion of Cunningham was also expressed indirectly:

> Randolph Churchill had suggested we should not ask too-awkward questions, as Cunningham had small experience of the Press and might get scared. So two or three of us had been deputed to ask a question each. But Cunningham appeared very ready to help. He was asked if sandstorms would hinder us. He said that, apart from the actual fighting, they might help us.[41]

Overall, Hodson provided a plethora of details but little cohesive narrative.[42] Like other correspondents, he repeatedly noted the involvement of Randolph Churchill in reorganizing press coverage to speed the flow of reporting, usefully humanizing an otherwise shapeless or caricatured figure. Regarding Willoughby Norrie, Churchill 'quoted somebody as saying that in the old days you found an able man and made him a general; now you make a man in general and hope to God he turns out to be an able man'.[43] And unlike most correspondents, Hodson noted freely problems with morale as well as British propaganda, noting importantly that 'the common view is that Winston started off this campaign by pitching it on too high a note; that we ought to have begun more modestly and waited for hard results before shouting.'⁴⁴ Overall, however, his description of the battle was kaleidoscopic: individual tales of fighting amidst chaos, the inferiority of British tanks and reversal of fortune, with a rare emphasis on British casualties as well as German supply problems.

But Hodson's characterization of Cunningham's view that the 'objective is to destroy the enemy armoured divisions – territory doesn't matter much. (A marked change of outlook from the last war)' hints at the operational conception in a more positive sense. Like almost the entirety of the British command, which had seen the titanic bloodshed of the Great War, Cunningham was casualty averse. Drawing Rommel into decisive armour battle in open territory, naïve from a tactical or logistical point of view, had a humane rationale. Still, he makes no mention of Cunningham's supersession. Perhaps he was unsurprised.⁴⁵

Russell Hill was correspondent for the *New York Herald Tribune* and had previously reported from Europe, including Germany from which he had been expelled. Later with other correspondents Hill had escaped from Yugoslavia on a sardine boat and sailed to Athens and then Alexandria, despite the loss of their pilot, killed by a German plane. His *Desert War*, published in early 1942, provided another eyewitness account of Operation *Crusader*, only from a distinctly American perspective. For Hill, meeting Auchinleck gave him the 'impression that "the Auk" was a man of ability as well as charm, although he might not possess the extremely rare quality which is military genius'.⁴⁶ For Hill Cunningham 'had a brilliant record' whose

> reputation stood higher than that of any general in the Middle East. There was no reason to believe that he would not do well in the Western Desert, unless it were that his experience had been with an entirely different types of warfare, and that he was pitted against a man who was an expert tank general. Also he was suffering from poor health.⁴⁷

With this underwhelming introduction, the first half of which regarding Cunningham's reputation was certainly untrue, Hill, too, attended Cunningham's briefing, commenting, 'Even as he greeted us I could see he was very confident.'⁴⁸ But details were vague: 'His object was to find Rommel and beat him. By Rommel he meant the German armored forces. He would try to find these forces and knock them out.' Cunningham acknowledged the numerical superiority of Rommel's forces but believed that 'the morale of the British, Imperial, and Allied troops was superior. Also, and this counted for a lot, we had more tanks and planes'.⁴⁹ Hill appears to have been impressed by Cunningham's confidence in his troops and in himself: 'He had always won. Now he expected to win, too, in the same way. But he had never before fought against Germans. He had never before fought against large numbers of tanks. He had never before fought in the open desert.'

Hill's Hemingway-esque prose notwithstanding, his account of the desert focused largely on the novelty of American tanks in battle for the first time. His interlocutors were full of praise for the speed and manoeuvrability of American tanks but not their guns. The reality of the weakness of British weapons became a kind of rhetorical trope and historical axiom. Another trope was the appearance of 'Miss Curie' and 'what she did about certain natural needs which are felt by even the most charming and attractive women'.[50] Like all correspondents, Hill reported that Randolph Churchill drove her into the desert and turned his back.

Hill spent many pages discussing his movement in the desert during its different phases, including the route back to the border of Egypt. He also expounded at length regarding the performance of American tanks, seemingly confident that American readers would find this informative and perhaps even inspirational. But Cunningham's relief was merely 'a dramatic piece of news' delivered by Randolph Churchill, on which the correspondents later speculated 'as we sat on our camp beds looking up at the myriad stars and arming ourselves with our last half-bottle of Cyprus brandy'.[51]

But Hill added one interesting detail. On 3 December, after a command conference, Hill and another correspondent were given five minutes with the new army commander, Neil Ritchie:[52]

> He gave us the "official" reason for his appointment, which he said might only be temporary. It was that General Cunningham was in bad health and could not continue at present on such an active job. He would probably be granted sick leave. General Auchinleck had appointed Ritchie because he did not wish to change one of the corps commanders in the middle of the campaign. This was said no doubt because one might wonder why a major-general had been chosen when there were lieutenant-generals already in the field.

How much to read into the quotation marks around 'official' is a matter of conjecture, but here again understatement as a cultural norm and rhetorical device may be at work. But it demonstrates that while the narrative of Cunningham's illness was being generated in correspondence between Auchinleck and London, it was already a fact in the desert. And for correspondents like Hill, long accustomed to being under fire, this was barely newsworthy.

In contrast to the understated Hill, American Quentin Reynolds of *Collier's Weekly* was touted as 'a man who goes everywhere, knows every one, and remembers everything.'[53] Married to movie star Virginia Pine, the former football star and future screenwriter's 1943 book *Only the Stars Are Neutral* followed up his evocatively titled *The Wounded Don't Cry* and *London Diary*.[54] His style was hard-boiled and breathless, and like most correspondents he took for granted both unfettered access to political and military leaders and his readers' interest in such accounts.

Urged to Cairo from Teheran at the instigation of Walter Monckton, Director General of the Ministry of Information and Under Secretary of State for Foreign Affairs, Reynolds joined other correspondents at the Shepherd's Hotel, whereupon they discussed at length the meaning of the word 'poon' and its application to various women. This was followed by a high-stakes poker game between the correspondents and Randolph Churchill, the 'visiting fireman', who won $2000. With Anglo-American relations thus cemented Reynolds flew to Fort Maddalena.

It is unclear exactly when Reynolds arrived, but from his description it appears that it was on 24 or 25 November. Reynolds's description of Cunningham's relief is so odd that it deserves to be quoted at length:

> The "Auk" was the one to take chances and to make sacrifices of men, if need be. Some generals lose battles trying to save men. Not the "Auk." He didn't like the way Cunningham had hesitated. Cunningham was driving at Tobruk, and was well on his way to taking the battered old city. But then he slowed down. He kept worrying about his railhead some sixty miles away, and he diverted part of his attacking forces to the East to protect it. That is like stopping to tie your shoelace when you're fighting Joe Louis. Rommel moved in, divided Cunningham's forces, and for the moment disrupted the British advance. The "Auk" immediately fired Cunningham. It was a courageous thing to do. To begin with, the success of the whole Libyan campaign depended on the co-operation between the Army and the British Navy, commanded by Admiral Sir Andrew Cunningham, brother of Alan. By firing Alan, the "Auk" risked the personal antagonism of the Admiral. But Alan Cunningham had committed the major military blunder; he had looked over his shoulder. Jockeys don't win Derbies by looking over their shoulders. You don't win battles that way either, so General Cunningham had to take the rap. He was replaced by General Ritchie, whom the "Auk" called a "thrusting General."[55]

Reynolds's grasp of military operations was weak, even long after the battles had ended. His description of Wavell, whose successes against the Italians were remarkable, was galling. Reynolds's description of Cunningham's relief was equally weak on details but captured the heart of the matter, at least for

American audiences. Moreover, it suggested that to an outsider writing for an audience far removed from specifically British concerns, Cunningham's relief was a minor detail: he was a blunderer who deserved to be replaced.

More interesting indeed, shockingly effective, was Reynolds's story of his time in the desert, which escalated from fairly conventional descriptions of battle to Reynolds under terrifying attack by German planes, screaming hysterically for his mother. He received minor injuries and was evacuated to Cairo at the end of November or beginning of December, after perhaps a week in the desert. Overall, one can only agree with a reviewer of Reynolds's book who noted the 'irrepressible American journalist and feature writer enjoys the war in Britain, Russia and the Near East in spite of its inconveniences'.[56]

Edward Kennedy of the Associated Press had been present in Egypt and Crete during Wavell's years, but he was most famous for having been expelled from Germany by the Allies for announcing the German surrender one day early. His memoir was written in 1950 but was not published until after his death.[57]

Kennedy's perspective was especially scathing:[58]

> The desert force, which had borne the newspaper-given name of "the Army of the Nile," was designated the Eighth Army. Lieutenant General Alan Cunningham, the conqueror of Ethiopia, was made its commander. Cunningham, of rosy face and clear blue eyes, looked like a healthy English squire. At press conference in Cairo on his departure for the desert, he exuded confidence to a point of foolishness. He saw little difference between desert warfare and the bush warfare he had waged successfully in Ethiopia; in fact, he saw no serious problems at all. He seemed to overlook the circumstance that he now was not pitted against a demoralized Italian colonial force, but against the best-organized and best-led Panzer force the German army had.

His account of Cunningham's supersession was equally harsh:[59]

> Auchinleck hurried to the desert to find out what was going on. Cunningham confessed he didn't know; he did not know his own dispositions, let alone the enemy's. The bewildered commander of the Eighth Army recommended giving the whole thing up as a bad job, withdrawing, and starting again later. Auchinleck sacked him on the spot. To avoid an adverse effect on the morale of the troops, it was decided to attribute Cunningham's removal to illness, and he agreed to enter a hospital. He made the story true by suffering a nervous breakdown in the hospital. Invalided to England, he recovered and filled home commands later in the war. Churchill would never give him a field command again, but when the Labour Party came to power, Cunningham was assigned the thorny Palestine commissionership-general.

The selection of Ritchie, a 'black-moustached and colourless figure who looked like a London bobby', did not improve the situation.

Kennedy's rather garbled account could be easily dismissed were it not for his critique of the 'fantastic claims of victory [that] emanated from the "Cairo spokesman", which meant Army Public Relations'.[60] Even before the battle Kennedy had clashed with a very specific spokesman, Brigadier Shearer. According to Alexander Clifford, on 22 October a number of journalists including Kennedy had been summoned by Shearer and admonished for 'breaches of trust and tendentious reporting'. Kennedy stormed out of the room and refused to stop when shouted at by Shearer, who then stated: 'Well that ends all relationship between us!'[61]

Later, as Rommel went back on the offensive in January 1942, Kennedy knew who was to blame: 'Brigadier Eric James Shearer who was responsible for a large part of the misinformation made public from the Middle East.'[62]

Ironically, Kennedy's contempt for Shearer was obviously shared by Alan Cunningham; at the moment Kennedy was observing Shearer's apparent mendacity, Cunningham was making his case in London to Brooke and others.

But the disparity between public expectations generated by officers in the rear, including intelligence heads like Shearer, does not explain command failures in the field. Intelligence sources, especially *Ultra*, show that Auchinleck and thus presumably Cunningham were well informed regarding German supply problems as well as Rommel's tactical objectives.[63] Shearer's mistaken and misleading assessments of German tank strength and resupply were made in December and January, after Cunningham had returned to London.[64] And it is conceivable that correspondents and even Cunningham had become caught up in Shearer's multiple roles as head of intelligence as well as deception operations, and a public face to the press. The fact that in March 1942 Auchinleck's new Chief of Staff, Brigadier Thomas Corbett, relieved Shearer – in a move that was heartily endorsed by the CIGS – suggests that in the end Shearer had crossed himself up.[65]

Eve Curie's 1943 account, *Journey among Warriors*, has been mentioned earlier. The novelty of a woman correspondent accounted for part of her popular appeal, as did her parentage. But Curie's account is valuable not only because of her graceful style and keen eye but because her unexpected presence elicited unusual responses. Curie, too, described the rout of British forces but with particular sympathy for foreign forces fighting the Germans, expatriates like herself.

Upon reaching Advanced Headquarters 'the presence of another commander – a strong, sun-burned man with light brown hair and blue eyes, who sat near me in complete silence-simply petrified me with timidity. The same presence had rendered Randolph Churchill, for once, absolutely mute and motionless, which will appear as a remarkable result to anybody who knows the turbulent son of the Prince Minister'.[66] To this penetrating description Curie then added her much repeated quote from Auchinleck; '"He [meaning the enemy] is making a desperate effort, but he will not get very far. That column of tanks simply cannot get supplies. I am sure of this." The way he said "I am sure of this" gave me, suddenly, a great tranquility.'

But Curie then added several curious details. She departed from Coningham and Auchinleck but learned later in Cairo that Auchinleck's[67]

> unannounced visit to the air vice-marshal had a serious motive. General Auchinleck had decided, that very night, to relieve the commander of the Eighth Army, his close friend Lieutenant General Alan Cunningham, and to replace him by Lieutenant General Neil M. Ritchie, whom he was to relieve a few months later, at the time of Rommel's great push into Egypt-before being, to everybody's surprise, relieved of command by Winston Churchill. Auchinleck had come to see Air Vice-Marshal Coningham (what a mixture of similar names!) in order to announce to him Ritchie's appointment.

Auchinleck and Cunningham were not friends of any sort, and where Curie could have picked this improbable notion up is unknown. And the idea that Auchinleck made his decision to replace Cunningham before returning to Cairo and had informed Coningham before departing is unlikely but not impossible, given his conversations with Galloway. Curie may more accurately reflect rumours in Cairo after the fact that exaggerated the certainty of Auchinleck's observations at Advanced Headquarters and directly or by implication, Cunningham's debilitated condition and reputation.

Like those of other British correspondents, Alaric Jacob's 1944 account of *Crusader* in *A Traveller's War* was mixed. Jacob had been at Cunningham's pre-offensive brief and found him 'smiling and confident, pink-faced and healthy. He looked like a foxhunter. But the particular fox he was after proved to be wilier than he'.[68] The *Daily Express* writer went on to observe that it was 'easy to look back on that evening with wisdom and pronounce General Cunningham's plan, or rather lack of planning, faulty from the start; but I do not remember any one doing so at the time'.

Having damned commanders with faint praise, Jacob turned to the issue of the quality and quantity of weapons, specifically American-supplied tanks and British anti-tank guns, and added how 'Brigadier Shearer and Randolph Churchill were emphatic that what material Washington *had* sent us out to get a good showing in our despatches'.⁶⁹ Jacob's remorse about the inaccuracy of his reporting – 'misleading, inaccurate nonsense! But, of course, we did not realize it then'⁷⁰ – echoed Cunningham's private complaints to Brooke at the end of 1941 regarding both the equipment and the overly optimistic briefings by Shearer.

Jacob's observations regarding the relative material weakness of Auchinleck's army compared to Montgomery's were canny, as was his comment that 'the student of war will find Auchinleck's campaign a more interesting one that Montgomery's. Auchinleck fought a real desert war'.⁷¹ But his picture of Auchinleck's relative material privations, sprawling front and tactical difficulties may have heightened the unfavourable comparison with Montgomery in the reader's mind. Though not the brilliant shoestring improvisations of Wavell's battles, Auchinleck's was an equivocal story where the initial promises of politicians and the army commander were unfounded, and where bravery and limited success in the face of desperation did not redeem a sense of disappointment.

The *Daily Express* correspondent's description of the rout of 24 November hardly improved the picture, with its lament regarding the 'crowning ignominy! Even the Italian trucks joined in the chase'.⁷² Jacob described the event as similar to 'the exaggerated chase scenes in the early Movies when the Villains giving chase seem to be catching up on the Hero all the time'. His account of the retreat and the turn of the battle, only to be followed by the British withdrawal to the Gazala Line in February, rounded out a story of courage but not clear victory. After Jacob's adventures, Cunningham's supersession was not deemed worthy of mention.

Canadian Matthew Holton was with Jacob and Fielding during *Crusader* and his 1944 book *Ten Years to Alamein*⁷³ was another vivid retelling of the battle. He was no more impressed by Cunningham's pre-operation briefing and the juxtaposition with the actual events: '"What is your plan?" we asked. "To seek out Rommel's armour and destroy it," he replied. Thirty five days later we were in Benghazi. Rommel's forces were destroyed. So were ours.'⁷⁴ Holton also echoes the complaints about the relative strength of British and German tanks: 'So it was a man with a dirk fighting a man with a sword.'⁷⁵ But unlike Jacob, Holton addressed the issue of Cunningham directly, saying, 'The situation was too much for General Cunningham. He wanted to call of the whole operation, retire to Egypt and admit defeat. But not General Auchinleck.'⁷⁶ Holton adds, perhaps imaginatively, that Auchinleck instructed Ritchie 'that the Eighth Army must go to Benghazi or die. I believe the exact words were: "You and the army must win, or never come back."'⁷⁷

With the entry of the United States into the war, Holton lost interest in the desert. But his descriptions bear consideration in terms of their reception. By the time Holton's book was published (1944) Egypt was long a backwater and Allied operations, and Western attention, had shifted to the Italian campaign and to the impending invasion of Europe.

But Holton, like many correspondents, was scathing regarding what he had seen in Cairo, especially the corruption of the natives, another elements that shaped readers' minds about this phase of the war.

For Holton, Cairo as the headquarters of British forces was 'cosmopolis' become 'bedlam'.[78] Moorehead and Clifford, residents for long periods in Cairo, drew it as a languid and corrupt backdrop to their stories but Halton provided a pithy description of heterogeneous city, with 'women of all complexions from negroid to Caucasian blonde. Touts cried their wares down, the streets and small boys offered to lead you to ineffable delights for fifty piastres ("very sweet, very clean, very beautiful"). Each time the enemy won a victory and neared the western approaches several night clubs closed and each time we won a battle new ones opened.'[79] Holton's assessment of a city where 'rich and callous pashas drove past beggarwomen sprawling on the pavements and half-naked babies too diseased or enervated to claw the flies from their eyes' was clear. But curiously, and in sharp contrast with others, Holton was defensive regarding British rear echelons, even the censors.

The alienness of the desert, and of the Egyptians, uniformly depicted as greedy, corrupt and of low morality, almost incidentally resident in a theatre of war where remarkable British feats of arms were being attempted, complicated narratives and is unlikely to have produced a sense of closeness or sympathy from readers. Most correspondents, even Americans, appear to have tapped an underlying sense of Victorian morality; yet, they were not inventing what they saw. Their revulsion, or resignation, was palpable. As a class, correspondents were deeply earnest about the honesty of their reporting and belief in the values that drove the fight against fascism, but the absurdity of war and warriors could not be easily reconciled. And however much they might have reluctantly enjoyed the many pleasures of Cairo, they were not above moralizing about it.[80]

Highlighting the absurdity of war through humour was one approach. Richard Busvine's 1944 book *Gullible Travels*[81] is a prime example. One day Busvine was the managing director of a fashionable London dressmaker, the next, by dint of slim but influential connections and being too old to serve, he was a correspondent for the *Chicago Times*. Drinking his way to expertise and then across every theatre of war was the foundation of Busvine's approach, as it might be argued it was for many other correspondents then and now, but his ear for hard-boiled dialogue and absurdity was unique.

Seen off from London by one woman he calls The Screwball (and who called him Butch) and attended to in Cairo by another he called The Doll, Busvine's war had the flavour of a *Thin Man* film. In contrast to other correspondents, Busvine revelled in the high life of Cairo ('Smelly, blatant, irresponsible Cairo. Cairo, the glamorous city of the Orient! Cairo, your kindly, fussy maiden aunt. Whatever you want to find in Cairo you *can* find. But doughnuts will get you dollars that in the end it will prove to be phony'),[82] and his descriptions of the dining and clubbing have a rueful sense of high times lost rather than a lament over the waste so emphasized by Moorehead and Clifford, with whom he experienced *Crusader*.

Summoned by Randolph Churchill to meet Cunningham, Busvine and the other correspondents trudge across 'sand with the sheen of snow' in a scene that reminded him of his experience during the Finnish War of 1939–40. Cunningham 'gave an outline of our plan of attack, which seemed to be based chiefly on the assumption that the German Armoured Forces would not stand and fight, but must be cornered and brought to battle. A strange theory, I thought to myself, if based on Rommel's strategy up to date. I little knew how strange and how costly that theory was going to prove'.[83] But as for the battle itself Busvine demurred and referred readers to Moorehead's and Clifford's 'exciting and amusing works'. For his part, with the bombing of Pearl Harbor Busvine immediately sought to travel east to Singapore, 'which seemed to me of far greater importance to an American public'.[84]

Australian Chester Wilmot brought a very different sensibility to the desert. His book *Tobruk 1941* was published in 1944. Wilmot's perspective was on the Tobruk garrison, where he reported on Australian forces from August to September 1941, and then with British forces in November during *Crusader*. Regarding 1942 and the fall of Tobruk, Wilmot claimed there was 'no valid' comparison with the prior year since Rommel's forces were stronger and there was no British offensive underway to bring relief to the garrison.[85] By 1942 Wilmot had moved to Southeast Asia and in 1944 was employed by the BBC covering the European theatre.

Wilmot's Tobruk narrative resembled a military history more than a war correspondent's account. Indeed, in 1952 Wilmot published his influential *The Struggle for Europe* and was intending to write the official Australian history of the Desert War before his death in 1954. In his account of Tobruk, individual soldiers are mentioned, as befitting an account discussing a relatively smaller force, and their contributions are praised but there is little fulsomeness. Moreover, there is little of Wilmot himself in the narrative: almost no accounts of experiences under fire, few personal reactions to witnessing combat and death, and no expressions of either fear or joy. In this sense it does not resemble any other report from the field.

Wilmot's comments regarding the position of the press, however, are similar to those of other correspondents, particularly 'the tendency to regard the war correspondent as first cousin to a fifth columnist'.[86] But beyond this there was little direct criticism of military or political leaders. Even Cunningham is laconically and incorrectly described as 'an infantry commander with little experience of armoured warfare and none of the Western Desert'.[87] Still, Wilmot's description of Cunningham's tactical approach is subtly devastating; he quotes Rommel's comments to a captured British tank commander to condemn the practice of splitting up armoured formations to be smashed one after another.

Yet for all Wilmot's tactical perspicacity regarding Cunningham's conduct of the battle, his description of the supersession is flat:[88] 'By this time, however, Cunningham was convinced that there was no chance of relieving Tobruk. He recommended to Auchinleck that the Eighth Army should withdraw to its former positions in Egypt, regroup and refit. Auchinleck would not hear of this. He flew at once to Cunningham's H.Q., bringing with him a new Army Commander, Major-General N. M. Ritchie.'

Wilmot went on to claim that Auchinleck stayed in the desert and directed the battle himself. Australian readers were thus given an account that was strong on tactics but weak on personalities and framed in strategic terms by a preface and epilogue that reflect the perspectives of 1943. The Australian accounting for the fall of Tobruk would come later.

Other correspondents reported from the desert, including the *New York Times*' Sam Pope Brewer, Arthur Merton of the *Daily Telegraph* (who had reported on the opening of King Tutankhamun's tomb and killed in a car accident in 1942 that injured Randolph Churchill), and Paul Holt, Richard Dimbleby of the BBC, and Christopher Lumby of *The Times*. All were influential in their own way but none produced books discussing the desert.

How can we sum up the many overlapping perspectives of war correspondents? For one, with the exceptions of Moorehead and Clifford, most gave short and superficial treatment to the Wavell era, treating Richard O'Connor's immense victories against Italian forces in a respectful but offhand manner. Their lack of respect for the Italian military and its commanders was uniform and appears to have been shared by British commanders. In the words of one British officer quoted by Reynolds, '"It would be very silly," he said thoughtfully, "to be killed by the Italians." "It would be very silly to be killed at all," I told him. "But especially silly to be killed by Eyeties," he persisted.'[89] Only the supplies lavished on Italian officers, and subsequently looted by war correspondents, rated praise. A cloud of pathos was hung over Italian conscripts, who, if not cowardly, were depicted as downtrodden and simply outmatched by British troops. Most simply wanted to go home.

In contrast, German forces were praised for their fighting abilities but damned for brutality and sullen fanaticism. In years to come, as the focus was directed on German commanders, particularly Rommel, this hard edge was smoothed over, with many, especially Basil Liddell Hart, taking Rommel's own self-serving lead in describing North Africa as a 'war without hate'.

But the place of the Desert War in the larger narrative arc of war reporting is important. Few correspondents were actually in the theatre during the Wavell years, understandably, since the battle for France and the defence of Britain were the most compelling stories for British and American readers, along with the Finnish War. These events were quickly followed by the German attack on the Soviet Union from June through December 1941 and followed by the Japanese attack on Pearl Harbor.[90] In this sense the disappointments of Wavell's final operations in Libya and in Greece set a depressing tableau not only for Auchinleck but for the suddenly enlarged number of correspondents in the desert in the later 1941.

For American correspondents in particular, the political leanings of their newspapers and networks, from interventionist to neutral, also played a role shaping accounts for the public. Much hyped by Churchill, military representatives in Cairo (not least of all Shearer) and the correspondents themselves, *Crusader* was – until Alamein – ultimately cast as a sideshow to much larger events taking place elsewhere. And for those writing in retrospect during and after Alamein, the middling results of Operation *Crusader*, and its command failures, appeared that much more dubious.

Some of the negative perceptions of British operations were shaped by habitually poor relations between journalists and military press officers and by censors. Public relations head Col Philip Astley in Cairo is mentioned positively and contrasted with Brigadier Shearer and especially the witless Captain Berrick, who failed to recognize the explicit sarcasm of calling the Italians 'charming' in a passage discussing their booby traps.[91]

But for all their wide-ranging perspectives and worldliness, war correspondents were an insular group, many of whom literally shared the same experiences in the desert, no doubt worked out while sipping brandy beneath the stars. None moved independently and, despite Randolph Churchill's efforts to speed the movement of their dispatches and lighten the hand of censorship, none could present accounts that significantly critiqued operations in the desert. Even their books published without censorship months to years later, they presented fairly homogeneous accounts. To them, Operation *Crusader* was not a success.

Measuring public awareness

Journalists had shaped public perceptions during and immediately after the war regarding Operation *Crusader* and Alamein. Newspapers continued to do so after the war, if only by omission. There were scant references to *Crusader* or its commanders, or even to Richard O'Connor or Wavell, and newspaper items that mention Cunningham in his role of High Commissioner in Palestine cite his role in the desert in passing. Despite the first memoirs that cast him in poor light, Cunningham's public rehabilitation was effectively complete.

At the same time, public memory of Operation *Crusader* and the first two years of the Desert War were fading from view. While newsreels had covered *Crusader* and its predecessors, documentaries were few. *Desert Victory* and other full-length documentaries made by the Ministry of Information during the war were by their nature 'obviously inspirational and celebratory productions'.[92] But there were also few feature films that emphasized the early phase of the war. One exception was the 1943 film *Nine Men*, in which a flashback shows British troops fighting off Italian forces. Another is the 1944 film *The Way Ahead*, also set in the desert but which shows British troops fighting Germans. Both focus on the travails and heroism of small groups of soldiers without reference to 'political' issues such as battles and commanders.

Humphrey Bogart's starring role in the 1943 film *Sahara* sets the action in the Battle of Gazala in July 1942 but is properly a film by and for Americans. It would not be until the 1950s that British filmmakers returned to the Desert War, with films such as *The Desert Fox: The Story of Rommel* (1951) and *Sea of Sand* (1958).[93] The positive representation of Rommel in *The Desert Fox*, based on Desmond Young's biography, had Liddell Hart as technical advisor, and his mythology of a clean 'war without hate' in the desert was given immense support and an agreeable face, in the ironic form of James Mason – a conscientious objector who did not serve during the war.

The mythos was further enshrined in the film *Ice Cold in Alex* (1958), which closed with the German spy claiming that all were 'against the desert, the greater enemy'. But Houghton has recently made the important observation that British memoirists who fought both in the desert and in Europe pointed to the former as an arena where war did far less damage to civilians and represented relatively 'cleaner' contest of wills.[94] If the desert was a clean war, it was in terms of collateral damage as much as chivalry or against the desert itself.

But memories were malleable. The famous Alamein reunion illustrates the process of Desert War commemoration and its emphases. The October 1946 reunion saw some 5000 'Desert Rats' assemble in the Albert Hall to hear Montgomery and Churchill, while the next year, with the addition of RAF veterans, over 7000 attended. In his call for veterans to turn out, Montgomery flattered the men of the 8th Army who 'fought at Alamein and in the Desert for the standards of honesty, team work, hard work, and a high sense of duty; it is these standards which we all need today at this time of crisis, and the men of the Eighth Army can be a strong force in these respects on the side of true democracy'.[95] Alamein was thus imbued, however successfully, not only with a specific historical significance but with a sense of future political obligation. Prior battles went unmentioned.

The next year, in 1949, Montgomery went on to further articulate the linkages between past and future, stating that the true symbol of the 8th Army was the tow-rope by which 'a broken down vehicle and its crew were pulled to safety', arguing that a 'glorious prospect of peace, understanding and happiness' and 'true understanding' between all peoples had been lost in the postwar period: a 'tow-rope philosophy was needed'.[96] Montgomery's idiosyncratic philosophy likely owed more to the intersection of his own upbringing as the son of a minister and his position of CIGS viewing the collapse of British power at home and abroad. But Alamein as a military operation – and what came before it – was lost.

Montgomery's messages at later reunions would be similarly hortatory, and Churchill's regular appearance cemented the importance of Alamein as a concept as well as their monopoly on the event as history and commemoration. More than 8000 attended the 1953 reunion but by 1962 the number had dropped to 3000, at which point, in the aftermath of memoir wars and revisionist histories, Montgomery exhorted that 'there are enough troubles in the world today without arguing about what happened 20 years ago'.[97]

The reunion continued for a time after Montgomery's death in 1976 but with different emphases, including British–German reconciliation and remembrance of, as one British attendee put it, a 'clean war, fast-moving, almost sporting war'.[98] This is a far cry both from the reality and from contemporary reporting, which for example in July 1942 reported frankly that New Zealand troops had bayoneted 500 Germans at Merseh Matruh.[99] It appears then, as far as remembrance went,

Liddell Hart's conception of the Desert War was triumphant, clean, chivalrous and with little trace of stupidity, brutality and waste, much less earlier battles such as *Crusader*.

What remained was memory, telescoped personal experience that, at its most intense,

> left such a deeply etched impression, that the whole spectrum actually re-inhabits my being with such remarkable freshness that the weight of the nostalgia is almost too much to bear, feelings that I had incurred towards people, incidents, nature, which I thought of as almost trivial, were really of Titanic proportions, and ones, that I now realize were to stay fresh and become more poignant as the years passed, and the desire to experience them all once again, be they good, bad or indifferent became a haunting spectre that suddenly, during the course of a day, takes you unawares, a particular word, a scent, a colour, or song could trigger it off.[100]

Memoir wars

History: Money, vindication, restoration

The postwar rush to publish memoirs had many different purposes. For Churchill the effort was the natural continuation of his life's work to prolong the Late Victorian world with him at the centre. But for many former generals an even more important motivation was economic. Retired officers' pensions were low and lower still for retired Field Marshals, who remained on the list of active officers only at half pay. Another was to present testimony, commemorating personal achievement and that of others for purposes as varied as self-aggrandizement, memorialization of sacrifice and self-vindication.

Most famous memoir was the result of CIGS Alan Brooke's reluctant decision to permit publication of his wartime diaries, in part the result of financial pressures that forced him to sell off his beloved collection of ornithology books.[101] Brooke's diary, bowdlerized and converted into text by historian Arthur Bryant, was published in two volumes in 1957 and 1959. In it he described Operation *Crusader* as something hyped by Churchill as 'a page to history that would rank with Blenheim and Waterloo'.[102] But the actual course of the battle and Cunningham's supersession went unmentioned, overshadowed by Pearl Harbor. His actual diary mentions neither.

Other Field Marshals and senior officers found themselves in similar situations, pulled by financial need and the impulse to make a statement in an environment where interest was receding. Harold Alexander's ghost-written memoirs were serialized in the *Sunday Times* in 1961 and published the next year as a book. Hastings Ismay, Churchill's chief military advisor and part of the syndicate that had helped Churchill write his version of the war, published his own memoir in 1960. His account of *Crusader* may reflect the perspective of Churchill's circle in London: 'Auchinleck went to the front himself, and found that General Sir Alan Cunningham, who had done so brilliantly in East Africa, and whom he had personally selected for the command of the Eighth Army, seemed on the verge of a nervous breakdown. He had been deeply affected by his losses in armour and was inclined to break off the battle.'[103]

But it was Montgomery's memoir that caused the largest firestorm. Commissioned in 1954, the book was serialized in a newspaper and published in 1958, the year he retired. The book, which began with a remarkably frank and self-critical tone regarding his upbringing, quickly devolved into a lengthy recitation of score-settling and self-glorification. It was a tremendous success and launched Montgomery's late in life career as a military commentator.[104]

In his memoir Montgomery cast the issue of Cunningham's supersession in terms of Auchinleck's poor judgement regarding personnel:[105] 'Again, nobody in his senses would have sent Ritchie to succeed Cunningham in command of the Eighth Army; Ritchie had not the experience or qualifications for the job and in the end he had to be removed, too.' Montgomery's subtle misrepresentations of the situation he found when appointed to command the 8th Army in August 1942 echoed those he had published in 1946 in his shadow memoir *El Alamein to the River Sangro,* particularly with respect to defensive preparations around Alamein and contingency plans to withdraw the army to the Nile Valley in the case of a German breakthrough.

The preface for the eruptions surrounding Montgomery's memoir had begun much earlier in 1951 when Eric Dorman-Smith, by then renamed Dorman-O'Gowan, had threatened a lawsuit against Churchill for the latter's depiction of Auchinleck's defensive preparations prior to Alamein and their dismissal in August 1942. The affair, which dragged on for three years and involved Churchill's solicitor, entailed consultations with Brooke, Montgomery, Alexander and others, resulting in an agreement to use Dorman-Smith's friend Liddell Hart as an impartial arbiter of the conflicting accounts and ultimately Churchill's assent to include a footnote correcting his initial account.[106]

In 1958 Auchinleck's response to Montgomery was a letter to the *Sunday Times* denying he had planned to withdraw from the Alamein position, followed by the threat of a lawsuit. Behind the scenes solicitors were again consulted and intermediaries drawn into the fray to find an acceptable solution to a situation that had potential to embarrass not only the ageing participants and their legacies but the Establishment, including the BBC where Montgomery was scheduled to give a broadcast discussing his most famous battle. Without apologizing or conceding the point, Montgomery was induced to insert a note into future editions crediting Auchinleck with 'stabilizing the British front on the El Alamein position'.[107] Satisfied, Auchinleck withdrew his threat and Montgomery's second career continued unabated.

Montgomery's publisher, Denis Hamilton, the father of his biographer Nigel Hamilton, perceived the later 1950s as the period when British voices finally pushed back against misrepresentations of British wartime strategy and conduct in American memoirs and histories.[108] This might be true, but Commonwealth Official Histories had already contributed to the negative impression of British leadership in North Africa prior to Montgomery that had been constructed by journalists.

This public antagonism towards commanders riled feathers, at least within a certain rarified segment of retired generals. In 1955, after the publication of the New Zealand account of Alamein, *Battle for Egypt*, editor Howard Kippenberger reported to his South African counterpart John A.I. Agar-Hamilton that Bernard Freyberg, former commander of New Zealand's forces and by then a member of the House of Lords, was upset:[109] 'Why he should be concerned that his disapproval of Middle East Command is not made public I don't know. He was at considerable pains to express his views then and ever since. But he says that Alex thinks it was in bad taste and others are pained and the less said of these things the better.'

Apparently Freyberg himself understood the explanation, as did the editors:[110] 'As General Freyberg used to say, people are not interested in the details of battles but in the quarrels between generals. That is quite true, though he was not so pleased when his own quarrels were related.' Behind the scenes Alexander Galloway was drawn into the fray, commenting to I.S.O. Playfair that 'I have been very heavily involved recently over this idiotic battle between the Two Field Marshals, and hope that all is now calm enough to see them out. It seems undignified that this sort of thing happens and the only beneficiaries are the lower grade sections of the press'.[111]

Montgomery's memoir was nonetheless a turning point, which extended the mythos of his leadership and the repurposing of Alamein into a mode of commemoration directed at politics outside the realm of history. These factors pushed *Crusader* and preceding events further into the background. But this culmination of the memoir wars, the apotheosis of Montgomery's self-aggrandizement and the abstraction of Alamein into symbol, overshadowed the actual publication of the Official History of *Crusader* and laid the foundations for revisionism, namely that of Correlli Barnett's *The Desert Generals* in 1960. Hubris had bred nemesis. It would also cast new and harsh light on Cunningham.

Crusader participants looking back through time

The history of *Crusader* began to be written immediately after the events but each account must be evaluated on the basis of their timing and proximity to the actual battle. A few, like 4th Indian Division commander Lt General Francis Tuker, would write an entire account of the Desert War including *Crusader* without even mentioning Cunningham or his supersession.[112]

Other factors also shaped perceptions of the earlier phases of the Desert War. The firings of generals after Cunningham created a subtle and unfounded sense that British commanders were inferior, a sense cultivated after the war by Liddell Hart's celebration of Rommel and other German generals. The resignation of Lt General Reade Godwin-Austin in January 1942 after an order was countermanded by 8th Army Commander Neil Ritchie bookmarked Cunningham's dismissal, particularly in Churchill's eyes. The earlier relief of Major General Michael Creagh in September 1941 from command of the 7th Armoured Division, and the dismissal of Willoughby Norrie, Frank Messervy and then Ritchie, after the first Alamein battle in the summer of 1942, and finally of Auchinleck and Dorman-Smith in the 1942 'Cairo Purge', all fed the impression. In a sense this early phase of the Desert War resembled the first years of the American Civil War, where a succession of Union generals was tried and found wanting.[113] Unfairly or not, this helped set the tone for later history as well as memory of this stage of the war. Memoirs would continue to do so.

de Guingand

As noted earlier, the first and arguably the most influential account of *Crusader* came in 1947 from Frederick de Guingand in his book *Operation Victory*. de Guingand had been on the Joint Planning Staff in Cairo and took over as Director of Military Intelligence after Shearer and was appointed 8th Army BGS in July 1942. Long a protégé of Montgomery's, de Guingand survived the 'purge' at the end of the summer of 1942 and became Montgomery's invaluable Chief of Staff throughout the North Africa campaigns and beyond. After retirement he proved a canny businessman, who helped manage Montgomery's finances, as well as an engaging writer.

de Guingand's 1946 account of the critical days of *Crusader* was important in that it presented in effect Galloway's version of the events. Since de Guingand was based in Cairo, it may be assumed that he ascertained matters from Auchinleck, Tedder, Lyttelton and probably Galloway himself. In a second memoir published in 1964 de Guingand's account again lauded Galloway but was much more concise:[114]

> Then he acted with great courage and determination during a critical phase of the 'Crusader' battle. General Cunningham lost heart when Rommel's mobile forces looked like threatening his communications. He ordered a withdrawal of the Army Headquarters back behind the wire into Egypt, It was then that Sandy Galloway, B.G.S. Eighth Army, showed great foresight and initiative, for he pretended to pack up many vehicles, but did so with the firm intention of staying put until the Commander-in-Chief arrived. On Auchinleck's appearance he took him aside and expressed his alarm at the proposed backward move, and Auchinleck lost little time in canceling the orders and relieving Cunningham of his command.

For de Guingand, eighteen years after his first account, Cunningham's 'doubts' had become an equally vague 'loss of heart', but Galloway's role remained pivotal.

John Connell Robertson

Auchinleck had refrained from becoming publicly involved in the memoir wars of the 1950s and the controversy around *Crusader*. But he was drawn in thanks to Dorman-Smith's conflict with Churchill in the early 1950s and then his own with Montgomery. Auchinleck's 1959 authorized biography by 'John Connell', the journalist John Connell Robertson, devoted over 400 pages to Auchinleck's year in the desert and had the benefit of full access to his then private files, including official correspondence with superiors. Though not written by Auchinleck himself, it is very nearly his own account.

Titled *A Critical Biography* the book veers between hagiography and operational history, with an endless recitation of command decisions and telegrams.[115] Framing the scene heavily with the South African Official History and other published accounts, Connell's description of Cunningham's supersession relied on Auchinleck's first letters to Cunningham. Published in full for the first time, they provided Auchinleck's rationale as 'defensive thinking' and Cunningham's 'strain'.[116] These gave no medical justification and made no mention of Cunningham going into the hospital for examination. By allowing private documents selected from a much longer series of exchanges to apparently speak for themselves, Connell depicted Auchinleck as decisive and firmly focused on the battle itself, rather than focused on the messy politics of the affair.

Lyttelton

Oliver Lyttelton, by then Viscount Chandos, published his account of the Cunningham supersession in 1962. It tracks with his 1941 note to David Margesson but adds a few new details:[117]

> Auchinleck told me that he and Tedder were going at once to the front, and that he would be back shortly. The news was a shock to me, and I felt the grip of anxiety.
>
> Two days later I was told that Auchinleck and Tedder were on their way back, and would be at the conference at G.H.Q in the evening.
>
> At the usual time I went round, and in the corridor leading to the map room I ran into Tedder. He stopped, and in the most marked and significant tones, spacing his works with care, said, 'It is most unfortunate-a great mistake-that the Auk has come back to Cairo'. 'Please don't talk to me in riddle', I said. 'You mean that Cunningham is not confident of winning the battle?' 'Yes'. 'Then he must be relieved tonight'. I hurried into the C. in.-C's room, and asked him the obvious question outright.
>
> He said he was more than glad that I had asked it and had expressed myself forcibly: the command of the Eighth Army was a War Office appointment, and he would have to ask me to support any action on which he determined. I said, 'You must not give this aspect of your authority a moment's consideration. This is a battle, and I will take the full responsibility for what you decide, but you must act tonight.' He then told me that Cunningham had talked of withdrawing behind the frontier but that he, Auchinleck, had ordered him to continue the attack.
>
> In the event, it turned out that Cunningham had fought himself to a standstill, and that his physical resilience had given out.
>
> I sent a telegram to the Prime Minister. I had certainly acted in haste, but I thought I knew what his attitude would be. I could not sleep for thinking of poor Cunningham, the brilliant commander with so many victories to his credit.

Tedder's role did not appear in Lyttelton's December 1941 letter to Margesson, and in the published account Lyttelton's own words were bowdlerized for public consumption even as his forcefulness was emphasized. But rather than a breakdown, Cunningham's 'physical resilience' was named as the source of his vacillation.

Tedder

The last major memoir by a principal who was on the scene at 8th Army Advanced Headquarters was that of Marshal of the Royal Air Force, 1st Baron Tedder, published a year before his death in 1966:[118]

> The following day, 23 November, I received a message from Coningham asking me to go up to the Desert as soon as possible. Shortly afterwards, Auchinleck received a similar message from Alan Cunningham, saying that vital decisions might be called for, and we decided to fly to the Desert together.
>
> General Auchinleck and I, Alan Cunningham and 'Mary' reviewed the situation carefully, then I went off to confer with our Air commanders.
>
> Meanwhile, Auchinleck was assessing the land situation. Alan Cunningham told him that on account of recent losses we were now probably inferior to the enemy in fast tanks.
>
> After breakfast on 25 November, I had a quiet talk with Auchinleck. I had felt uneasy about Alan Cunningham for some time. Again and again he had struck me as taking counsel of his fears. He seemed to be obsessed by the counting of heads, and gave me the impression of feeling completely at sea in matters of armoured warfare. General Cunningham himself remarked to me: 'I wish I knew what Rommel means to do.' This impressed me as being a strange outlook for the commander of a superior attacking force. Once the battle had begun, he fluctuated between wishful optimism and the depths of pessimism until after a day or two 'Mary' Coningham had become so worried that he had signaled me to come. Although Auchinleck's arrival had produced an immediate tonic effect, and although matters now seemed to be working satisfactorily again, I urged that the Commander-in-Chief should stay the in the Desert a while longer. I felt that Alan Cunningham would inevitably relapse. I think that Auchinleck had probably made up his mind already that he would stay; at all events he agreed. I made no secret of my grave misgivings about the direction of the Eighth Army.
>
> After lunch I returned to Cairo in the Lockheed, landing as the sun sank low behind a lovely golden blaze over the Nile. I wondered what was happening

in the Desert. The next day, Auchinleck returned to Cairo. Alan Cunningham had again relapsed. I learnt that Auchinleck had discussed the affair with 'Mary' Coningham, whom I had told to speak frankly, and with the B.G.S., General Galloway, who was level-headed and sound but felt that he must be loyal to General Cunningham. Auchinleck and I discussed the situation. He told me that he had decided that an immediate change in command was needed. I assured him of my whole-hearted support. That night I met Oliver Lyttelton in the corridor leading to the Map Room. I told him that it was a great mistake for Auchinleck to have come back to Cairo. He asked: 'You mean that Cunningham is not confident of winning the battle?'

'Yes', I replied.

'Then he must be relieved tonight,' said the Minister of State. He urged this course on Auchinleck, offering to support him fully in London.

Tedder's account agreed with the private accounts he sent Portal at the time, including about Coningham's doubts regarding Cunningham, and with those of Lyttelton and Galloway. At the end of his life, with little to gain from a skewed account, Tedder's account appears definitive.

Belchem

David Belchem had been GSO 2 (Ops) assisting Galloway in Greece and was chosen by him as GSO 1 (Staff Duties) for the 8th Army. He was present at the Advanced Headquarters until 25 December, departing only hours before Auchinleck returned to Cairo. He may therefore be regarded as a first-hand observer, albeit one not fully privy to conversations between the commanders.

In his 1978 book Belchem noted: 'Cunningham looked the figure of a general, but he remained remote, showing no warm personality; he made no attempt to exude confidence, nor to encourage us, and he was unnecessarily sharp-tempered.'[119]

Belchem's account of Cunningham's supersession is the most Galloway-centric of all:[120]

> There are various versions published about the next phase of the story, but as I was on the spot at Fort Maddalena with Sandy Galloway I will put the record straight.
>
> In the early morning of 23 November, Sandy Galloway told me that *he* had spoken that morning with General Auchinleck in Cairo, by field telephone, and

asked him to fly urgently to Maddalena. He had explained that Cunningham was ordering disengagement and that he appeared ill. As we were talking, Cunningham was pacing up and down outside his caravan, and then came across to us. He curtly demanded of Sandy why the Command Post was not being packed up: he had ordered Galloway to move us back to Landing Ground 75, and had drafted signals to his senior subordinates to withdraw to the frontier. Sandy confided in me that General Auchinleck, with Air Chief Marshal Tedder, was airborne and should arrive soon and that meanwhile he had *not* passed the Commander's signals to the cipher people, nor did he intend to order us (of the Command Post) to pack up and move back. For the Chief Staff Officer of an Army to take upon himself such as responsibility must be exceptional indeed, but Sandy alone knew how deeply disturbed mentally, and unwell physically, our Commander was. And he knew of the pressures on Auchinleck from Prime Minister Churchill to relieve Tobruk and its gallant defenders under General Morshead (of the Australian Army). And so the time passed slowly with Galloway anxiously watching the sky for the sign of aircraft coming from Cairo.

General Auchinleck surveyed the situation rapidly. He consulted the Corps commanders, who were adamant that the operation should continue, and then gave Cunningham a written directive to attack with greater vigour the enemy who, in his view, was almost certainly even more exhausted than our own troops. Tobruk was to be relieved, and the enemy chased to the west. Auchinleck stayed two days with us, and upon his return to Cairo sent Major-General Neil Ritchie to relieve General Cunningham, who retired exhausted to hospital.

Belchem's description added useful colour to the scene at Advanced Headquarters, in particular Cunningham's state and Galloway's response, but is notably wrong about Galloway calling Auchinleck directly, as opposed to Whiteley. It is difficult to judge whether this small but telling mistake compromises his other recollections. But since there is no evidence of later correspondence between Belchem and Galloway, much less any friendship, it should be regarded as a genuine, and perhaps even correct, recollection.

More valuable than Belchem's published account, however, are his earlier private observations related to Basil Liddell Hart in 1954 during the complex debates over the South African Official History. In one Belchem noted:

Cunningham said, after the disastrous outcome of the initial armoured battle, that it was no use continuing, because even if Tobruk were relieved, we should not have adequate strength to achieve decisive results. Therefore, he aimed to avoid further losses, by disengaging – as a preliminary to a new defensive period, designed to cover fresh acquisition of strength. The Auk arrived (at Sandy Galloway's instigation) just in time to countermand the orders.[121]

Liddell Hart had pressed Belchem on the question of Cunningham's orders to withdraw, and on this point Belchem stated a point which did not clarify the matter:[122]

> Cunningham had definitely issued orders for withdrawal of the Headquarters 8th Army, before the Auk arrived on the scene. I remember him sending several times for Sandy Galloway to ask why there were no signs of the H.Q. troops packing up. Whether he had ordered withdrawal of the fighting formations or not, I cannot remember. It may have been his intention to pull H.Q. back and then to break off the offensive.

The Harding interview, 1984

John Harding was BGS to 13 Corps Commander Willoughby Norrie. In a 1984 interview he recounted several aspects of the battle including disobeying direct orders he received from Cunningham to not move his headquarters by telling the communications officer to cut the telephone wires. He also noted that 'Cunningham collapsed, had a breakdown, soon after the incident I referred to, and he was replaced by Neil Ritchie who had been on the staff at GHQ'.[123]

If Cunningham had won the battle for Official History, he had lost the memoir war as well as the battle for memory among his fellow generals. He would lose again during the revisionist turn.

The revisionists

By the later 1950s, as the memoir wars were reaching their peak, with threats of lawsuits on the one hand and letters in the newspapers between ageing retirees on the other, a new genre of analyses was about to come to light. Historian Correlli Barnett and journalist Reginald William Thompson were the most notable examples of a revisionist turn in British military history. Both were veterans of the British Army, Barnett having served in Palestine from 1945 to 1948 and Thompson in the Intelligence Corps during the Second World War.

In the introduction to the 1983 edition of his book, Barnett states that his impetus was the Montgomery myth, which 'unjustly neglected, indeed, scorned, the achievements of the British Commonwealth forces in the Desert in the hard campaigns before Montgomery's advent'.[124]

In addition to restoring O'Connor to history, Barnett sought redress for Auchinleck, who had been done a personal injustice by Churchill and Montgomery, had been denied credit for stopping Rommel in July 1942, as well as recognition that Montgomery had faced the Germans later using a plan and defensive positions prepared by Auchinleck and his principal assistant, Dorman-Smith. These views were heterodox if not heretical in 1960 when the book first appeared and 'accounts for the polemical sharpness of the narrative that so enraged Montgomery's fans. Were I writing the book today, with Montgomery reduced as he is to life-size, a Plumer rather than a Wellington and an eccentric rather than a genius, the tone would no doubt be cooler and more detached'.

Barnett had the advantage of being able to interview most of the British officers, as well as the newly appeared South African Official History, *The Sidi Rezeg Battles*, and the volumes of Playfair's history.[125] As was so often the case, Liddell Hart had a quiet role in the background as a consultant and reader of drafts. *Ultra* intercepts were out of reach but were consulted for the second edition published in 1983.

Barnett's interpretation of *Crusader* was framed in both military and social terms. For one thing his description of the battle came after long chapter exploring Richard O'Connor's early successes and Wavell's subsequent failures in Operations *Brevity* and *Battleaxe* under the command of Generals Beresford-Peirse and Creagh. The themes of under-gunned and undertrained British troops and overbearing interference by Churchill loomed large in his narrative, as it had for Galloway.

But Cunningham himself was depicted sympathetically, a talented and popular officer given the nearly task of 'leaping into the saddle of a moving horse and taking control of it', a problem compounded by the alien environment of the desert, the immense, indeed unprecedented, scale of the operation, 'rather like the successful owner of a village shop suddenly put in charge of a London department store', along with his own complete unfamiliarity with armoured warfare.[126]

Barnett's sympathy for Cunningham was broad but was tinged with a critique, for the man but more fundamentally for the army:[127]

> He was to control a swiftly moving armoured battle against Germans who had been practising tank warfare in the field since 1936; yet when he first reached the desert he so little understood radio-telephony that he is remembered fumbling helplessly with a radio-telephone, trying to use it like an ordinary telephone.

Sureness of command depends on professional knowledge and experience. However great the qualities of leadership in a man, he cannot make use of them unless he is a master of the technical details of his profession – unless he knows his subordinates' jobs at least as well as they. Otherwise his orders, made in partial ignorance, must be given and received with underlying diffidence. In the desert, in command of a large tank army, Cunningham was the green newcomer, the outsider, in the presence of many officers to whom the desert was a familiar thing, a friend; who had seen Western Desert Force grow into Eighth Army; and whose military mind had grown with it. Slight though their knowledge might be, it was yet more than that of their army commander. Thus, though it was no fault of his, Cunningham found himself in a difficult and embarrassing position of learning and at the same time giving orders to his teachers. The result was a weakening of his authority and, personally, an added emotional strain. As General Godwin-Austen, who served under Cunningham both in East Africa and the Desert, wrote later: "I felt he was not as happy in Egypt ... he did not dominate conferences as he had in East Africa.

In his evocative prose, Barnett described Galloway as both a boon and hindrance to Cunningham, since

> daily association with him could only bring home constantly to Cunningham his own inexperience. Galloway himself was a forceful personality, crisp in speech, impatient, and, like his Army Commander, inclined to short temper. Though he supplied some of the knowledge of desert warfare that Cunningham lacked, he was hardly the man to make Cunningham feel any more easy and comfortable in his headquarters.[128]

Barnett emphasized the parallels and contrasts between Cunningham and Galloway throughout his narrative.

The structure of Barnett's narrative, as well as his marvellous prose, should be emphasized. His description of the planning for *Crusader* has a decided story arc: Cunningham, a man out of his depth, an army facing unprecedented challenges – scale, tactics, weapons – for which it was mentally and culturally unprepared, a flawed plan with vague aims, and back to Cunningham:

> Thus after two months of exhausting work, and of the emotional strain of trying to establish personal ascendancy over more experienced men, in a strange and over-aweing environment, Cunningham found himself on the eve of battle with a compromised plan that seemed quite likely to produce no desired results, but instead a wide choice of unpleasant possibilities. It was not a situation conducive to buoyant confidence or calm resolution. It was aggravated for Cunningham by a personal matter. He had always been a very heavy pipe smoker; but he

had recently stopped smoking altogether, because he had slight trouble with one of his eyes, said by his occulist to be caused by smoking. But he concealed his anxieties; General Freyberg even thought him over-confident. In his eve-of-battle press conference his voice was hoarse, perhaps with strain, but his talk was resolute enough: 'I am going to seek old Rommel out and destroy him and his armour.'[129]

After a discussion of British weapons and their overstated weaknesses, Barnett proceeded to the battle itself. The battle itself was framed by a remarkable statement:[130]

> Cunningham it now seems clear, was not fit enough to bear the weight of commanding a major battle. Since February he had been under pressure almost without a pause. This pressure had culminated in ten weeks of over-work and emotional strain. His physical strength, his nerves and his capacity for clear judgment and decision had all suffered. On the eve of Crusader he seems to have already reached that stage of mental and physical fatigue when even ordinary tasks and decisions loom immense and daunting to a man. Yet Cunningham would never admit it, not even to himself; his duty lay in leading Eighth Army into battle, as it was his brother's duty to lead the Fleet; he could not go sick on the eve of action. While the army marched into Libya, therefore, Cunningham fought a private battle against the effects of overstrain.

Out of sight, the battle raged, at first indecisively and then with illusions of success, and finally on 22 and 23 November, a dawning realization of disaster. But it is here that Barnett in effect offers a lengthy digression, on 'a much more profound meaning than the miscarriage of a particular battle. The unfortunate Cunningham had picked up the bill for twenty years of military decadence'. The British Army was 'the army of a twentieth-century social democracy and a first-class industrial power, it was nevertheless spiritually a peasant levy led by the gentry and aristocracy'.[131]

Unprepared to deal with technocracy, the modest and chivalrous army leaders were trained to prize amateurism. Barnett spends pages excoriating the regimental system, reviews the history of the cavalry from the eighteenth century onwards as it conditioned attitudes towards mechanization and armour, interwar competition between the army and the RAF for money and responsibilities, the entire history of British armour and its profound contrasts with the German system, and comparisons between British and German anti-tank weapons. Far more than merely a military or even industrial critique of Britain is the kernel of a profound cultural critique: British conservativism in war, rooted in outdated methods to defend the Empire, was the origin of overall British decline.

Cunningham the man and commander was a product, perhaps even a victim, of trends and forces far beyond his grasp, with which he was especially ill-prepared to cope: 'One of the most terrifying of emotions is a sense of impotence in the presence of unfolding disaster, an awareness that events are slipping beyond the limits of one's technique.'[132] Framed by a nuanced description of the pressures bearing down on Cunningham, the lighter version of medical explanation was critical to Barnett's narrative. But importantly, it was counter-posed against a description of the British Army's phlegmatic core – centred on Galloway himself – as what turned the tide. He described the fateful meeting at which Galloway rallied commanders in terms of[133]

> the gentlemen who led the British army displayed those virtues which were as much a part of their social and intellectual order as the shortcomings that had got them into the present mess. They had defied reason in the interwar years; they defied it now with an instinctive faith that the right thing to do was the most dangerous and difficult. They had been bred to provide leadership; they prized bravery and resolution above any kind of cleverness and expertise; and they were to fight their way out of catastrophe, as had their country in 1940, by treating facts as less real than willpower.

Auchinleck's arrival at Advanced Headquarters was aided by 'some strange events occurred to keep the army in place until he arrived: tents and caravans at Eighth Army headquarters took an astonishing time to be struck, telephone lines were cut so that orders to retire or cease advancing, should they be issued, could not be received'. The human situation was momentarily as dangerous as the military situation: 'Cunningham was a spent man … he had driven himself past the limit.'[134] Fortunately, in that moment, when 'the course of the history of the war in the Middle East, perhaps world history, thus turned on the character of a single man', it was good fortune that Auchinleck was now on the scene and in command.

The remainder of Barnett's narrative used familiar elements: Auchinleck's meeting with Cunningham and Galloway, the inevitable appearance of Eve Curie and the confident order for the Eighth Army to proceed. Auchinleck returned to Cairo 'resolved to relieve Cunningham, who, it was plain to all observers, was mentally and physically exhausted with battle fatigue'.[135] After consultations with Lyttelton, the decision was made. Ritchie and Smith arrived the next day and the latter escorted Cunningham back to Cairo.[136]

> '"He was," said Smith, "a grand chap." How sad it was that at this critical time and because of his health he lost grip He was not himself-he was not Cunningham.

Even now, with the Army's battle fading behind him, Cunningham did not give up his own battle with himself. 'He was absolutely tired,' said Sir Arthur Smith, 'but was fighting against it with tremendous courage. I had great difficulty persuading him to enter hospital for a check up'. After Cunningham had been in hospital some days, his doctors found that he was suffering from severe overstrain.

Barnett's second edition makes note of evidence on Cunningham that had been published in Nigel Hamilton's biography of Montgomery, specifically the Top Secret CIGS file on the supersession that contained the correspondence between Auchinleck and Cunningham. As for Cunningham himself:[137]

While it appears that in hospital Cunningham recovered his poise within a few days, and while noting the opinion of the consultant physician that he had not suffered a nervous breakdown (whatever the clinical definition of that may be), there is still absolutely no question from the oral evidence given to me by General Galloway and others of Cunningham's senior subordinates partially cited in this book that in non-medical terms Cunningham by 24th November was a spent man, incapable of decision and resolute leadership. I therefore interpret Auchinleck's letter to Cunningham in hospital as a white lie proceeding from Auchinleck's characteristic kindness and humanity.

Barnett's description of the scene at Advanced Headquarters tracks with those of other witnesses but adds details that could only come from Galloway, Tedder or Belchem. The book was poorly received at the time but has proven influential. His interpretation of Cunningham as a spent man experiencing 'battle fatigue' grasped the situation almost as precisely as possible. But his critique of *Crusader* and the decadence of British leadership may be the more important, if understated contribution. Indeed, from *The Desert Generals* Barnett expanded his critique of the British officer class and educational system and leadership of the British military in the First World War in a series of articles, before launching his four-volume series on the 'pride and the fall' – British decline – in 1972.[138]

For his part Thompson's work was less original, in terms of its research, and was more straightforward iconoclasm directed at Montgomery and subsequently at Churchill. Sourced exclusively from published materials – and from Dorman-Smith and Liddell Hart's files – the book recapitulated the defences of Auchinleck and Dorman-Smith better articulated by Barnett. Thompson characterized Montgomery as a general whose 'invincible bloody-mindedness and his sense of infallibility'[139] appealed directly to Churchill, but who otherwise lacked charm, grace or penetrating insight. Operation *Crusader* is discussed only cursorily and

Alan Cunningham is not mentioned. Though iconoclastic towards Montgomery, Thompson's work inadvertently bolstered the narrative that everything that came before Alamein was of lesser interest.

With the appearance of a monumental three-volume biography of Montgomery, his image has been very much reduced to something more appropriately scaled, a gifted but flawed officer with an odd and cramped personality. In this much revised conception Montgomery's command abilities are not in question but his strategic insights are, and for this reason a slow but steady stream of books debating the matter continues to appear. The question of Montgomery as military genius or average commander is unlikely to be resolved. But his centrality to the mythos of the Second World War and to history cannot be avoided. Perhaps his nemesis, Eric Dorman-Smith, perceived the matter correctly in 1943:[140] 'But that is Monty. He is grand so long as he can swing sledgehammers at nuts preferably in the presence of the press.'

Operation *Crusader* and the Desert War as a whole continue to be objects of fascination. Books appear on a regular basis but most recapitulate the standard views. Without new data to review or participants to interview, the same pieces are turned over and over to produce accounts that tout Auchinleck, Montgomery or Rommel, which depict Cunningham as having had a breakdown or becoming 'defensively minded', and which describe the operation as a whole as a success or a failure. The place of *Crusader* in the larger scope of the Desert War is generally neglected even as the bravery of its soldiers is praised. But the audience for these books is limited to academics or to war history enthusiasts. As a matter of history, *Crusader* is given a reasonable place for specialists but not the general public, but as memory it had faded from view, along with the Desert War as a whole, save the vague and ambiguous icon of Alamein.

8

Crusader between History and Memory

The history of Operation *Crusader* has three enduring points of relevance:

1. It sheds light on the competence of British commanders and their subordinates during the early period of the war, including the willingness of subordinates to bypass the chain of command to get superiors to remove the incompetents.
2. Writ large, *Crusader* illustrates the ways in which history, especially uncomfortable episodes, is written, especially the inclusions and elisions to protect institutions, individuals and reputations.
3. As history writing, it illustrates the dialectic between official and unofficial histories in creating streams of understanding in historical writing and contributing to the construction of cultural memory.

The story of *Crusader* as a military operation demonstrates the importance of battlefield leadership and the ambiguities of historical documentation. The story of *Crusader* as Official History shows how ambiguities are sifted and rearranged according to the criteria of sponsoring institutions and, in turn, how these contrast with personal narratives. Fundamentally, it shows how both individuals and society were concerned with fitting the details of war, including insubordination and command, into a large sense of identity and memory.

A letter from Hastings Ismay to Claude Auchinleck captured some of the contradictions. Ismay reassured the Auk that he had 'faithfully kept my word and destroyed practically all the strictly confidential letters that you wrote me from Cairo as soon as I had read and digested them'.[1] Sources are inevitably shaped, and issues elided, without thought to history.

But Ismay had retained an extract from one of the Auk's letters, written on the eve of the battle, which he planned to include in his forthcoming memoir. The Auk's excerpt captured the essence of *Crusader* far better than anything written before or since, at least from a command perspective: 'But I wonder if you and those others who sit at the council table with you realize what a peculiar battle it is to be, and how everything hangs on the issue of one day's fighting, and on one man's tactical ability on that one day.' Indeed, for all the Official History's emphasis on machines and tactics, most subsequent historiography has focused on the peculiarities of men, their tactics and personalities.

Arthur Tedder, writing to Basil Liddell Hart, captured another aspect of the conundrum, as it related to writing the history of the Second World War:

> I wonder if it has struck you that there is a remarkable likeness between Monty and Winston in their respective attitudes towards history. In other words, each of them determined, so far as lay within his own power, to make sure 'his story' should record his own version of the events rather than history. It was in quite early days of the Desert War – even before – Monty arrived – that one saw this process of adjustment in motion, and it was early days when I was forced to the conclusion that the chances of a true history being recorded of that campaign were very slight indeed. Nothing that has happened since has made me any less pessimistic on that subject. Indeed, while it is evidence that Winston's story will in due course be disentangled, on the other hand as regards Monty the record was so skillfully adjusted at the time that I see little, if any, prospect of the truth being disentangled from the story![2]

Tedder was both right and wrong. Explanations for the failures of *Crusader* were worked out in a few weeks after the events. Churchill's political needs to downplay the question of leadership meshed with Cunningham's need for vindication. And over time both Churchill's and Montgomery's narratives have been comprehensively 'disentangled'. But at least with regard to *Crusader,* Cunningham's story of machines and Liddell Hart's story of the gifted Rommel and the chivalrous Desert War have endured, even as Cunningham's mental state has been a persistent subtext.

How much did these narratives matter in the long term? On the one hand there remains a persistent narrative regarding a 'clean' or 'chivalrous' war in the desert. This largely top-down perspective only partially masked the true consequences of battle, which were revealed in memoirs as well as in physical and mental scars, such as those that marked Howard Kippenberger and Harry B. Latham.[3] But perhaps the myths of a clean war and of the incredible 'success' of Alamein served another strategic purpose, as psychological protection from an otherwise unrelentingly grotesque reality.

Literary critic and Second World War infantryman Paul Fussell described the tragic misapprehensions that accompany the beginning of war, which also apply to its aftermath[4]: 'No one wants to foresee or contemplate the horror, the inevitable ruin of civilized usages, which war will entail. Hence the defensive exercise of the optimistic imagination.' When coupled to the equally human instincts to protect reputations and to avoid admitting error, the results of the 'defensive exercise of the optimistic imagination' are histories shaded towards exculpation, and memories that emphasize individual heroism while walling off failure. The optimistic imagination thus partitioned the two halves of the Desert War, pre- and post-Alamein, separating 'failure' from 'success', 'good' generalship from 'bad'. In this sense the best collective memories of *Crusader* were individualized and disaggregated from the larger, unhappy whole.

Churchill's frequently quoted words from November 1942, after the final battle of Alamein, drew the line clearly: 'Now this is not the end. It is not even the beginning of the end. But it is, perhaps, the end of the beginning.' He amplified them in 1951 and drove home the message: 'Before Alamein we never had a victory. After Alamein we never had a defeat.' Though unfair and incorrect, as with so many of his aphorisms Churchill was able to capture and then shape the spirit of the moment.

But Fussell offered another important hint regarding the shape of postwar history and memory, the perspective of the returned soldier, 'the conviction that optimistic publicity and euphemism had rendered their experiences so falsely that it would never be readily communicable'.[5] Literature and film tried to make sense of 'sacrifice' but few depicted the mutilation and horror that were the inevitable to combat and its aftermath, as well as the boredom and stupidity of military life at the front lines and in the far larger rear areas. Here, too, the optimistic imagination focused on success over failure, the dashing pilot and the daring Commando, and by the 1950s had swung towards a conservative conception of heroism and sacrifice, typified by the 'Myth of the Blitz'. Inadvertently, or presciently, in 1941 Keith Douglas had already captured what would become the operative postwar psychology in the opening lines of his most famous poem: 'Remember me when I am dead and simplify me when I'm dead.'

Coupled with the understandable desire to get on with lives interrupted by boredom, stupidity and mayhem, the general impulse among veterans was parallel to that of their civilian brethren, with their own distinct sense of having been very much put out by the war, to commemorate but also to forget. For both communities, past and future were bound together by uncertainty. As Evelyn Waugh's character Virginia Crouchback put it in the final volume of his *Sword of Honour* trilogy, 'As she ate her greasy bread in the kitchen she did not contrast her present lot with her past. Now, as it had been for the past month, she was aghast at the future.'[6]

How then does the past shape the future? In this we might make reference to the penetrating comments of a now neglected British historian, Lewis Namier:[7]

> One would expect people to remember the past and to imagine the future. But in fact, when discoursing or writing about history, they imagine it in terms of their own experience, and when trying to gauge the future they cite supposed analogies from the past: till, by a double process of repetition they imagine the past and remember the future.

Writing coincidentally at the beginning of 1941, Namier captured in one stroke the essential paradox about how the past structures the future and the reverse. The 'Myth of the Blitz' and the 'tow-rope philosophy' of Alamein were means to 'remember' the future and to clear it of uncertainty. Putting Namier another way, Spike Milligan asked 'Is it because with the future unknown, the present traumatic, that we find the past so secure?'[8]

Walter Benjamin famously carried this one step further:[9]

> There is happiness – such as could arouse envy in us – only in the air we have breathed, among people we could have talked to, women who could have given themselves to us. In other words, the idea of happiness is indissolubly bound up with the idea of redemption. The same applies to the idea of the past, which is the concern of history. The past carries with it a temporal index by which it is referred to redemption. There is a secret agreement between past generations and the present one.

The secret agreement between Britain and its history and memory of the war brought a measure of redemption at a cost. This entailed forgetting the years of failure including the Desert War, or describing it in the familiar, sardonic terms of the soldier. As Neddie Seagoon, brainchild of 8th Army veteran Spike Milligan, put it to the even more dim witted character of Eccles – who had stayed at his post long after the war was over – in The Goon Show's 1955 broadcast 'Rommel's Treasure', 'Eccles you upheld the flag, you never questioned the order. You stayed out here alone. You, without food or water. You, without money. You, without anything to stop you walking away. You – you IDIOT!'[10] The places of loyalty and failure in these processes of remembering and redemption are far from simple.

The impact of the war and remembrance on British culture and identity were thus transformative, but not necessarily positive. This study suggests that Operation *Crusader* and the Desert War played an important role, but far from bolstering confidence, the ambiguities and failures tempered British confidence in themselves and in their leaders. Even the rallying point of Alamein was ambiguous and after the war overburdened with additional meanings and responsibilities. And when set into the postwar contexts of economic hardship and imperial collapse, the impact on British culture was significant.

The corollary questions of postwar identity and 'national character' are broad but it has been suggested here that the decline thesis as articulated by Barnett has an important part of its origin in the Desert War. Whether Britain in fact 'declined' is beside the point: from the simple perspective of imperial retreat the answer is clear, although other metrics, not least the eventual success of postwar reconstruction and the establishment of a consumer culture, argue the opposite. Certainly in the eyes of military professionals like Alexander Galloway decline was unquestionable: 'Fortunately that is over now for Grand Mother Britain.'

Can any more be said about the relationship of the Desert War and the question of 'national character?' As conservative culture of the 1950s gave way to nostalgic 'heritage' culture of the 1960s – and spreading youth culture – the stoic 'Little Man' incarnation British 'national character' was preserved only in corners of the 'Establishment' even as the 'myth of national destiny' gradually disappeared. British national character was redefined on the one hand by the welfare state (more in the sense of entitlement than socialist ideology or class), and on the other, it was characterized by two countervailing tendencies, relentless commercialization of the present and commodification of the past.

But in the postwar generation a tension also emerged between fathers and sons, between those who served and those who did not. For all their rebellion Mods like Ray Davies (born 1944) would use elements of wartime speeches in the Kinks' 'Mr. Churchill Says' as ambiguous cues, at once satirical and envious, while Pete Townshend (born 1945) would construct worlds of heroes and anti-heroes that bridged war and peace. As David Bowie (born 1947) put it, 'We can be heroes just for one day.' The song itself refers to the fall of the Berlin Wall but the aspiration appears addressed as much to the past as to the present. But perhaps it was not coincidence that the B-side of 'Heroes' was the song 'V-2 Schneider'.

Arguably, British national character has never come to grips with the Second World War. What is failure and what is loyalty?

The aftermaths of Crusader

Alexander Galloway's reward for his acts of insubordination was promotion to acting Major General in December 1941. He was made Deputy Chief of the General Staff in Cairo, admitted to the Distinguished Service Order in December 1941, awarded the Military Cross in April 1942 and then sent to the United States to select equipment for the 8th Army. But then General Sir Alan Brooke, Chief of the Imperial General Staff, ordered Galloway to London to become Director of Staff Duties at the War Office 'much to his vexation'.[11] Fellow Cameronian and Deputy Director of Staff Duties Eric Sixsmith stated that Galloway was 'furious. All his hopes were centred on getting command of a division in the forthcoming renewal of the desert battles. For several days he did his duty in the War Office dressed in his tropical khaki drill as if to establish the fact he did not belong there'.[12]

The timing of Galloway's reassignment is puzzling. On the one hand, he had considerable desert experience and could have remained there in some capacity. His association with Auchinleck was strong but he was also close with Montgomery, under whom he would serve later in the war. Indeed, before Montgomery went to Egypt he sought out Galloway, who advised him to 'buy the biggest thermos you can find!' and more substantively to 'organize your force so that you can really control it' from the army command down.[13]

On the other hand, his War Office assignment brought him close to the army's military and political heart. His tenure as Director of Staff Duties (DSD) saw him responsible for overseeing key aspects of the immense jigsaw puzzle of the army as a whole, including its equipping and training, as it prepared for an entirely new scale of global and coalition warfare. Most of the DSD's files are prosaic records of units, equipment and training, but overall statements on how to design, man, equip and command a truly modern army are mostly absent. Galloway's role was central to transforming the British Army into the entity that went on to victory but it remains uncharted.

Here, in addition to his advice to Montgomery, reference should be made to Pile's May 1942 report to Liddell Hart about his meeting with Grigg and then Galloway, where the latter advocated the development of airborne forces, better army-air force cooperation, prioritizing weapons development along with command.[14] Galloway's view was amplified further by Pile to Liddell Hart, where he 'insisted that infantry plus tanks was the only way of fighting in the desert'.[15] Perhaps behind the scenes Galloway had a larger role in restructuring the army for victory than is generally known.

But his attitude was also summed up in 1942 to Auchinleck, after the August purge. In it he explained about the army's plans to expand weapons research, expressed confusion at why Tobruk had ever been invested in the first place, but most famously (in an excerpt published by Connell) related his experience as Director of Staff Duties:[16]

> This is not to say that I don't find being D.S.D. here interesting: it is very interesting but it isn't soldiering and I go home at night dead-tired with vexation because a third of every day is spent in the building fighting battles which are not against the Axis powers and I cannot see that it is necessary. We have a hundred examples of the bad effects upon military conception of operations and upon their carrying out by political influence, wangling, ogling, jockeying and the like and yet every time that any military operation takes place it still suffers from the same thing, and as long as we go on as we do now we shall continue so to suffer. It is a very great tragedy for it has cost the lives of thousands of men, prolonged the last two wars by at least two years and has lost us, and will continue to lose us, numbers of our best officers. It is pathetic to think that in peace time the Army struggles along stinged in every way so that even its thought is affected and that this all due to political misconceptions and vote-catching on an enormous scale, while when the war breaks out the Army has to stand the hardest knocks as the result, until, indeed, it is a wonder that it survives at all and when everything does not go perfectly it is the subject of severe criticism from high-ups and even ridiculed by the man in the street.

Galloway's fate was to be the man called upon to do unglamorous jobs. In 1944 he was briefly given command of the 1st Armoured Division in North Africa and then the 4th Indian Division, mired at Monte Cassino, before falling ill and returning to the 1st Armoured Division and finally being sent back to Britain. But in early 1945 at the request of Montgomery he was then assigned to the staff of the 21st Army Group and given the task of organizing relief for the Netherlands. Finally, at the end of the war he was made Chief of Staff of the 21st Army Group. From there he commanded 30 Corps before being assigned as Commander-in-Chief of British forces in Malaya.

His last military command, from 1947 to early 1950, was as High Commissioner and head of British forces in Austria. After retirement he became the representative of the United Nations Relief and Works Agency for Palestine Refugees in Jordan.[17] He was sacked from that position at the demand of the Jordanian government after refusing to replace international personnel with locals.

Cunningham's career was more straightforward, from Staff College, to Ireland, Eastern Command, and finally Palestine. But why was Cunningham protected and by whom? Some of the features have been mentioned here: his famous brother, the network of gunners and possibly Conservative politicians whom he tried to activate in his defence, none of whom seem influential enough to have made much of a difference to save a tarnished career. There are few mentions of Cunningham in military memoirs by contemporaries and it is thus difficult to assess how he was viewed within the military establishment and beyond. His association with Brooke and Smuts, which remains difficult to characterize in personal terms, was far more consequential.

Ultimately, Cunningham was the source of his own salvation: the letters he sent to the CIGS that were preserved in the special file and his own archive demonstrate his efforts to restore his reputation, including the core of the Official History. Whatever his failures in the desert as a battlefield commander and leader, these efforts to shape history and his own career must be judged a success.

Cunningham's final rehabilitation came in November 1945 when he was appointed to one of the most sensitive positions in the Empire, High Commissioner in Palestine.[18] Cunningham had no experience in the region or background in colonial administration or imperial policing. Judging from his letters, his wartime experience in Ireland was mostly low key and uneventful and thus slight preparation for a momentous assignment.[19] In the end, Cunningham had won the war for history and for his own career. His tenure in Palestine, however, fixed his place in history.

The Desert War: Failure and loyalty

The Desert War is simultaneously inflated, romanticized and under-internalized in military history: history began with Montgomery and his victories that were backed by overwhelming force and traditional tactics. The earlier improvisational victories of the Wavell era under O'Connor were offset by the failures of Greece. The Auchinleck era is difficult to characterize, on the border between the freewheeling and improvisational O'Connor but not fully set-piece warfare and mechanical victories of Montgomery. Auchinleck and Cunningham were thus largely ignored in the larger view because their results were ambiguous and their methods 'untraditional'; they represented the culmination of inter-war tactics, rather than the fully relearnt 'tradition' exemplified by Montgomery, above all in the use of massive force, especially artillery. In retrospect, when measured, even unconsciously, against this 'tradition' the failures especially of command, training and materiel were heightened. In this sense as well, the historical fascination with 'private armies' in the Desert War, especially the nascent Special Air Service, was a counternarrative that highlighted individual daring in an era of increasingly impersonal mechanized warfare, regardless of limited results.

The ambiguities of the Wavell and Auchinleck eras, and *Crusader*, must also be set into another critical context, the last months of Britain Alone. The American entry into the war came during *Crusader*, and the battle's up and down narrative (along with the more consequential fall of Singapore and Tobruk) was a far cry from the unequivocally heroic Battle of Britain. Coalition warfare would offer many examples of ambiguity and failure, as well as scenes of overwhelming heroism and success. *Crusader* fell deeper into a grey area. But history is filled with such moments of equivocation and ambiguity. In years to come *Crusader* was exceptionally well analysed from a military standpoint but it was not commemorated. It became history but not memory.

Had *Crusader* been treated more immediately and honestly, would it have mattered to the larger British perception of the Desert War, its successes and failures? Or was the British public just fed up with it all? More honest assessments of failures and successes probably would not have changed the shape of postwar politics or culture, dominated by much larger forces.

In the writing of Official History British authorities fretted about details until suddenly realizing it no longer mattered and that the forms of history were of little relevance. South African and New Zealanders were more frank because they had to explain their losses but the gradual collapse of their Official History projects reflected the declining importance of wartime history and experience as a whole to political authorities and to their nations. Fate was especially cruel to the South African project, which was unceremoniously closed and its files locked away for decades.

But as a whole British society moved rapidly away from concerns about history and more slowly away from unhappy wartime memory, regardless of what officialdom was writing about (or not). It was creating its own memories through popular media that emphasized bravery and success, selective acts of loyalty and self-preservation.

The political utility and historical impact of Official Histories were far less than unofficial accounts, which were subjective but more frank and readable, and which correctly pointed to issues of command and personality, especially the role of Galloway. But all these details were effectively lost in the elision of *Crusader* from British memory in the postwar period.

The British military learned much from *Crusader* in a strategic and tactical sense about air support and logistics, the vital need for communications among widely dispersed units, combined arms battles and massed artillery, in retrospect all either obvious new lessons or lessons relearned from the First World War. But while lessons were also learned by the military about command and competence, planning and tactical improvisation, the more fraught questions of character and mental stability appear not to have been addressed, except in the important sense of wartime assessment of new personnel for assignment. For commanders already within the military it was simply a matter of evolution: those who could not cope with the pace and intensity of fast paced mechanized warfare fell by the wayside.

In some respects, perhaps British society as a whole and individual combatants learnt these lessons better. Sandy Galloway put it this way to Eric Sixsmith:

> What is loyalty?
> May I suggest that the two questions:-
>
> 1. 'What is failure?'
> 2. 'What is loyalty?'
>
> Can give you much food for thought. Much more important for our future generations including Prime Minister, Angels and Ministers of Grace than stating that some armoured Brigade was sent to the wrong place and fell over a precipice, 27 years ago.

Though uncharacteristically oblique, Galloway cut to the heart of the matter. How are success and failure in war defined, and by whom? What are accurate measures: objectives on a map, reached according to timetables, losses in men and materiel, the functioning of the military itself or something else? And what is the role of loyalty? To whom are soldiers loyal, to the chain of command, the ultimate objectives, or again, something else? In the twilight of his life he echoed his earlier comments to Eric Sixsmith, about strategic and command inevitabilities: 'But we were learning + we had to LEARN quickly + reinforce our tactics + equipment: + gain confidence in ourselves.'[20] Confidence is in effect loyalty to one's self.

Galloway's formulation may also be applied in another, larger sense. What is loyalty between a military and its society and what are the roles of history and memory in generating and sustaining it? Is the writing of history contingent on measures of military success or failure defined at the time or later? To whom are historians loyal, to the 'facts' as they perceive them and resulting narratives, or to larger goals of creating memory that serves society in some cohesive or other sense? And in these regards, was *Crusader* a success or failure? Moreover, was the remembering of *Crusader* a success or failure?

What is failure and what is loyalty can give you much food for thought.

And what of Sandy Galloway? His postwar conception of loyalty is instructive. In correspondence he was friendly but often deferential to his former command superiors, addressing men he had known as near equals for fifty years like Bernard Montgomery and Harold Alexander as Field Marshal. In turn, they addressed him as Sandy, but with few exceptions they did not preserve his letters in their archives.

Galloway's primary historical concerns were quelling conflicts between Field Marshals, making sure that *Crusader* received proper recognition as an immense and necessary learning experience for the British Army, and seeing that its participants were properly recognized. In 1960 he articulated this concern to the *Daily Telegraph* and also expressed his attitude towards the memoir wars:[21]

> Must we, after all these years, go on raking the ashes of past battles, to the embarrassment of some and the edification of none? Can we now accept the fact that all generals tried their best and that all were equal in this respect, even if were more equal than others?
>
> And what of the private soldier, the rifleman, who generally has to bear no ordinary brunt; who invariably carries the can of blood, sweat and sometimes even tears of mortification, no matter what? If he was in the Eighth Army before Alamein, but not in the October battle or afterwards, he cannot wear the figure '8' on his campaign medal, no matter how hard he tried during the 12 months from September, 1941, and goodness knows he tried.
>
> There is still a chance to correct this deliberate omission and to remove the implied stigma from the soldiers of many nations who played their full part at any rate-no matter what the generals or the politicians did or did not do.
>
> Therefore let all the field-marshals and the generals get together and cause this wrong to be put right. For here at any rate is one closed shop which can be opened.

The letter launched a two-year effort that culminated in 1962 with a series of exchanges with Montgomery regarding the Africa Star decoration:[22]

> But I have come to the conclusion that this injustice did take place. In the turmoil and heat of the War it would have been stupid to attempt to get such a decision revoked or put right. But after all the years, when most of the things that had to be said and written are now on record, I feel that it is perfectly obvious that this injustice amounted to a slight – and no means slight – upon the soldiers of the Eighth Army at the time in question. Most people seem to accept the state of

affairs or to have forgotten it. I do neither. And therefore I think it only fair to tell you that if I possibly can I will continue to try to get this put right until I am completely satisfied that I have done all I can.

My philosophy about such things is that if an injustice has been done, resulting in a slight to people who do not deserve it (i.e. the ordinary soldiers), in circumstances over which they had no control whatever, it is wrong not to try as hard as one can to get this put right, however late in the day.

The effort eventually reached Buckingham Palace but no decision was taken. What is loyalty?

Finally, with regard to *Crusader* and the supersession of Cunningham, it is fitting to conclude with a professional assessment. On 20 December 1969 Montgomery wrote one of his final notes to Galloway:[23]

> My dear Sandy,
>   Your letter and card received, with great joy.
>   It is pretty cold down here – snow, sleet, fronts, etc. Maybe it is worse with you up north!
>   I keep very well. Do please come and see me when next you come south. But I will be away all January, in Bournemouth – where I go every year for a change, and to sniff the ozone.
>   Dick O'Conner visited me not long ago and we had a most interesting talk on the Desert war in his days. I put it to him that when the Auk removed Alan Cunningham from command, he made a great error in giving command of the Army to Ritchie – who was quite unfit for the job of handling three difficult Corps Commanders. The right man to take command at that moment was you. Dick agreed.
>   Yrs. Ever
>   Montgomery of Alamein

Loyalty cuts many ways and may sometimes be acknowledged too late.

Notes

Introduction

1 Simon Ball, *Alamein* (Oxford: Oxford University Press, 2016).

Chapter 1

1 Michael Howard, *The Uses of Military History*. Shedden Paper, No. 1 (Canberra: Australian Defence College, 2008), 5. http://www.defence.gov.au/ADC/Publications/Shedden/2008/Publctns_ShedPaper_050310_TheUseofMilitaryHistory.pdf
2 For comments on Official History see Jeffrey Grey, 'A Commonwealth of Histories: The Official Histories of the Second World War in the United States, Britain and the Commonwealth.' In *Trevor Reese Memorial Lecture*. London: Sir Robert Menzies Centre for Commonwealth Studies, Institute of Commonwealth Studies, 1998.
3 Peter J. Beck, 'Locked in a Dusty Cupboard, Neither Accessible on the Policy-makers' Desks Nor Cleared for Early Publication: Llewellyn Woodward's Official Diplomatic History of the Second World War.' *English Historical Review* 127, no. 529 (2012): 1438.
4 Ian van der Waag and D. Visser, 'Between History, Amnesia and Selective Memory: The South African Armed Forces, a Century's Perspective.' *Scientia Militaria* 40, no. 3 (2012): 1–12.
5 Beck 2012, 1444.
6 For Churchill's approach to history, see generally David Reynolds, *In Command of History: Churchill, Fighting and Writing the Second World War* (New York: Random House, 2005). For comments regarding Montgomery, see especially Nigel Hamilton, *Monty, Final Years of a Field Marshal, 1944–1976* (New York: McGraw-Hill, 1987), 857–902.
7 For summaries of the North African theatre in the early years of the war, see Correlli Barnett, *The Desert Generals* (London: Cassell, 1983, originally published 1960), 1–80; William G.F. Jackson, *The North African Campaign, 1940–43* (London: B.T. Batsford, 1975), 1–133.
8 For the Greek campaign and the defence of Crete generally, see Robin Higham, *Diary of a Disaster* (Lexington, KY: University of Kentucky Press, 1986) and Antony Beevor, *Crete, The Battle and the Resistance* (London: John Murray, 1991).

9   Auchinleck's semi-official biography is John Connell (aka John Henry Robertson), *Auchinleck, A Critical Biography* (London: Cassell, 1960). Other biographies include his former aide-de-camp Alexander A. Greenwood, *Auchinleck* (Aldershot: Pentland, 1990) and Philip Warner, *Auchinleck, The Lonely Soldier* (London: Buchan and Enright, 1981).

10 No biography of Cunningham exists. The best short analysis is in Richard Mead, *Churchill's Lions, A Biographical Guide to the Key British Generals of World War II* (Stroud: Gloucestershire: Spellmount Press, 2007), 109–12.

11 For the development of the Crusader plan and its flaws, see Barnett 1983, 87–90 and Eric K.G. Sixsmith, *British Generalship in the Twentieth Century* (London: Arms and Armour Press, 1970), 219–22.

12 I.S.O. Playfair, *The Mediterranean and the Middle East, Volume III – British Fortunes Reach Their Lowest Ebb* (London: HMSO, 1960), 36. See also John Ferris, 'The British Army, Signals and Security in the Desert Campaign, 1940-1942.' In J. Ferris, *Intelligence and Strategy, Selected Essays*, 181–238. London: Routledge, 2005.

13 Sixsmith 1970, 217–19.

14 See especially Barnett's comments (1983, 103–10) on 'twenty years of military decadence'. For comments on the imaginative trio military thinkers, Basil H. Liddell-Bart, John Frederick Charles 'Boney' Fuller and Percy Cleghorn Stanley Hobart, and their 'vivid metaphors and similes', see Shelford Bidwell and D. Graham, *Fire-Power, The British Army Weapons and Theories of War, 1904–1945* (Barnsley, S. Yorkshire: Pen & Sword, 2004), 193.

15 Frederick H. Hinsley et al., *British Intelligence in the Second World War*, vol 2 (New York: Cambridge University Press, 1981), 302–4, 976. See also John Ferris, 'The "Usual Source": Signals Intelligence and Planning for the Eighth Army "Crusader" Offensive, 1941.' *Intelligence and National Security* 14 (1994): 106–7; Ralph Bennett, *Ultra and the Mediterranean Strategy* (New York: William Morrow, 1989), 89.

16 Hinsley et al. 1981, 307–11.

17 David I. Hall, *Strategy for Victory: The Development of British Tactical Air Power, 1919-1943* (Westport, CT: Greenwood, 2008), 104–13; Brad W. Gladman, 'Air Power and Intelligence in the Western Desert Campaign, 1940-43.' *Intelligence and National Security* 13 (1998): 144–62.

18 Mark Harrison, *Medicine & Victory, British Military Medicine in the Second World War* (Oxford: Oxford University Press, 2004), 82–127.

19 Hans-Otto Behrendt, *Rommel's Intelligence in the Desert Campaign, 1941-1943* (London: William Kimber Ltd, 1985), 96–145.

20 The impact of these purloined American reports was extremely significant in 1942 but their role in shaping the German response to *Crusader* has not been assessed. See Behrendt 1985, 145–7. See also Christopher J. Jenner, 'Turning the Hinges of Fate: "Good Source" and the UK–US Intelligence Alliance, 1940-1942.' *Diplomatic History* 32 (2008): 165–205 and John Ferris, 'Assessing the Impact of Intelligence:

The "Good Source" and Anglo-American Intelligence in the Second World War and After.' H-Diplo. https://issforum.org/reviews/PDF/Ferris-Jenner.pdf (4 November 2008).
21 Playfair 1960, 30.
22 Barnett 1983, 88–90.
23 Sebastian Cox, "'The Difference between White and Black": Churchill, Imperial Politics, and Intelligence before the 1941 Crusader Offensive.' *Intelligence and National Security* 9, no. 3 (1994): 405–47.
24 Kevin Jeffreys, *The Churchill Coalition and Wartime Politics, 1940–1945* (Manchester: Manchester University Press, 1995), 22–5, 87–9.
25 Hansard, House of Commons debate, 1 July 1942, vol 381. cc224-476. http://hansard.millbanksystems.com/commons/1942/jul/01/central-direction-of-the-war-1#S5CV0381P0_19420701_HOC_554 (accessed 5 April, 2017).
26 John Connell, *Auchinleck, A Critical Biography* (London: Cassell, 1959), 249.
27 John Dill to Claude Auchinleck, 26 June 1941, quoted in J. Connell, *Auchinleck, A Critical Biography* (London: Cassell, 1959), 247.
    Connell adds (p. 248) that Auckinleck did not receive this letter until 21 July, well after a contentious exchange with Churchill. He also comments 'Churchill was incapable of acting upon Dill's wise advice-to back or sack.' The notion that Churchill contemplated sacking Auchinleck in the summer of 1941 immediately after his appointment is not indicated by documentary evidence.
28 James R.M. Butler, *History of the Second World War. Grand Strategy, Volume II September 1939–June 1941* (London: HMSO, 1957), 448.
29 Winston S. Churchill, *The Grand Alliance* (New York: Houghton Mifflin, 1950), 404.
30 The National Archives (TNA), FO 954/5A/61. Miles Lampson to Anthony Eden, 12 April 1941.
31 Churchill Archive Centre (CAC), CHAR 20/41/112, Claude Auchinleck to Winston S. Churchill, 16 August 1941.
32 The only biography of O'Connor is John Baynes, *The Forgotten Victor: General Sir Richard O'Connor, KT, GCB, DSO, MC* (London: Brassey's, 1989).
33 Liddell Hart Centre for Military Archives (LHCMA), LH 15/4/22. Eric-Dorman-Smith to Basil H. Liddell Hart, 6 June 1946.
34 Connell 1960, 285.
35 In his diary entry for 19 November Lt General Sir Henry Pownall, Vice Chief of the Imperial General Staff, notes that 'The reason for announcing all this – today – was to keep it clear of 'Crusader, which started yesterday in the Western Desert. They didn't want Dill's discharge to be connected with that event if it fails (which God forbid).' Brian Bond (ed.), *Chief of Staff, The Diaries of Lieutenant-General Sir Henry Pownall, Volume Two, 1940–1944* (London: Leo Cooper, 1974), 53.

36 Alex Danchev and D. Todman, *War Diaries, Field Marshal Lord Alanbrooke* (Berkeley: University of California Press, 2001), 199–208. Dill's conflicts with Churchill were extensively documented in John Noble Kennedy, *The Business of War* (New York: William Morrow and Company, 1958). Characteristically, Churchill misrepresented his efforts to retire Dill, saying only that Dill had been replaced by Brooke after the Japanese attack on Pearl Harbor. See Winston S. Churchill, *The Grand Alliance* (New York: Houghton Mifflin, 1950), 626.

37 John Maurer, '"Winston Has Gone Mad": Churchill, the British Admiralty, and the Rise of Japanese Naval Power.' *Journal of Strategic Studies* 35, no. 6 (2012): 775–97.

38 The best description of Churchill's relationship with Andrew Cunningham remains Stephen Roskill, *Churchill and the Admirals* (New York: William Morrow, 1977), especially chapter 10. See also Richard Ollard, *Fisher and Cunningham, A Study in the Personalities of the Churchill Era* (London: Constable and Company, 1991), 82–136; Christopher M. Bell, *Churchill and Sea Power* (Oxford: Oxford University Press, 2013), 202–11.

39 Michael Simpson, *A Life of Admiral of the Fleet Andrew Cunningham, A Twentieth Century Naval Leader* (London: Frank Cass, 2004), 82.

40 David French, *Military Identities, the Regimental System, the British Army, & the British People c. 1870–2000* (Cambridge: Cambridge University Press, 2005), 165.

41 Vincent Orange, *Tedder, Quietly in Command* (London: Frank Cass, 2004), 155–60.

42 Portal's 25 November 1941 letter to Auchinleck (Christ Church College Library, Portal Papers, Box C, Folder 4) shows that Churchill's October efforts to supersede Tedder were only temporarily quelled. Auchinleck's reply of 11 December 1941 indicates that Tedder's position was finally secure only after the battle.

43 Claude Auchinleck Papers, John Rylands Library, University of Manchester, number 289. Claude Auchinleck to John Dill, 21 July 1941.

44 Paul Hasluck, *The Government and the People, 1939–1941* (Canberra: Australian War Memorial, 1952), Appendix 10, The Withdrawal from Tobruk, 616–24. See also James de la Billière, 'The Political–Military Interface: Friction in the Conduct of British Army Operations in North Africa 1940–1942.' *Defence Studies* 5 (2005): 247–70.

45 Angus Calder, *The People's War, Britain 1939–1945* (London: Jonathan Cape, 1969), 249.

46 Jeremy A Crang, *The British Army and the People's War 1939–1945* (Manchester: Manchester University Press, 2000), 5–15.

47 Calder 1969, 250–60.

48 Calder 1969, 265–83.

49 For strategic planning of the war economy, see Michael M. Postan, *British War Production* (London: HMSO, 1952), 115–22. There is a contentious literature regarding British war production but the salient disagreements are well covered

in Paul Edgerton, *Britain's War Machine, Weapons, Resources, and Experts in the Second World War* (Oxford: Oxford University Press, 2011).

50 Masculinity has generated a vast literature. See generally George Mosse, *The Image of Man, The Creation of Modern Masculinity* (Oxford: Oxford University Press, 1996), 107–53. With respect to the British military in the Second World War and the themes of fear, damage and masculinity, see the discussions in Martin Francis, *The Flyer, British Culture and the Royal Air Force, 1939–1945* (Oxford: Oxford University Press, 2008), 107–52 and Sonya O. Rose, *Which People's War? National Identity and Citizenship in Wartime Britain* (Oxford: Oxford University Press, 2003), 151–96. Neither address the unique conditions of the army or higher command.
51 David French, *Raising Churchill's Army, The British Army and the War against Germany 1919–1945* (Oxford: Oxford University Press, 2000), 12–47.
52 French 2005, 125–8.
53 Gary D. Sheffield, *Leadership in the Trenches: Officer–Man Relations, Morale and Discipline in the British Army in the Era of the First World War* (London: Macmillan, 2000), 2.
54 For the period prior to the First World War, see Andrew George Duncan, *The Military Education of Junior Officers in the Edwardian Army*. Unpublished PhD diss., University of Birmingham, 2016, 2–12.
55 David French, 'Officer Education and Training in the British Regular Army, 1919–39.' In *Military Education: Past, Present, and Future*, edited by Gregory C. Kennedy and Keith Neilson, 106. Westport, CT: Praeger, 2002.
56 Correlli Barnet, *The Collapse of British Power* (New York: William Morrow & Company, 1972), 31.
57 Barnett 1983, 103.
    As a complement to Barnett (born 1927), we should also take note of the assessment by South African historian, and wartime Lt Colonel, John A.I. Agar-Hamilton (born 1895): 'My experience with British officers gives me an impression of their ingrained schoolboyishness-which makes them easy to chat to, but fills one with distrust of their reactions to any really serious business of life. I believe firmly that the level of congenital intelligence is as high among British officers as in any other category of the population-indeed of any other population-but I feel that they train themselves to replace intelligence by heartiness and a few catch words.' Archives New Zealand (ANZ), R12325670, John A.I. Agar-Hamilton to W.E. Murphy, 27 October 1955.
58 Keith Douglas, *Alamein to Zem Zem* (London: Faber and Faber, 1946), 44.
59 Peter Mandler, *The English National Character: The History of an Idea from Edmund Burke to Tony Blair* (New Haven: Yale University Press, 2006), 165.
60 French 2002b, 108.
61 See generally Christopher B. Otley, *The Origins and Recruitment of the British Army Elite, 1870–1959*. Unpublished PhD diss., University of Hull, 1965.

62 Correlli Barnett, 'The Education of Military Elites.' *Journal of Contemporary History* 2 (1967): 21.
63 French 2002b, 117.
64 Lavinia Graecen, *Chink, A Biography* (London: Macmillan London, 1989), 96–103.
65 Tim Travers, 'The Hidden Army: Structural Problems in the British Officer Corps 1900–1918.' *Journal of Contemporary History* 17 (1982): 524, 525.
66 On this point Galloway's frank contrasts between Auchinleck and Montgomery are of great significance, particularly how the former's 'long (+not unimportant) time in India did not much qualify him for modern mechanical war in the Western Desert or anywhere else'. Letter from Alexander Galloway to Kenneth Startup, 2 July 1973.
67 W. Sorley Brown, *War Record of the 4th Bn. King's Own Scottish Borderers and Lothian and Border Horse* (Galashiels: John McQueen & Son, 1920), 31.
68 Edgar Jones and Simon Wessely, *Shell Shock to PTSD, Military Psychiatry from 1900 to the Gulf War* (New York: Psychology Press, 2005), 17–43.
69 Jones and Wessely 2005, 13–15, 119–23.
70 Harrison 2004, 58–62. See also Alan Allport, *Browned Off and Bloody-Minded: The British Soldier Goes to War 1939–1945* (New Haven: Yale University Press, 2015), 254–6; Edgar Jones and Simon Wessely, '"Forward Psychiatry" in the Military: Its Origins and Effectiveness.' *Journal of Traumatic Psychiatry* 16 (2003): 411–19.
71 Jones and Wessely 2005, 64.
72 Harrison 2004, 122.
73 Robert H. Ahrenfeldt, *Psychiatry in the British Army in the Second World War* (New York: Columbia University Press, 1958), 92–5; Harrison 2004, 120–25.
74 Charles McMoran Wilson (Lord Moran). *The Anatomy of Courage* (Boston: Houghton Mifflin, 1967).
75 Moran 1967, 183, 188.
76 Moran 1967, 197.
77 Moran 1967, 201.

Chapter 2

1 The most concise description of the battle is Jackson 1975, 145–83, while Barnett's is the best written.
2 Playfair 1960, 41, 48.
3 TNA, WO 169/998/59.
4 There is no record of this signal in operational documents.
5 There is no record of this signal in operational documents.
6 There is no record of this signal in operational documents. Several sources indicate Tedder kept a diary, which he likely consulted for his 1966 memoir, but it remains

in the hands of Lord Trenchard's family and is inaccessible. More information may become available when papers belonging to Tedder's (and Coningham's) biographer, the late Vincent Orange, become available at the RAF Museum (personal communication, Nina Hadaway, 28 July 2016).

7   TNA, AIR 41/25, 157.
8   TNA, WO 201/631 93a. CAC, CHAR 20/45/97. Oliver Lyttelton to Winston S. Churchill, 25 November 1941. Shearer appears to have left no papers but a number of sources report a memoir based on a diary. In an email to the author (28 March 2014) the late Robin Higham, who consulted the document for his piece in *Balkan Studies* 8 (154, note 27), suggested the document had been deposited in the University of Cambridge Library, but I could not locate it there. A copy may exist in the papers of the late historian Vincent Orange.
9   Alexander Clifford's diary noted that an 'Ann Shearer' was Auchinleck's secretary (IWM Documents 16727, Alexander Clifford collection, Box 1–2, 16 March 1942). But the identity of this woman is problematic since Eric Shearer apparently married a woman named Phyllis Muriel Mules in 1919 (https://www.familysearch.org/search/record/results?givenname=Phyllis%20Muriel&surname=Mules&collection_id=1584967&count=20). The inconsistency in names cannot currently be resolved.
10 TNA, WO 169/998, 440A, Box 59.
11 This passage in the original report is noted with a pencil mark.
12 TNA, CAB 106/702, A.R. Godwin-Austen to Harry B. Latham, 4 October 1950.
13 IWM Documents 16727, Alexander Clifford collection, Box 1–2, 25 November 1941.
14 Auchinleck Papers, number 454. Gist of conversation between Auchinleck and Lt General Alan Cunningham, 23 November 1941.
15 TNA, WO 106/5826. As will be explained below, the file was transferred to the Cabinet Office Historical Section in 1949 and became CAB 106/665, originally designated AL 804. A copy is also found in the Bernard Law Montgomery Archive at the Imperial War Museum.
16 National Army Museum (NAM) 8303/104.
17 CAC, CHAR 20, 45/87. Claude Auchinleck to Winston S. Churchill, 24 November 1941.
18 TNA, WO 169/998, 487. Copies are also preserved in Cunningham's papers, NAM 8303/104, Auchinleck Papers, number 456, and in CAB 106/655.
19 Barnett 1983, 114. See also Playfair 1960, 54–5.
20 US National Archives, Record Group 165, Entry 77, Box 760. Notes on Naval Intelligence Data, Enclosure A, Notes made on the Western Desert dated November 21, 1941 by Lt. (j.g) Richard Scott Mowrer, I-V(S), U.S.N.R, Correspondent for the Chicago Daily News.
21 Playfair 1960, 55. See also AIR 41/25, 152–4.
22 TNA, WO 169/995, serial 173. Barnett 1983, 114. The events are vividly described in George Clifton, *The Happy Hunted* (London: Cassell & Co., 1952), 131–2.

23 TNA, WO 169/995, serial 151.
24 TNA, WO 169/998, 330–333; WO 169/995, Serial 103.
25 TNA, WO 169/998.
26 Auchinleck Papers, number 463a. Cipher message from Claude Auchinleck to John Dill, 23 November 1941.
27 Auchinleck Papers, number 464. Cipher message from Claude Auchinleck to Winston S. Churchill, 25 November 1941 (=CHAR 20/45/106).
28 CAC, CHAR 20/45/97-99. Oliver Lyttelton to Winston S. Churchill, 25 November 1941.
29 TNA, CAB 106/655, Appendix E. Copies also appear in Auchinleck's and Cunningham's papers.
30 Auchinleck Papers, number 459. Claude Auchinleck to Alan Cunningham, 25 November 1941.
31 Auchinleck Papers, number 470. Andrew Cunningham to Claude Auchinleck, 26 November 1941.
32 NAM 8303/104-19.
33 IWM Documents.8469, Ralph Blewitt collection, Alan Cunningham to Ralph Blewitt, 24 January 1940.
34 IWM Documents.8590, James Blewitt collection, James Blewitt diary.
35 One additional note regarding Blewitt and Cunningham is found in the Imperial War Museum oral history provided by Corrie Alexander Halliday, ADC to Godwin-Austin. He recounted a visit by Cunningham to Godwin-Austin (possibly 24 November), at which time he was greeted by his old school friend Blewitt, who whispered to him 'tell your man not to pay much attention to what my man says.' Whether this referred to Cunningham's state or that the battle going on was beyond the control of either general is unknown. Halliday added that he passed Blewitt's advice to Godwin-Austin who did not respond (IWM 15260, Corrie Alexander Halliday oral history, reel 25).

Chapter 3

1 Auchinleck Papers, number 476a, b. Claude Auchinleck to John Dill, 27 November 1941.
2 Smith's reply to Churchill in Auchinleck's name raises the question of whether he spoke in his own voice rather than his commander's. This possibility is given limited support by a 27 January 1942 letter from Smith to Auchinleck (Auchinleck Papers, number 658) in which Smith noted: 'I quite agree about not normally answering the Prime Minister's telegrams to you, and now that your letters have started to arrive regularly there should be no undue delay in his getting

information.' Smith also noted that at Auchinleck's request he was sending copies of all of Auchinleck's 'telegrams to the Prime Minister and letters to myself on the present "phase,"' presumably to the Advanced Headquarters. This suggests that Auchinleck wanted to review communications to Churchill sent in his name by Smith. A later note from Auchinleck to Brooke, however, makes it clear that Smith was 'due for a change though he will be missed here as he has served MIDEAST and myself very well' (Auchinleck Papers, number 725). This question cannot be answered with certainty. Smith returned to Britain in March to take command of London District.

3   Auchinleck Papers, number 481. Cipher message from John Dill to Claude Auchinleck, 28 November 1941.
4   Kennedy 1958, 181.
5   Auchinleck Papers, number 484. Cipher message from Claude Auchinleck to John Dill, 28 November 1941.
6   CAC, CHAR 20/45/126. Claude Auchinleck to Winston S. Churchill, 28 November 1941.
7   CAC, CHAR 20/46/1. Winston S. Churchill to Claude Auchinleck, 30 November 1941.
8   CAC, CHAR 20/46/10. Claude Auchinleck to Winston S. Churchill, 1 December 1941.
9   CAC, CHAR 20/46/12. Winston S. Churchill to Claude Auchinleck, 2 December 1941.
10 CAC, CHAR 20/46/36. Claude Auchinleck to Winston S. Churchill, 7 December 1941.
11 CAC, CHAR 20/46/37. Winston S. Churchill to Claude Auchinleck, 7 December 1941.
12 CAC, CHAR 20/46/45. Winston S. Churchill to Claude Auchinleck, 8 December 1941. On 12 December *Sydney Morning Herald* ran two articles, one of which mentioned Churchill's statement in the House of Commons about Cunningham's 'over-strain' while the other discussed his 'sacking' by his 'military friend' Auchinleck after 'something apparently misfired' ('Libya Army Change', 12 December, p. 8).
13 CAC, CHAR 20/46/57. Claude Auchinleck to Winston S. Churchill, 9 December 1941.
14 Hansard, House of Common debate 11 December 1941, vol 376, cc1686-700. http://hansard.millbanksystems.com/commons/1941/dec/11/war-situation#S5CV0376P0_19411211_HOC_283 (accessed 5 April, 2017).
15 Auchinleck Papers, number 542. Cipher message from Claude Auchinleck to Alan Brooke, 11 December 1941.
16 TNA, CAB 106/655. Short Account of Operations in Libya November 18–25th, 1941 by Lt Gen Sir Alan Cunningham. CAB 106/655, Appendix B. See also British Library, Andrew B. Cunningham Papers, Add MS 52570.

17 Efforts to locate additional information on Cunningham's medical condition were unsuccessful. Such information is conceivably included in his confidential file, which is inaccessible to non-relatives.
18 TNA, CAB 106/655, Appendix G. Note by General Cunningham on Medical Aspect of Case. Undated.
19 Auchinleck Papers, number 497. Medical report on the health of Lt General Alan Cunningham by Col W.D.D. Small, Consultant Physician.
20 University of Edinburgh, Faculty of Medicine, Official List of Passes, *Scottish Medical and Surgical Journal*, vol 20, January to June (1907): 485; University of Edinburgh. Degrees. *The British Medical Journal*, vol 2, No. 2795 (25 July 1914): 208. A clinician, Small (1889–1964) was later a faculty member and dean of the Edinburgh medical school, and president of the Royal College of Physicians in Edinburgh from 1947 to 1949.
21 Lieutenant Colonel J. Cunningham, C.I.E., M.D., F.R.S.ED., I.M.S. (RET.), *British Medical Journal*, 1968, 503.
22 *Former Fellows of the Royal Society of Edinburgh, 1783–2002, Biographical Index, Part One* (Edinburgh: Royal Society of Edinburgh, 2006), 107. https://www.royalsoced.org.uk/cms/files/fellows/biographical_index/fells_indexp1.pdf
23 IWM Documents.8469, Ralph Blewitt collection, Alan Cunningham to Ralph Blewitt, 26 December 1941.
24 With one exception, both Auchinleck and Cunningham retained copies of these letters, but the latter began a practice of making hand copies of his letters and reports.
25 NAM 8303/104-19. Claude Auchinleck to Alan Cunningham, 27 November 1941. This letter is not present in Auchinleck's papers.
26 Auchinleck Papers, number 485. Alan Cunningham to Claude Auchinleck, 28 November 1941.
27 Auchinleck Papers, number 486. Alan Cunningham to Claude Auchinleck, 28 November 1941. This letter is only summarized in the Cunningham papers.
28 Auchinleck Papers, number 487. Andrew Cunningham to Claude Auchinleck, 28 November 1941.
29 Auchinleck Papers, number 492. Claude Auchinleck to Andrew Cunningham, 29 November 1941.
30 Auchinleck Papers, number 491. Claude Auchinleck to Alan Cunningham, 29 November 1941.
31 Auchinleck Papers, number 493. Claude Auchinleck to Alan Cunningham, 29 November 1941.
32 Auchinleck Papers, number 498. Alan Cunningham to Claude Auchinleck, 30 November 1941.
33 Auchinleck Papers, number 490. Cipher message from Claude Auchinleck to Winston S. Churchill, 29 November 1941.

34 Cunningham's papers include a series of letters exchanged with Auchinleck in 1966, prompted by the publication of Arthur Tedder's book. Cunningham's aggrieved tone and Auchinleck's tone of sadness are evident.
35 NAM 8303/104-19. Arthur Smith to Alan Cunningham, 29 November 1941.
36 Auchinleck Papers, number 500. This letter does not appear in Cunningham's papers. Alan Cunningham to Claude Auchinleck, 30 November 1941.
37 Auchinleck Papers, number 518. Arthur Smith to Claude Auchinleck, 4 December 1941.
38 Auchinleck Papers, number 524. Claude Auchinleck to Arthur Smith, 6 December 1941.
39 NAM 8303/104-19. Arthur Smith to Alan Cunningham, 12 July 1942.
40 Smith (1890–1977) apparently left no papers save those items preserved in Auchinleck's collection. I am grateful to Brigadier Ian Dobbie, who knew Smith late in life, for his enlightening comments.
41 Ian Dobbie, 'Lieutenant General Sir Arthur Smith (1890–1977)'. http://www.evangelical-times.org/archive/item/7060/Historical/Lieutenant-General-Sir-Arthur-Smith-1890-1977-/
42 In contrast, Eric Dorman-Smith's assessment of Arthur Smith was as a '"genius of stupidity," one of the most stupid men I've ever met, though cunning, in a pious guardsman, mitre in Mayfair way.' LHCMA, LH 15/4/22, Eric Dorman-Smith to Basil H. Liddell Hart, 6 June 1946.

Chapter 4

1 TNA, CAB 106/655, 10. Cunningham also retained handwritten copies of these files in his papers, NAM 8303/104-19.
2 TNA, CAB 106/655, 11.
3 TNA, CAB 106/655, 12.
4 TNA, CAB 106/655, 13.
5 TNA, CAB 106/655, 19.
6 Auchinleck Papers, number 491. Claude Auchinleck to Alan Cunningham, 29 November 1941.
7 TNA, CAB 106/655, 24.
8 TNA, WO 106/2204.
9 TNA, WO 106/5826.
10 TNA, CO 967/100. Bernard Law Montgomery to George H. Hall, 6 August 1946.
11 British Library, Andrew B. Cunningham papers, Add MS 52570. Alan Cunningham to Andrew Cunningham, 1 January 1942.
12 NAM 8303/104-19. Andrew Cunningham to Alan Cunningham, 14 February 1942.

13 NAM 8303/104-19. Andrew Cunningham to Alan Cunningham, 4 April 1944.
14 NAM 8303/104-19. Alan Cunningham to Jan Smuts, 5 December 1941.
15 NAM 8303/104-19. Jan Smuts to Alan Cunningham, 14 December 1941.
16 NAM 8303/104-19. Alan Cunningham to Jan Smuts, 10 February 1942.
17 Sarah Quail, *Portsmouth in the Great War* (Barnsley, South Yorkshire: Pen & Sword Books Ltd, 2014), 29–30.
18 NAM 8303/104-19. Alan Cunningham to Ralph Blewitt, 26 December 1941.
19 Hansard, House of Commons debate, 9 July 1941, vol 373, cc165-7. http://hansard.millbanksystems.com/commons/1941/jul/09/minister-of-state-duties-middle-east (accessed 5 April, 2017).
20 NAM 8303/104-19. Robert H. Haining to Alan Cunningham, 1 December 1941.
21 NAM 8303/104-19. Robert H. Haining to Alan Cunningham, 5 December 1941.
22 NAM 8303/104-19. Robert H. Haining to Alan Cunningham, 11 February 1942.
23 Alex Danchev and D. Todman, *War Diaries, Field Marshal Lord Alanbrooke* (Berkeley: University of California Press, 2001), 208. Arthur Bryant's novelization of Brooke's diaries elided the matter of Cunningham and other uncomfortable issues completely.
24 Danchev and Todman 2001, 211.
25 Danchev and Todman 2001, 236, 238, 252.
26 Danchev and Todman 2001, 258.
27 Danchev and Todman 2001, 261.
28 Danchev and Todman 2001, 331.
29 Hansard, House of Commons debate, 8 January 1942, col 377, cc43-174. http://hansard.millbanksystems.com/commons/1942/jan/08/war-situation#S5CV0377P0_19420108_HOC_398 (accessed 5 April, 2017).
30 Brian Montgomery, *Shenton of Singapore: Governor and Prisoner of War* (London: Leo Cooper, 1984), 118.
31 CAC, David Margesson Papers, MRGN 1/6, Duff Cooper to David Margesson, 1 October 1941. See also Ong Chit Chung, *Operation Matador: Britain's War Plans against the Japanese 1918–1941* (Singapore: Times Academic Press, 1997), 226.
32 Hansard, House of Commons debate, 27 January 1942. http://hansard.millbanksystems.com/commons/1942/jan/27/lieut-general-sir-alan-cunningham#S5CV0377P0_19420127_HOC_117 (accessed 5 April, 2017).
33 Hansard, House of Commons debate, 10 February 1942, vol 377, cc1370-1. http://hansard.millbanksystems.com/commons/1942/feb/10/military-operations-libya#S5CV0377P0_19420210_HOC_43 (accessed 5 April, 2017).
34 Hansard, House of Commons debate, 10 March 1942, vol 378, c912. http://hansard.millbanksystems.com/commons/1942/mar/10/lieut-general-sir-alan-cunningham#S5CV0378P0_19420310_HOC_84 (accessed 5 April, 2017).
35 Hansard, House of Commons debate, 1 July 1942, vol 381, cc224-476. http://hansard.millbanksystems.com/commons/1942/jul/01/central-direction-of-the-war-1#S5CV0381P0_19420701_HOC_371 (accessed 5 April, 2017).

36 For Lyttelton's account of the debate, see *The Memoirs of Lord Chandos* (London: Bodley Head, 1962), 301–3.
37 Richard Stokes's papers were on loan to the Bodleian Library but were withdrawn by family members in 2008. It was reported that they were being used for a biography and would then be deposited at the Ipswich Public Record Office (now part of the Suffolk Records Office). There is no record of the papers having been deposited again. Colin Harris of the Bodleian kindly provided a box list (20 April 2017).
38 http://hansard.millbanksystems.com/commons/1942/may/19/war-situation#S5CV0380P0_19420519_HOC_449 (accessed 5 April, 2017).
39 CAB 65/25/31. Conclusions of a Meeting of the War Cabinet, 9 March 1942.
40 CAB 65/26/25. Conclusions of a Meeting of the War Cabinet, 18 May 1942.
41 CAB 65/28/13. Conclusions of a Meeting of the War Cabinet, 20 October 1942.
42 NAM 8303/104-19. Alan Cunningham to the Undersecretary of State, 28 May 1942, 25 June 1942.
43 NAM 8303/104-19. H.C.B. Wemyss to Alan Cunningham, 26 June 1942.
44 NAM 8303/104-19. H.C.B. Wemyss to Alan Cunningham, 3 August 1942.
45 NAM 8303/104-19. Alan Cunningham to the Military Secretary, 10 June 1943, H.C.B. Wemyss to Alan Cunningham, 11 June 1943.
46 NAM 8303/104-19. H.C.B. Wemyss to Alan Cunningham, 23 October 1943.

Chapter 5

1 Viscount Portal Papers, Box C, Folder 8. Arthur Tedder to Charles Portal, 4 December 1941.
2 Andrew M. Pollock, *Pienaar of Alamein: The Life Story of a Great South African Soldier* (Cape Town: Cape Times Limited, 1943), 69–70.
3 South African National Defense Force Documentation Centre, Acquisitions Group, Boxes 38 and 39, 'Military Information Bureau, Pretoria. F.H. Theron Collection', Liaison 49, GOA/2/L, U.D.F. Administrative H.Q., General Headquarters, Middle East Forces.
4 CAC, David Margesson Papers, MRGN 1/6, Oliver Lyttelton to David Margesson, 21 December 1941.
5 IWM, Documents.6786, Charles Miller collection, CHM/1 1940–1945, Administration in the Western Desert campaigns 1940–1941. Compare WO 201/1961.
6 NAM 8303/104-19. Alan Cunningham to Murray, Beith & Murray, 16 November 1943.
7 TNA, WO 201/631, p. 93a.

8   NAM 8303-104/18. Comments by Gen Sir Alan Cunningham, GCMG, KCB, DSO, MC, on draft Chapters 40 and 41 of vol III, dated December 1955, I.S.O. Playfair to Alan Cunningham, 16 December 1955, 'A note for record', November 1943.
9   Auchinleck relieved Shearer in February 1942 in effect for underestimating German strength, overstating German losses, and for general overconfidence. See Ferris, 'The "Usual Source,"' especially pages 87–90.
10 See especially Hermione, Countess of Ranfurly, *To War with Whitaker: The Wartime Diaries of the Countess of Ranfurly 1939-1945* (London: William Heinemann, 1994) and Artemis Cooper, *Cairo in the War* (London: Hamish Hamilton, 1989), 143–51.
11 A fuller biography of Galloway helps set his documents in context. He was born in the Scottish Lowlands at Minto Manse, Hawick, on 3 November 1895, the second son and youngest of four children of the Presbyterian minister of Minto, Reverend Alexander Galloway, and Margaret Rankin Smith (*The Times*, 1 February 1977, 16; Eric K.G. Sixsmith, 'Lieut. General Sir Alexander Galloway, K.B.E., C.B., D.S.O., M.C.' *The Covenanter* (1977) Summer Number: 3–4; A. Farrar-Hockley, 'Sir Alexander Galloway,' *Oxford Dictionary of National Biography*; R. Mead, *Churchill's Lions: A Biographical Guide to the Key British Generals of World War II* (Brimscombe Port Stroud Gloucestershire: The History Press Ltd, 2007), 156–61. Educated at King William's College, Isle of Man, Galloway was about to go up to Cambridge as the First World War broke out. Galloway first saw active service with 4th Battalion King's Own Scottish Borderers at Gallipoli, and then took part in the campaigns in Egypt and Palestine before being assigned to the Western Front. He became a regular army officer in 1917 and was awarded the Military Cross in 1918. He ended the war with the rank of captain and joined the Cameronians (Scottish Rifles).

Galloway married Dorothy Hadden in 1920 and they had three sons. After serving in Ireland and then Hong Kong, in 1925 he succeeded Richard O'Connor as Adjutant of the 1st Battalion of the Cameronians at Aldershot. Citing a letter from Captain E.B. Ferrers, O'Connor's biographer notes that Galloway was a 'somewhat frightening person' whose nickname in the Battalion was the 'PR' for 'perpetual rage' (Baynes 1989, 34; cf. Sixsmith 1977, 4).

Galloway entered the Staff College at Camberley in class of 1928. His instructors and classmates included many officers who were to lead the British Army during the Second World War and with whom he would serve closely. On the staff were Bernard Law Montgomery and Richard O'Connor. Fellow students included two future Field Marshalls, John Harding and Gerald Templer, and the iconoclastic and temperamental Eric Dorman-Smith. In 1932 Galloway became Brigade Major to Brigadier Sir Frederick Alfred (Tim) Pile in the Canal Brigade in Egypt. Galloway returned to the UK at the end of 1934 and worked in staff positions in the War Office. He returned to Camberley as an instructor in February 1937 before being assigned as a Lieutenant Colonel to command the 1st Cameronians in Calcutta in August 1938.

The Calcutta assignment was short-lived when Galloway became the first commander of the new Middle East Staff College at Haifa in February 1940, established to train officers who could not reach England because of wartime conditions. When Galloway was assigned as Wilson's BGS the Staff College at Haifa was handed over to his Camberley classmate and Auchinleck confidant Eric Dorman-Smith.

The small number of Galloway's papers, housed at the Churchill Archive Centre, is puzzling. From internal evidence it appears that he corresponded occasionally with figures such as Bernard Law Montgomery and others. It is also curious that Galloway's correspondence is not preserved in Montgomery's otherwise voluminous archive. Similarly, there are no letters to or from Galloway in the collections of Claude Auchinleck, Frederick Pile or Basil H. Liddell Hart, despite evidence showing they were in contact.

One partial explanation regarding Galloway's own small archive is that he suffered from Alzheimer's disease in his last years and there is reason to think that his wife, Lady Dorothy, kept certain letters from him in order not to cause upset (Dorothy Galloway to Kenneth Startup, 13 May 1977). I am grateful to Kenneth Startup for sharing his correspondence with the Galloways. Family members also suspect that after his death Lady Galloway culled his letters and presented only a sample to the Churchill Archive Centre (personal communication, Bruce Galloway).

12 Sixsmith 1970, 213–42.
13 CAC, Alexander Galloway Papers, GLWY 1/6. Comments on the Draft Chapter on the Western Desert battle CRUSADER – vide Eric Sixsmith book 'Generalship XXth Century (British)'.
14 IWM 8179, Neil Ritchie oral history, reel five.
15 LHCMA, LH 4/39. 'BHLH Notes on a Draft of S.A. Official History of The Winter Battle ("Crusader").' Cover letter dated 6 August 1954.
16 LHCMA, LH 4/30, Basil H. Liddell Hart to Harry B. Latham, 4 February 1954.
17 South African Defence Force Documentation Centre. PMH 2.2.2. Publications – *The Sidi Rezeg Battles*, 1941. vol 1. John A.I. Agar-Hamilton to H.B. Latham, 26 October 1955.
18 James Marshall-Cornwall, *Wars and Rumours of Wars* (London: Leo Cooper, 1984), 190–1.

Chapter 6

1 Baynes 1989, 266. One indication that senior commanders, aside from Montgomery, viewed O'Connor's resignation with dismay is found in a letter from Alexander Galloway to O'Connor: 'I can only say that it is a first class calamity, for everyone had the greatest confidence + understanding for + in you + without prejudice to Jas. (Lt. General James Stuart Steele), it was quite evident what you

were doing on the "A" work for us all which is by far the most sticky I think these days!' LHCMA O'Connor 7/20. Alexander Galloway to Richard O'Connor, 28 August 1947.
2 See generally Alan Allport, *Demobbed, Coming Home after World War II* (New Haven: Yale University Press, 2009). See also French 2012, 36–40.
3 See generally Christopher J. Bartlett, *A History of Postwar Britain, 1945–7* (London: Longman, 1974); David Childs, *Britain since 1945, A Political History* (London: Routledge, 1992), 1–70; David Kynaston, *Austerity Britain, 1945–1951* (London: Bloomsbury, 2007).
4 See generally Peter Clarke, *The Last Thousand Days of the British Empire* (London: Bloomsbury, 2008).
5 David French, '"An Extensive Use of Weedkiller": Patterns of Promotion in the Senior Ranks of the British Army, 1919–39.' In *The British General Staff, Reform and Innovation c. 1890–1939*, edited by D. French and B.H. Reid, 132–45. London: Frank Cass, 2002.
6 Crang 2000b, 35–9.
7 See generally Alan Allport, *Browned Off and Bloody Minded, The British Soldier Goes to War 1939–1945* (New Haven: Yale University Press, 2015); Frances Houghton, *The Veterans' Tale: British Military Memoirs of the Second World War* (Cambridge: Cambridge University Press, 2019).
8 Baynes 1989, 260.
9 French 2012, 20.
10 Nick Hayes, 'An "English War," Wartime Culture and "Millions Like Us."' In *'Millions Like Us'? British Culture in the Second World War*, edited by Nick Hayes and Jeff Hill, 18–22. Liverpool: Liverpool University Press, 1999.
11 James E. Cronin, *The Politics of State, Expansion War, State and Society in Twentieth-Century Britain* (London: Routledge, 1991), 135–42; Hayes, 1999, 22–5.
12 Angus Calder, *The Myth of the Blitz* (London: Jonathan Cape, 1991); John Baxendale, '"You and I – All of Us Ordinary People": Renegotiating "Britishness" in Wartime.' In *'Millions Like Us'? British Culture in the Second World War*, edited by Nick Hayes and Jeff Hill, 295–322. Liverpool: Liverpool University Press, 1999.
13 Penny Summerfield, 'Dunkirk and the Popular Memory of Britain at War, 1940–1958.' *Journal of Contemporary History* 50 (2010): 788–811.
14 See the discussion of 'right' and 'left' declinism in Jim Tomlinson, *The Politics of Decline, Understanding Post-War Britain* (New York: Routledge, 2014).
15 On the parallel historiographic question regarding the irresponsible creation and abandonment of the Empire, brought about by failure of British resolve, it is worth mentioning the work of Anglo-Iraqi historian Elie Kedourie. His critique, articulated most famously in *The Chatham House Version and Other Middle*

Eastern Studies (London: Weidenfeld & Nicolson, 1970), is both the antithesis and complement to Barnett's approach to decline.

Kedourie's attack on the Establishment's post-colonial consensus, typified by Arnold Toynbee, that regarded British abdication of the Empire as wise and just, was also an attack on a school of history writing. In this sense it dovetailed with Barnett's critique of the smugness of the postwar 'New Jerusalemites', who directed British energies and wealth towards an unnecessary prolongation of the Empire and oversized military forces, and a National Health System that was predicted to be a limitless consumer of resources, while shortchanging both urban reconstruction and industrial development. In both cases, however, self-satisfaction among policymakers and historians alike were the targets. See Malcolm E. Yapp, 'Elie Kedourie and the History of the Middle East.' *Middle Eastern Studies* 41 (2005): 665–87.

16 'Decline' has generated a huge literature. See the insightful analysis of Barnett in David Edgerton, 'The Prophet Militant and Industrial.' *Twentieth Century British History* 2 (1991): 360–79.
17 Barnett 1983, 99.
18 Correlli Barnett, *The Lost Victory, British Dreams, British Realities 1945–1950* (London: Macmillan, 1995), 46–102.
19 See the essays in Jeffrey Grey (ed.), *The Last Word, Essays on Official History in the United States and the British Commonwealth* (Westport, CT: Praeger, 2003).
20 David Reynolds, 'Official History: How Churchill and the Cabinet Office Wrote *The Second World War*.' *Historical Research* 78 (2005): 400–22.
21 Winston S. Churchill, *The Grand Alliance* (New York: Houghton, Mifflin, and Company, 1950), 569. For how Churchill's view of Auchinleck and *Crusader* was softened by his syndicate of advisors, see Reynolds 2005a, 258.
22 For example, LHMCA, Ismay 2/3/122, Henry Pownall to Hastings Ismay, 1 December 1948.
23 TNA, CAB 140/53. Anthony Head to Norman Brook, 13 January 1953.
24 Nigel Hamilton, *Monty, Final Years of a Field Marshal, 1944–1976* (New York: McGraw-Hill, 1987), 605.
25 Harry C. Butcher, *My Three Years with Eisenhower: The Personal Diary of Captain Harry C. Butcher, USNR, Naval Aide to General Eisenhower, 1942 to 1945* (New York: Simon and Schuster, 1946). For Churchill's reaction to Butcher's book, see Reynolds 2005a, 40–1.
26 Nigel Hamilton, *Monty, Final Years of the Field-Marshal, 1944–1976* (New York: McGraw-Hill, 1987), 734–40.
27 Hamilton 1987, 795–7.
28 *Eighth Army: El Alamein to the River Sangro* (Printing and Stationery Services, British Army of the Rhine, 1946).
29 Compare Montgomery's comments regarding the alleged lack of army cooperation with the RAF (1946, 5) with James M.A. Gwyer and J.R.M. Butler, *Grand Strategy*,

vol III, June 1941–August 1942 (London: Her Majesty's Stationary Office, 1964), 220–3.
30 Nigel Hamilton, *Monty, Final Years of a Field Marshal, 1944–1976* (New York: McGraw-Hill, 1987), 634, quoting Montgomery's letter to the Principal Undersecretary of War.
31 Alan Moorehead, *Montgomery, A Biography* (London: Hamish Hamilton, 1946), 16.
32 Alan Moorehead, *Mediterranean Front* (London: Hamish Hamilton, 1941), *A Year of Battle* (London: Hamish Hamilton, 1943, originally published as *Don't Blame the Generals*), and *The End in Africa* (New York: Harper, 1943). The three volumes were published together as *African Trilogy* (London: Hamish Hamilton, 1945).
33 Alan Moorehead, *Eclipse* (London: Hamish Hamilton, 1946).
34 See Moorehead 1946a, especially 114–27. The best discussion of Moorehead's relationship with Montgomery and the book is Thornton McCamish's *Our Man Elsewhere: In Search of Alan Moorehead* (Melbourne: Black, 2017), who describes their 'warm rapport, largely based on the high opinion both men had of Montgomery' (unpaginated).

See also Ann Moyal's *Alan Moorehead, A Rediscovery* (Canberra: National Library of Australia, 2005), 35–7. Curiously, neither Moorehead's autobiography *A Late Education* (London: Soho Press, 2003, originally published 1970), nor the fascinating collective biography of journalists Moorehead, Alexander Clifford and Christopher Buckley by Richard Knott, *The Trio, Three War Correspondents of World War II* (The Mill, Brimscombe Port: The History Press, 2015), discuss the Montgomery biography in any detail. Simon Ball's *Alamein* similarly omits discussion of the book.
35 Francis de Guingand, *Operation Victory* (London: Hodder & Stoughton, 1947).
36 de Guingand 1947, vii. He also credits Alan and Lucy Moorehead for proofreading the book (see viii). As noted, Lucy Moorehead was a personal secretary to Auchinleck and later to Lieutenant General Thomas Corbett, chief of general staff Middle East Forces (see Ball 2016, 66).
37 de Guingand 1947, 98–9.
38 Claude J. Auchinleck, 'Operations in the Middle East from 1st November 1941 to 15th August 1942.' *Supplement to the London Gazette* Number 38177, 309–400, Thursday, 15 January 1948.
39 TNA, WO 201/500.
40 Auchinleck 1948, 309.
41 Auchinleck 1948, 311.
42 Auchinleck 1948, 310.
43 Auchinleck 1948, 312.
44 Auchinleck 1948, 312.
45 In his 1987 biography of Lt General George Brink, commander of the 1st South African Infantry Division, journalist and war correspondent Carel Birkby

recounted how his account of the Sidi Rezeg battle and South African casualties was rejected by censors until being unexpectedly approved by Auchinleck himself. The report was then transported to Cairo over the objections of an RAF officer thanks to the improbable intervention of Randolph Churchill who threatened, 'If you don't give me that aeroplane I'll tell Daddy.' It then caused a sensation in South Africa and a minor political crisis for Smuts, with instructions eventually reaching Birkby to 'lay off this grim war stuff'. Carel Birkby, *Uncle George, The Boer Boyhood, Letters and Battles of Lieutenant-General Geeorge Edwin Brink* (Johannesburg: Jonathan Ball Publishers, 1987), 242–4.

46 Paul Addison, *The Road to 1945: British Politics and the Second World War* (London: Random House, 1994), 195–209.
47 TNA, CAB 103/142, John A.I. Agar-Hamilton to Harry B. Latham, 14 May 1948.
48 Karen Horn and David Katz, 'The Surrender of Tobruk in 1942: Press Reports and Soldiers' Memories.' *Scientia Militaria* 44 (2016): 190–208.
49 For a recent military analysis of the fall of Tobruk that largely blames Klopper, see David Katz, 'The Greatest Military Reversal of South African Arms: The Fall of Tobruk 1942, an Avoidable Blunder or an Inevitable Disaster?' *Journal for Contemporary History* 37 (2012): 71–104.
50 See Andrew Stewart, '"The Klopper Affair": Anglo-South African Relations and the Surrender of the Tobruk Garrison.' *Twentieth Century British History* 17 (2006): 516–44 for an analysis of the background of British–South African military relations, the impact of the Tobruk surrender on South African politics. The description here is derived from his important analysis.
51 See generally Leonard Thompson, *A History of South Africa* (New Haven: Yale University Press, 2001), 177–86.
52 See especially Jeffrey Grey, '"Standing Humbly in the Ante-chambers of Clio": The Rise and Fall of the Union War Histories.' *Scientia Militaria* 30 (2000): 253–66; Ian van der Waag, 'Contested Histories: Official History and the South African Military in the 20th century.' In *The Last Word? Essays on Official History in the United States and British Commonwealth*, edited by Jeffrey Grey, 27–52. Westport, CT: Praeger, 2003; David Katz, 'A Case of Arrested Development: The Historiography Relating to South Africa's Participation in the Second World War.' *Scientia Militaria* 40 (2012): 280–317. See also Stewart 2006 and Andrew Stewart, 'The "Atomic" Despatch: Field Marshal Auchinleck, the Fall of the Tobruk Garrison and Post-war Anglo-South African Relations.' *Scientia Militaria* 36 (2008): 78–94.
53 Robert J. Crawford, R.A.S.C., as Narrated to Major John Dalgleish, *I Was an Eighth Army Soldier* (London: Victor Gollancz, 1944).
54 Robert Crisp, *Brazen Chariots: An Account of Tank Warfare in the Western Desert, November–December 1941* (London: Frederick Muller, 1959).

55 See especially Spike Milligan, *Adolf Hitler: My Part in His Downfall* (London: Michael Joseph Ltd., 1971) and *'Rommel?' 'Gunner Who?': A Confrontation in the Desert* (London: Michael Joseph Ltd., 1974).
56 These included 'Notes from the Theatres of War', 'Current Reports from Overseas', and 'Operational Research Reports', most of which were produced by for individual units or commands.
57 James R.M. Butler, 'The British Military Histories of the War of 1939-1945.' In *Official Histories, Essays and Bibliographies from around the World*, edited by Robin Higham, 511-14. Manhattan, KS: Kansas State University, 1970.
58 Keith Hancock, 'British Civil Histories of the Second World War.' In *Official Histories, Essays and Bibliographies from around the World*, edited by Robin Higham, 518-25. Manhattan, KS: Kansas State University, 1970.
59 Canadian historian Charles Perry Stacey provided the only account of that meeting, in which British and American historians denied Commonwealth historians access to Combined Chiefs of Staff records and produced an agreement between themselves while other historians were taken on a tour of Gettysburg. The controversy took two years to resolve and required the intervention of the Canadian Ministry of External Affairs and the involvement of Norman Brook. C.P. Stacey, *A Date with History, Memoirs of a Canadian Historian* (Ottawa: Deneau Publishers, 1980), 205-12.
60 A very useful summary is provided in Cat Wilson, *Churchill on the Far East in World War II* (London: Palgrave Macmillan, 2014), 138-41.
61 Hancock 1970, 521.
62 For example, the 1964 discussion regarding the timing of the *Crusader* operation presented by Gwyer and Butler could make no mention of *Ultra* intercepts regarding Rommel's proposed offensive. Gwyer and Butler 1964, 181-2.
63 Butler 1970, 513.
64 Geoffrey Elton, *Modern Historians on British History, 1485-1945, A Critical Bibliography, 1945-1969* (London: Methuen & Co., 1970), 157.
65 Jim Davidson, *A Three-Cornered Life: The Historian W. K. Hancock* (Kensington NSW: University of New South Wales Press, 2010), 186-227.
66 Noble Frankland, *History at War: The Campaigns of an Historian* (London: Giles de la Mare Publishers, 1998), 35-59. A query to Noble Frankland regarding Acheson and the Cabinet Office Historical Section was kindly transmitted via Gill Smith, Board Secretary of the Imperial War Museum. Frankland's response was that he had nothing to add to the account presented in his memoir (Personal communication Gill Smith, 22 August 2016).
67 Michael E. Howard, *Captain Professor: A Life in War and Peace* (New York: Continuum, 2006), 150-2, 188-91. Efforts to reach out to Sir Michael Howard for information regarding the Cabinet Office Historical Section were unsuccessful.
68 Herbert Butterfield, 'Official History: Its Pitfalls and Criteria.' In *History and Human Relations,* edited by H. Butterfield, 182-224. London: Collins, 1951.

69 Butterfield 1951, 183.
70 Butterfield 1951, 186.
71 Butterfield 1951, 191.
72 C.T. McIntire, *Herbert Butterfield, Historian as Dissenter* (New Haven, CT: Yale University Press, 2004), 168–70.
73 Noble Frankland, 'Some Thoughts about and Experience of Official Military History.' *Journal of the Royal Air Force Historical Society* 17 (1997): 5–15.
74 Frankland 1997, 6–7.
75 Frankland 1997, 13.
76 For example, Rachael Elizabeth Bell, *Memory, History, Nation, War: The Official Histories of New Zealand in the Second World War 1939–45*. PhD diss., Massey University, Palmerston North, 2012.
77 Sean Fielding, *They Sought Out Rommel: A Diary of the Libyan Campaign, from November 16th to December 31st, 1941* (London: Issued for the War Office by the Ministry of Information, 1942).
78 Fielding 1942, 4, 5.
79 Fielding 1942, 16–17.
80 Fielding 1942, 18, 19.
81 Fielding 1942, 27.
82 Fielding 1942, 33.
83 House of Commons, *Papers by Command*, vol 3 (London: HMSO, 1942), 29.
84 The Book of the Month Club had some 600,000 members in 1943. A. Keith Fowler, '"Anon."-Britain's Favorite Author.' *Saturday Review*, 19 June 1943, 13.
85 *The Battle for Egypt* (London: Issued for the War Office by the Ministry of Information, 1943).
86 *The Eighth Army, September 1941 to January 1943* (London: His Majesty's Stationary Office, 1944).
87 *The Eighth Army*, 20.
88 *The Eighth Army*, 21.
89 The question of commanders' personalities, the American Civil War, the role of technology and strategic context are all hallmarks of Basil H. Liddell Hart. There is, however, no indication he was involved in the production of *The Eighth Army* during what was an especially fallow period in his career.
90 NAM 8303/104-19. Cunningham copy of *The Eighth Army*.
91 NAM 8303/104-19. John N. Kennedy to Alan Cunningham, 3 April 1944.
92 NAM 8303/104-19. Alan Cunningham, handwritten note on letter from Henry Colville Barclay Wemyss, 5 May 1944.
93 NAM 8303/104-19. Henry Colville Barclay Wemyss to Alan Cunningham, 5 May 1944.
94 NAM 8303/104-19. Alan Cunningham to Henry Colville Barclay Wemyss, 11 May 1944.
95 NAM 8303/104-19. Henry Colville Barclay Wemyss to Alan Cunningham, 2 June 1944.

96 NAM 8303/104-19. Alan Cunningham to Henry Colville Barclay Wemyss, 8 June 1944.
97 TNA, CAB 44/91. Chapter G. General Auchinleck's Offensive and the Relief of Tobruk. Phase 1 – The Planning Period, June–November 1941, 20.
98 NAM 8303/104-19. John N. Kennedy to Alan Cunningham, 15 June 1944.
99 NAM 8303/104-19. Alan Cunningham to John N. Kennedy, 18 June 1944.
100 As discussed above, the earliest CIGS file, WO 106/5826, was transmitted to the Historical Section where it became CAB 106/655. Quotations here are from the later file.
101 TNA, CAB 106/655, 5.
102 TNA, CAB 106/655, 8.
103 IWM Documents 20500, BLM 54, Bernard Law Montgomery collection. See also Nigel Hamilton, *Monty, The Making of a General, 1887–1942* (New York: McGraw-Hill, 1981), 512.
104 TNA, CO 967/100. Bernard Law Montgomery to George H. Hall, 6 August 1946.
105 Higham 2012.
106 Gavin Long, *Greece, Crete and Syria* (Canberra: Australian War Memorial, 1953), especially 191–6.
107 W.G. McClymont, *To Greece*. Official History of New Zealand in the Second World War (Wellington: Department of Internal Affairs, 1959), especially 471–85.
108 Karl Hack and Kevin Blackburn, *Did Singapore Have to Fall? Churchill and the Impregnable Fortress* (London: RoutledgeCurzon, 2004). See also the essays in Brian P. Farrell (ed.), *Churchill and the Lion City, Shaping Modern Singapore* (Singapore: NUS Press, 2011).
109 Cat Wilson, *Churchill on the Far East in World War II* (London: Palgrave Macmillan, 2014).
110 Hack and Blackburn 2004, 2–9.
111 Hack and Blackburn 2004, 130–71. Kevin Blackburn and Karl Hack, *War Memory and the Making of Modern Malaysia and Singapore* (Singapore: NUS Press, 2012).
112 Butler 1970, 511.
113 Butler 1970, 512–13.
114 Butler 1970, 513.
115 Playfair 1960, 60–1.
116 Agar-Hamilton and Turner 1957, 313.
117 W.E. Murphy, *The Relief of Tobruk* (Wellington: War History Branch, 1961), 200.
118 Barton Maughan, *Tobruk and El Alamein* (Canberra: Australian War Memorial, 1966), 455.
119 TNA, WO 201/2770. Operations in Western Desert (17 Nov. 41–4 Feb. 42).
120 TNA, CAB 44/91, Chapter G. General Auchinleck's Offensive and the Relief of Tobruk, Part 1. CAB 44/92. General Auchinleck's Offensive and the Relief of Tobruk, 18 November–30 November 1941.

121 ANZ, R12325661, Harry B. Latham to Howard K. Kippenberger, 13 March 1954.
122 TNA, CAB 44/92, 138.
123 TNA, CAB 103/331, Ian Jacob to Andrew B. Acheson, 30 May 1956.
124 AIR 41/25, 151, no. 2. The Middle East Campaigns, vol II: Operations in Libya and the Western Desert, June 1941–Jan. 1942.
125 Denis Richards and Hilary St. George Saunders, *Royal Air Force 1939–1945, Volume 2, The Fight Avails* (London: HMSO, 1953), 175.
126 Clifton 1952, 134.
127 R.M.P. Carver, 'Desert Dilemmas.' *Royal Armoured Corps Journal* 2 (1948): 194.
128 Playfair 1960, 54.
129 TNA, WO 169/996, Serial 87, 1530 hours.
130 TNA, WO 169/996, Serial 103, 1700 hours.
131 The use of the term 'flap' also demonstrates the role of understatement when describing comportment, with respect to both individual incidents and broader temporal horizons. For example, South African historians also referred to the period of June–July 1942 as a 'flap' (TNA, CAB 103/144), John A.I. Agar-Hamilton to Harry B. Latham, 4 October 1951.
132 TNA, CAB 106/719, Alexander Galloway to Harry B. Latham, 22 October 1950.
133 TNA, CAB 106/719, Alexander Galloway, comments on letter from Harry B. Latham, 30 October 1950.
134 TNA, CAB 106/719, A.R. Godwin-Austen to Harry B. Latham, 4 October 1950.
135 TNA, CAB 103/147, Harry B. Latham, to Howard K. Kippenberger, 28 September 1950.
136 TNA, CAB 106/745, Alexander Galloway to Harry B. Latham, 27 September 1952.
137 TNA, CAB 106/745, Alexander Galloway to Harry B. Latham, 5 January 1953.
138 TNA, CAB 106/745, Alexander Galloway to Harry B. Latham, 5 January 1953.
139 TNA, CAB 106/745, Alexander Galloway to Harry B. Latham, 1 February 1953.
140 TNA, CAB 106/745, Harry B. Latham to John A.I. Agar-Hamilton, 19 February 1953.
141 TNA, CAB 106/745, Alexander Galloway to Harry B. Latham, 30 May 1953.
142 TNA, CAB 106/745, Alexander Galloway to Harry B. Latham, 27 July 1953.
143 TNA, CAB 140/129, Alexander Galloway to I.S.O. Playfair, 2 January 1954.
144 South African Defence Force Documentation Centre. PMH 2.2.2. Publications – The Sidi Rezeg Battles, 1941. vol 1, Harry B. Latham to John A.I. Agar-Hamilton, 1 December 1955.
145 Personal communication from Mrs Diana Evelyn Miller, 24 November 2014.
146 I am grateful to Richard Mead for information regarding Latham's military career.
147 See Johnston's correspondence notebook CAB 106/831 and interview notebook CAB 106/832. Latham often gave precise locations for various emplacements from memory.
148 TNA, CAB 106/745, Harry B. Latham to John A.I. Agar-Hamilton, 19 March 1953.

149 For example, TNA, CAB 103/331, Harry B. Latham, Comments on Page 1 to 159 (Crusader) of the draft history of 'The Mediterranean and Middle East – volume III', 18 December 1956.
150 TNA, CAB 140/45, J.R.M. Butler to Harry B. Latham, 4 June 1958.
151 NAM 8303/104-18, James Blewitt to Alan Cunningham, 31 January 1942.
152 ANZ, R12681219, Harry B. Latham to Howard K. Kippenberger, 16 July 1949. Excerpt.
153 Howard Kippenberger, *Infantry Brigadier* (London: Oxford University Press, 1949).
154 Quoted in Ian McGibbon, '"Something of Them Is Here Recorded": Official History in New Zealand.' In *The Last Word, Essays on Official History in the United States and the British Commonwealth*, edited by Jeffrey Grey, 53–68. Westport, CT: Praeger, 2003, 60.
155 McGibbon 2003, 60–1.
156 Rachael Bell, 'Evidence and Interpretation in New Zealand's Official History: The Battle for Crete, May 1941.' *War in History* 22 (2015): 367–8.
157 Kippenberger 1949, 210–21.
158 ANZ 12681219, Bernard Freyberg, Comments on Volume 1, Planning and Preparation, Second Libyan Campaign, 1941 – November–December. Undated but likely written 1950.
159 Glyn Harper, *Kippenberger, An Inspired New Zealand Commander* (Auckland: HarperCollins, 1997), 122–3.
160 ANZ 12681219, Bernard Freyberg, Comments on Volume 1, Planning and Preparation, Second Libyan Campaign, 1941 – November–December. Undated but likely written 1950. Present also in CAB 106/702.
161 ANZ R12325670, Howard K. Kippenberger to John A.I. Agar-Hamilton, 1 February 1956.
162 ANZ R12325670, John A.I. Agar-Hamilton to W.E. Murphy, 15 December 1955.
163 ANZ R12325661, Harry B. Latham to Howard K. Kippenberger, 26 January 1956.
164 Peter Dennis, Leonard Charles Frederick Turner, *Australian Dictionary of Biography*. http://adb.anu.edu.au/biography/turner-leonard-charles-frederick-15565
165 TNA, CAB 140/136, John A.I. Agar-Hamilton to I.S.O. Playfair, 11 March 1957.
166 Latham complained to Kippenberger as early as 1949 about Turner's approach, calling one of his narratives 'so violent in tone that I was quite unable to circulate it here for comment' (TNA, CAB 103/146, Harry B. Latham to Howard K. Kippenberger, 11 June 1949). In the letter Latham also thanked Kippenberger for food packages which helped sustain the Latham family.

Much later Latham commented to Agar-Hamilton: 'It was very lucky for Turner and for all of us that you were his "BOSS". Some of his original work that came here was a bit childish and only caused resentment.' (Rhodes University, Cory Library for Humanities Research, J.A.I. Agar-Hamilton Papers, Harry B. Latham to John A.I. Agar-Hamilton, 11 August 1961.)

Latham also wrongly complained that in defiance of the Official Secrets Act, Turner had used Admiralty records to write a popular book with Betzler that would apparently reflect badly on the Royal Navy and, in turn, on Turner. Contrary to Latham's allegations, no such book appeared, nor was Turner's career affected. I am grateful to Elizabeth de Wet for locating and examining Agar-Hamilton's papers at the Cory Library.

167 Frederick von Mellenthin, *Panzer Battles* (Norman, OK: University of Oklahoma Press, 1956).
168 See N. Southey and F.A. Mouton, '"A Volksvreemde Historian": J.A.I. Agar-Hamilton and the Production of History in an Alien Environment.' *South African Historical Journal* 44 (2001), 72–98.
169 TNA, CAB 106/745, John A.I. Agar-Hamilton to Harry B. Latham, 12 March 1953.
170 ANZ R12325661, Howard K. Kippenberger to Harry B. Latham, 26 March 1956.
171 TNA, CAB 140/133, Alan Cunningham to I.S.O. Playfair, 1 December 1955.
172 Murphy 1961, 307.
173 TNA, CAB 103/540, Memo by Andrew B. Acheson, 24 February 1949.
174 Astrid Eckert, *The Struggle for the Files. The Western Allies and the Return of German Archives after the Second World War* (Washington, DC: German Historical Institute and Cambridge University Press, 2012), 198–204.
175 Frankland 1998, 51, 53–4, 139–43.
176 TNA, CAB 103/543, Andrew B. Acheson to Llewelyn Woodward, 4 April 1957.
177 Tina Nelis, *Northern Ireland in the Second World War*. Unpublished M Phil thesis, University of Manchester, 2012, 161–88.
178 CAB 103/523, Harry B. Latham to Andrew B. Acheson, 26 January 1956.
179 South African National Defense Force Documentation Centre, PMH 2.2.2. Publications – *The Sidi Rezeg Battles*, 1941. vol 1, Andrew B. Acheson to John A.I. Agar-Hamilton, 8 May 1956.
180 South African National Defense Force Documentation Centre, PMH 2.2.2. Publications – *The Sidi Rezeg Battles*, 1941. vol 1, John A.I. Agar-Hamilton to Andrew B. Acheson, 17 May 1956.
181 South African National Defense Force Documentation Centre, PMH 2.2.2. Publications – *The Sidi Rezeg Battles*, 1941. vol 1, Harry B. Latham to John A.I. Agar-Hamilton, 22 May 1956.
182 South African National Defense Force Documentation Centre, PMH 2.2.2. Publications – *The Sidi Rezeg Battles*, 1941. vol 1, Andrew B. Acheson to John A.I. Agar-Hamilton, 2 June 1956.

183 'Mr. Andrew B. Acheson', *The Times,* 13 May 1959. Acheson's health was evidently in decline since at least 1955 and in 1957 he reported to Llewelyn Woodward that he was affected by a paralytic disorder.
184 LHCMA, LH 1/575, Frederick Pile to Basil H. Liddell Hart, 28 May 1942. Most of the document details Pile's conversation with Secretary of State for War P.J. Grigg. Perhaps for this reason the document is stamped Secret.
185 LHCMA, LH 1/575, Frederick Pile to Basil H. Liddell Hart, 3 April 1943.
186 LHCMA, LH 1/30, Claude Auchinleck to Basil H. Liddell Hart, 25 September 1951.
187 TNA, CAB 140/101, Basil H. Liddell Hart to I.S.O. Playfair, 11 September 1954, regarding comments from the 'Unknown Correspondent'. In addition to analysis, the comments themselves clearly describe Dorman-Smith's participation in Desert War operations. Dorman-Smith's attitude towards Official History is also succinctly summed up: 'The whole system of presentation of the history of the war as decided on by the Cabinet is a cover-up.'
188 ANZ, R12325661, Basil H. Liddell Hart, 'A Strategic Puzzle, Questions Raised by Rommel's Counterstroke in "Crusader" (24th Nov. 1941).' Dated January 1954.
189 ANZ R12325661, 'Notes on a Strategic Puzzle B.H.K.H. Jan. 54. Questions Raised by Rommel's Counterstroke in "Crusader" (24th Nov. 1941).' Howard K. Kippenberger to Harry B. Latham, 3 March 1954.
190 ANZ, R12325661, Harry B. Latham to Howard K. Kippenberger, 4 February 1954.
191 LHCMA, LH 1/108, Charles Broad to Basil H. Liddell Hart, 1 March 1954.
192 Union War History Histories, Administrative Files, P.MH. 206, II, Western Desert, Crusader, Nov, '41–Feb. '42, Correspondence with London. Michael Carver to John A.I. Agar-Hamilton, 10 June 1949.
193 Especially R.M.P. Carver, 'Desert Dilemmas.' *Royal Armoured Corps Journal* 2 (1948): 181–99, followed by accounts in later books.
194 LHCMA, LH 1/153, Michael Carver to Basil H. Liddell Hart, 10 February 1954. Carver coyly implied to Liddell Hart in 1953 that he had been given confidential access to the draft South African history. In fact he had corresponded extensively with Agar-Hamilton and Turner beginning in 1949, primarily on the questions of South African units and General Dan Pienaar's conduct during *Crusader*, specifically his difficulty cooperating with other units and refusal to 'over-train' his troops, which the historians were anxious to downplay. Carver went so far to admit that his earliest article 'was altered at the request of the Historical Section of the Cabinet Offices in order to ensure that there should be no misunderstanding about the part which 1st South Africa Division and Pienaar in particular had played' (IWM Documents.22500, Papers of Field Marshal Lord Carver, Box 5, File 1, Michael Carver to John A.I. Agar-Hamilton, 14 April 1949).

195 Michael Carver, *Dilemmas of the Desert War* (Bloomington: Indiana University Press, 1986), 42; *Out of Step, The Memoirs of Field Marshal Lord Carver* (London: Hutchinson, 1989), p. 86.

Carver's parallel career as a military writer should be examined closely since his shifting perspectives and loyalties are evident. For example, in 1959 he complained to Liddell Hart that the Cabinet Office had thwarted a proposed book on the El Alamein since it would preempt publication of the Official History (LHCMA, LH 1/153, Michael Carver to Basil H. Liddell Hart, 18 December 1959). But in 1962 he described this as the War Office 'desperately anxious not to rekindle all the flames of the feud between the Field Marshals, which only, in their opinion, brings discredit on the Army as a whole' (LHCMA, LH 1/153, Michael Carver to Basil H. Liddell Hart, 26 September 1962). In the 1979 foreword to the third edition of the book, however, Carver claimed that it was I.S.O. Playfair who feared 'adding fuel to the fire of the controversy between the advocates of the two Field-Marshals' (*El Alamein*, London: Wordsworth, 1979, 13).

In fact, Carver had requested and then been given permission to examine Cabinet Office historical files but his publication was vetoed on the not wholly specious grounds that 'we cannot hope to suppress the fact that you had access to the official records, and we have no grounds for defending this in the face of the War Office refusal to grant such access to anybody else. There have been several applicants; and high-powered ones at that' (IWM Documents.22500, Papers of Field Marshal Lord Carver, Box 40, Richard Fyffe to Michael Carver, 24 August 1961).

Carver also stated in *Dilemmas of the Desert War* that he was motivated by a desire to restore Neil Ritchie's reputation, which he regarded as having been unfairly sullied by Dorman-Smith and Barnett. His files indicate that he negotiated with Ritchie's widow for access to her husband's papers. Ritchie, however, had reported in 1956 that his papers had been lost 'having been sunk on their journey home' (TNA, CAB 140/135, Neil Ritchie to I.S.O. Playfair, 22 October 1956).

Whatever Ritchie papers Carver obtained much later resided for a time within his collection at the Imperial War Museum but at some point were transferred to the Black Watch Museum (Richard Mead, personal communication, 9 November 2015).

Carver's initial work was not well regarded by professional historians. Agar-Hamilton described Carver's earliest analyses of *Crusader*, in which Carver 'goes so far as to suggest that if the H.Q. in which he was serving a the time had been in charge of the operations things would have gone better!!' as reflecting a 'warped mentality' (TNA, CAB 103/142, John A.I. Agar-Hamilton to Harry B. Latham, 1 April 1949).

196 Alex Danchev, *Alchemist of War, The Life of Basil Liddell Hart* (London: Weidenfeld & Nicolson, 1998), 221–42.
197 Basil H. Liddell Hart, *The Other Side of the Hill: Germany's Generals, Their Rise and Fall, with Their Own Account of Military Events, 1939–1945* (London: Cassell, 1948).
198 Basil H. Liddell Hart, *The Tanks, A History of the Royal Tank Regiment and Its Predecessors*, Volumes I and II (New York: Praeger, 1959).
199 On the question of German manipulation versus Liddell Hart's alleged fabrications compare Danchev 1998, 232–3, and n. 75 with John Mearsheimer, *Liddell Hart and the Weight of History* (Ithaca: Cornell University Press, 1988), especially 178–217. Mearsheimer's study is suspect on this and a number of other points, not least of all thanks to the fact that it does not mention Eric Dorman-Smith.
200 Desmond Young, *Rommel: The Desert Fox* (New York: Harper & Brothers, 1950).
201 Basil H. Liddell Hart, *The Rommel Papers* (New York: Harcourt Brace, 1953).
202 Brian C. Etheridge, '*The Desert Fox*, Memory Diplomacy, and the German Question in Early Cold War America.' *Diplomatic History* 32 (2008): 207–38.
203 TNA, CAB 140/134, Claude Auchinleck to I.S.O. Playfair, 16 November 1956.
204 See, for example, Charles Messenger, *Rommel, Leadership Lessons from the Desert Fox* (New York: Palgrave Macmillan, 2009), and Patrick Caddick-Adams, *Monty and Rommel, Parallel Lives* (New York: Harry N. Abrams, 2013).
205 TNA, CAB 140/138, Edward Playfair to I.S.O. Playfair, 26 September 1958.
206 TNA, CAB 140/138, C.J.C. Molony to I.S.O. Playfair, 29 September 1958.

Chapter 7

1 Richard Titmus, *Problems of Social Policy* (London: HMSO, 1950), Table 10.
2 George MacDonald Fraser, *Quartered Safe Out Here: A Harrowing Tale of World War II* (London: Harvill, 1993), xi.
3 See generally Brian P.D. Hannon, *The Story behind the Stories, British and Dominion War Correspondents in the Western Theatres of the Second World War*. Unpublished PhD diss., University of Edinburgh, 2015.
4 Christopher Buckley, 'A Modern Blenheim in the Desert.' *Daily Telegraph and Morning Post*, 24 November 1941, 1.
5 A Student of War, 'Swift Success in Libya Tank Battle Would Have Decisive Effects.' *Daily Telegraph and Morning Post*, 24 November 1941, 4.
6 Moorehead is the subject of three useful biographies but the most trenchant observations are to be found in Moorehead's autobiography, *A Late Education: Episodes in a Life* (London: Hamish Hamilton, 1970), and in an essay by Clive

James in his book *Cultural Amnesia: Necessary Memories From History and the Arts* (New York: W. W. Norton, 2006), 515–23.
7   Alan Moorehead, *African Trilogy* (London: Hamish Hamilton, 1945), 185.
8   Moorehead 1945, 186.
9   Moorehead 1945, 186.
10 Moorehead 1945, 187.
11 Moorehead 1945, 187–8. Crang points out that new educational schemes for soldiers were implemented in late 1942 after earlier programmes demonstrated pervasive ignorance of 'British democratic, social, and economic institutions' (Jeremy Crang, 'The British Army as a Social Institution, 1939–45.' In *The British Army, Manpower and Society into the Twenty-First Century*, edited by Hew Strachan, 26. London: Frank Cass, 2000).
12 Moorehead 1945, 188.
13 Moorehead 1945, 209.
14 Moorehead 1945, 210.
15 Moorehead 1945, 210.
16 Danchev and Todman 2001, 225.
17 Moorehead 1945, 212.
18 Moorehead 1945, 211.
19 Moorehead 1945, 217.
20 Moorehead 1945, 227.
21 Moorehead 1945, 229.
22 Moorehead 1945, 230.
23 Alexander Clifford, *Crusader* (London: George G. Harrap, 1942).
24 Alexander Clifford, *Three against Rommel, The Campaigns of Wavell, Auchinleck, and Alexander* (London: George G. Harrap, 1943). The American edition of the same year was entitled *The Conquest of North Africa 1940–1943* (Boston: Little, Brown, and Company).
25 Clifford 1942, 47, 48.
26 Clifford 1942, 5.
27 Clifford 1942, 62.
28 Clifford 1942, 62.
29 Clifford 1942, 78.
30 Clifford 1942, 83.
31 Clifford 1942, 84–5. Historians would make similar calculations, along with the range and power of German guns and the thickness of armour, during the early 1950s. None cited Clifford or his informant.
32 Clifford 1942, 87.
33 Clifford 1942, 91.
34 Clifford 1942, 90.
35 Clifford 1942, 91.

36 Clifford 1942, 102–3.
37 Angus Calder's important studies relied heavily on Hodson's perceptions of the home front. He described Hodson's books as providing an 'honest commentary' (Calder 1969, 630).
38 James Lansdale Hodson, *War in the Sun* (London: Victor Gollancz, 1942), 201.
39 Hodson 1942, 201.
40 Compare Keith Douglas's comments regarding a briefing a year later during the Alamein battles from his colonel 'Piccadilly Jim', 'This speech, the first of Piccadilly Jim's resumes I had heard, impressed me without deceiving me. It was couched in a nice mixture of parliamentary and colloquial terms, magnifying what we had done, half belittling what remained to be done, half glorifying it.' (Douglas 1946, 39). This type of understatement would not have impressed war correspondents, cynical by both nature and experience.
41 Hodson 1942, 201.
42 Hodson's narrative switched at one point from his own experiences to a day-by-day reconstruction of various units in the battle itself. This is impossible to comprehend without a map, which the book does not include.
43 Hodson 1942, 198.
44 Hodson 1942, 217.
45 Illustrating the grey line between correspondents and propagandists, Hodson also co-wrote the 1943 film *Desert Victory* and travelled to the United States on a speaking tour on behalf of the British Ministry of Information. These activities, however, are well explained in a letter he sent to Randolph Churchill, decrying the censorship by different services and declaring that the correspondents' duties were not to the government but to the 'British Commonwealth as a whole'. See Hodson (1942, 268–9). In this same vein, Christopher Buckley of the *Daily Telegraph* wrote three popular books for the 'The Second World War 1939–1945, A Short Military History Series'. That series, published in the early 1950s and sponsored by His Majesty's Stationary Office, did not include a volume on Egypt or North Africa. Interestingly, two of Buckley's volumes dealt with military failures, namely Norway, and the campaigns in Greece and Crete.
46 Russell J. Hill, *Desert War* (New York: A.A. Knopf, 1942), 84.
47 Hill 1942, 85.
48 Hill 1942, 115.
49 Hill 1942, 116.
50 Hill 1942, 139.
51 Hill 1942, 181.
52 Hill 1942, 183.
53 'Thrilling Stories Done by Foreign Correspondents.' *Chicago Tribune*, 7 December 1941, 61.

54 Quentin Reynolds, *Only the Stars Are Neutral* (Garden City, NY: Blue Ribbon Books, 1943), 238–43.
55 Reynolds 1943, 244–5.
56 Robert Gale Woolbert, Review of Q. Reynolds, *Only the Stars Are Neutral*, *Foreign Affairs,* October 1942, 13.
57 Edward Kennedy, Julia Kennedy Cochran (ed.), *Ed Kennedy's War: V-E Day, Censorship, and the Associated Press* (Baton Rouge: Louisiana State University Press, 2012), 13.
58 Kennedy 2012, 67.
59 Kennedy 2012, 88.
60 Kennedy 2012, 87.
61 Knott 2015, 82.
62 Kennedy 2012, 89.
63 Hinsley 1981, 307–11.
64 Hinsley 1981, 315–24.
65 Hinsley 1981, 332–3.
66 Eve Curie, *Journey among Warriors* (New York: Doubleday, Doran and Company, 1943), 50.
67 Curie 1943, 50.
68 Alaric Jacob, *A Traveller's War* (New York: Dodd, Mead, 1944), 79.
69 Jacob 1944, 80.
70 Jacob 1944, 81.
71 Jacob 1944, 81.
72 Jacob 1944, 91.
73 Matthew Holton, *Ten Years to Alamein* (Toronto: S.J. Reginald Saunders, 1944).
74 Holton 1944, 192.
75 Holton 1944, 201.
76 Holton 1944, 211.
77 Holton 1944, 212.
78 Holton 1944, 188.
79 Holton 1944, 188–9.
80 Another example of this attitude is expressed in Frank Gervasi's *War Has Seven Faces* (Garden City, NY: Doubleday, Doran, and Company, 1942), 82–4. Gervasi, of *Collier's Weekly*, left Cairo after the appointment of Auchinleck but his account should be read closely for its absolute excoriation of the British organization of the Desert War and its commanders, with the exceptions of Wavell and Auchinleck.
81 Richard Busvine, *Gullible Travels* (London: Constable, 1945).
82 Busvine 1945, 315.
83 Busvine 1945, 266–7.
84 Busvine 1945, 267.

85 Chester Wilmot, *Tobruk 1941: Capture, Siege, Relief* (Sydney: Angus and Robertson, 1944), viii.
86 Wilmot 1944, 34.
87 Wilmot 1944, 292.
88 Wilmot 1944, 304.
89 Reynolds 1943, 259.
90 John Hohenberg, *Foreign Correspondence: The Great Reporters and Their Times* (New York: Columbia University Press, 1964), 207–9.
91 Gervasi 1942, 87.
92 Anthony Aldgate and Jeffrey Richards, *Britain Can Take It: The British Cinema in the Second World War*, 2nd edition (London: I.B. Tauris, 2007), 8.
93 It is worth noting the appearance of the films *The Dambusters*, *The Colditz Story (1955)*, *Reach for the Sky* (1956), *The Bridge over the River Kwai* (1957), and *Dunkirk* (1958).
94 Houghton 2019, 79–83.
95 'C.I.G.S. Appeals for Full Alamein Reunion.' *Sunday Times*, 5 October 1947, 6.
96 'Eighth Army Spirit.' *The Times*, 23 October 1948, 3.
97 'Stop Arguing over the Last War.' *The Times*, 20 October 1962, 8.
98 '"Tommy" and "Jerry" Bury Hatchet.' *The Sunday Times*, 29 October 1978, 1.
99 'Germans' Heavy Losses: 500 Bayoneted.' *Daily Telegraph*, 3 July 1942, 6.
100 Milligan 1976, 156–7.
101 Compare the delicate description of Brooke's financial situation and motivations for publishing his diaries in David Fraser, *Alanbrooke* (New York: Atheneum, 1982), 514–15, with the more frank discussion in Danchev and Todman 2001, xxiv–xxv.
102 Arthur Bryant, *The Turn of the Tide* (Garden City, NY: Doubleday & Co, 1957), 224.
103 Hastings Ismay, *The Memoirs of Lord Ismay* (New York: Viking Press, 1960), 271.
104 Hamilton 1987, 857–66, 885–902.
105 Bernard L. Montgomery, *The Memoirs of Field Marshal the Viscount Montgomery* (New York: World Publishing Company, 1958), 86.
106 See Graeen 1989, 304–9. Cf. Reynolds 2005b, 356–9.
107 Hamilton 1987, 897.
108 Hamilton 1987, 87.
109 ANZ, R12325670, Howard K. Kippenberger to John A.I. Agar-Hamilton, 19 August 1955.
110 ANZ, R12325670, Howard K. Kippenberger to John A.I. Agar-Hamilton, 8 November 1955.
111 TNA, CAB 140/139, Alexander Galloway to I.S.O. Playfair, 17 December 1958.

112 Francis Tuker, *Approach to Battle, A Commentary, Eighth Army, November 1941 to May 1943* (London: Cassel, 1963).
113 Bidwell and Graham 2004, 250.
114 Francis de Guingand, *Generals at War* (London: Hodder and Stoughton, 1964), 180.
115 For Connell Robertson's affectionate relationship with Auchinleck, see his letter to Ismay, LHCMA, Ismay 4/9/34, John Connell (Robertson) to Hastings Ismay, 4 October 1959.
116 Connell 1960, 370–71.
117 Lyttelton 1962, 266.
118 Arthur Tedder, *With Prejudice: The War Memoirs of Marshal of the Royal Air Force* (London: Cassell, 1966), 194–7.
119 David Belchem, *All in the Day's March* (London: Collins, 1978), 98.
120 Belchem 1978, 99.
121 LHCMA, LH 1/56/20, David Belchem to Basil H. Liddell Hart, 31 January 1954.
122 LHCMA, LH 1/56/20, David Belchem to Basil H. Liddell Hart, 16 June 1954.
123 IWM 8736, John Harding oral history, reel 18.
124 Barnett 1983, 7.
125 I am grateful to Correlli Barnett for permission to examine his files at the Churchill Archive Centre.
126 Barnett 1983, 85.
127 Barnett 1983, 85–6.
128 Barnett 1983, 86.
129 Barnett 1983, 90.
130 Barnett 1983, 94.
131 Barnett 1983, 103.
132 Barnett 1983, 110.
133 Barnett 1983, 111.
134 Barnett 1983, 112.
135 Barnett 1983, 116.
136 Barnett 1983, 118.
137 Barnett 1983, 120. Unfortunately, and ironically, I was unable to locate his interview with Alexander Galloway.
138 Barnett's many newspaper pieces in the *Daily Telegraph* in the early 1960s in which he discussed the British economy and the European Economic Community – as an economic alternative to the empire – should also be mentioned.
139 Reginald W. Thompson, *Churchill and the Montgomery Myth* (New York: M. Evans and Company, 1966), 251. Published in Britain with the title *The Montgomery Legend*.
140 LHCMA, LH 1/242, Eric Dorman-Smith to Basil H. Liddell Hart, 17 November 1943.

Chapter 8

1. LHCMA, Ismay 1/14/4, Hastings Ismay to Claude Auchinleck, 2 May 1960. See also Ismay 4/9/3, Extract of letter from Claude Auchinleck to Hastings Ismay, 19 November 1941.
2. LHCMA, LH 1/679, Arthur Tedder to Basil H. Liddell Hart, 7 March 1963.
3. Latham declined an MBE in 1962 for unknown reasons. He died in 1977.
4. Paul Fussell, *Wartime. Understanding and Behavior in the Second World War* (Oxford: Oxford University Press, 1988), 10.
5. Fussell 1988, 268.
6. Evelyn Waugh, *Unconditional Surrender* (London: Penguin Books, 1964), 81.
7. Lewis B. Namier, 'Symmetry and Repetition.' In *Conflicts: Studies in Contemporary History*, 69–70. London: Macmillan, 1942. Originally published in the *Manchester Guardian*, 1 January 1941.
8. Milligan 1976, 157.
9. Walter Benjamin, 'On the Concept of History.' In *Walter Benjamin, Selected Writings, Volume 4, 1938–1940*, edited by Howard Eiland and Michael W. Jennings, 389–90. Cambridge, MA: Belknap Press of Harvard University Press, 2006.
10. http://www.thegoonshow.net/scripts_show.asp?title=s06e06_rommels_treasure
11. Farrar-Hockley 2004.
12. Sixsmith 1977, 4.
13. LHCMA, LH 1/575, Frederick Pile to Basil H. Liddell Hart, 28 December 1942.
14. LHCMA, LH 1/575, Frederick Pile to Basil H. Liddell Hart, 28 May 1942.
15. LHCMA, LH 1/575, Frederick Pile to Basil H. Liddell Hart, 17 July 1942.
16. Auchinleck Papers, number 1000, Alexander Galloway to Claude Auchinleck, 31 August 1942.
17. Alexander H. Joffe and Asaf Romirowsky, 'A Tale of Two Galloways: Notes on the Early History of UNRWA and Zionist Historiography.' *Middle Eastern Studies* 46 (2010): 655–75.
18. The sudden resignation of Lord Gort as High Commissioner and Commander-in-Chief of British forces in Palestine was a shock. Widely respected by the British establishment, and trusted by both Jews and Arabs, Gort had brought immense political experience to Palestine after his position as Governor General of Malta and Gibraltar. His resignation at the end of October 1945 (kept secret until early the next month) set off a sudden and unexpected search for a successor.

    The choice focused instantly on soldiers. Curiously, some months before Zionist leader David Ben Gurion had mentioned in an interview with a Colonial Office official, 'Lord Gort was liked and trusted by everyone. He murmured that "our best High Commissioners have always been soldiers"' (TNA, CO 733/452/5, Note of interview with Mr. Ben Gurion, 2 May 1945). It is unclear whether this statement, made in passing, influenced the process or whether by parallel reasoning British officials turned to the military for suggestions.

The search for a replacement began before Gort's resignation was made public. In a meeting with Prime Minister Clement Attlee attended by Vice Chief of the Imperial General Staff Archibald Nye, Cunningham's name was mentioned, along with that of General Sir George Giffard, who had ended his army career somewhat acrimoniously as Commander-in-Chief of the 11th Army Group in Southeast Asia. In 1940 Giffard had briefly commanded British forces in Palestine and Transjordan, a fact mentioned by Attlee in his meeting with Nye (TNA, CO 967/99, Archibald Nye to Alan Brooke, 29 October 1945).

Brooke, then on an extended tour of the Middle East and Asia, responded quickly and reported that he had discussed the question with Gort and head of Middle East Command General Sir Bernard Paget, who agreed that Cunningham and Giffard were 'too old'. Instead, Brooke suggested retired Air Chief Marshal Charles Portal (TNA, CO 967/99, Alan Brooke to Archibald Nye, 1 November 1945). But Attlee rejected Portal as being 'very tired' and, impatient with Brooke's subsequent slow replies, offered the position to Giffard, who after an interview refused on the grounds of his wife's ill health (TNA, CO 967/99, Archibald Nye to Alan Brooke, 6 November 1945).

But the same day Brooke again telegraphed Nye to explain that he had thought the Cunningham being referenced was the admiral and acknowledged that Alan Cunningham would be a 'suitable choice'. His order of preference was Cunningham, Giffard, Paget and General Richard McCreery (TNA, CO 967/99, Alan Brooke to Archibald Nye, 6 November 1945). Whether before or after the receipt of Brooke's message, the decision to select Cunningham was made that day and announced immediately.

19 Cunningham is not mentioned by name in recent histories of Ireland during the war.
20 Alexander Galloway to Kenneth Startup, 15 July 1973.
21 *Daily Telegraph*, 10 October 1960, 12.
22 CAC, Alexander Galloway Papers, GLWY 1/6. Alexander Galloway to Bernard Law Montgomery, 15 May 1962.
23 CAC, Alexander Galloway Papers, GLWY 1/6. Bernard Law Montgomery to Alexander Galloway, 20 December 1969.

Bibliography

Archives

Archives New Zealand

R12325661
R12325670
R12681219

British Library, London

Andrew B. Cunningham Papers

Christ Church College Library, Cambridge

Viscount Portal Papers

Churchill Archive Centre, Cambridge

Alexander Galloway Papers
David Margesson Papers
Winston Churchill Papers

Imperial War Museum, London

IWM Documents.16727, Alexander Clifford collection
IWM Documents.8469, Ralph Blewitt collection
IWM Documents.8590, James Blewitt collection
IWM Documents.6786, Charles Miller collection
IWM Documents.20500, BLM 54, Bernard Montgomery collection
IWM Documents.22500, Papers of Field Marshal Lord Carver
IWM 8179, Neil Ritchie oral history
IWM 15620, Corrie Alexander Halliday oral history
IWM 8736, John Harding oral history

John Rylands Library, University of Manchester

Claude Auchinleck Papers

Liddell Hart Centre for Military Archives, London

Basil H. Liddell Papers
Hastings Ismay Papers
Richard O'Connor Papers

The National Archives, College Park, Maryland

Record Group 165, Entry 77

The National Archives, Kew

AIR 23
AIR 41
CAB 44
CAB 65
CAB 103
CAB 106
CAB 140
CO 733
CO 967
FO 954
WO 169
WO 201
WO 5826

National Army Museum, London

Alan Cunningham Papers

Rhodes University, Cory Library for Humanities Research

J.A.I. Agar-Hamilton Papers

South African National Defense Force Documentation Centre

Acquisitions Group, Box 38 and 39
PMH 2.2.2
PMH 206

Unpublished Papers

Kenneth Startup letters

Books and Articles

Addison, Paul. *The Road to 1945: British Politics and the Second World War*. London: Random House, 1994.
Agar-Hamilton, John A.I., and L.G.F. Turner. *The Sidi Rezeg Battles 1941*. Cape Town: Oxford University Press, 1957.
Ahrenfeldt, Robert H. *Psychiatry in the British Army in the Second World War*. New York: Columbia University Press, 1958.
Aldgate, Anthony, and J. Richards. *Britain Can Take It: The British Cinema in the Second World War*, 2nd edition. London: I.B. Tauris, 2007.
Allport, Alan. *Demobbed, Coming Home after World War II*. New Haven, CT: Yale University Press, 2009.
Allport, Alan. *Browned Off and Bloody Minded, The British Soldier Goes to War 1939–1945*. New Haven, CT: Yale University Press, 2015.
Ball, Simon. *Alamein*. Oxford: Oxford University Press, 2016.
Barnett, Correlli. 'The Education of Military Elites.' *Journal of Contemporary History* 2, no. 3 (1967): 15–35.
Barnett, Correlli. *The Collapse of British Power*. New York: William Morrow & Company, 1972.
Barnett, Correlli. *The Desert Generals*, 2nd edition. London: Cassell, 1983.
Barnett, Correlli. *The Lost Victory, British Dreams, British Realities 1945–1950*. London: Macmillan, 1995.
Bartlett, Christopher J. *A History of Postwar Britain, 1945–74*. London: Longman, 1974.
Baynes, John. *The Forgotten Victor: General Sir Richard O'Connor, KT, GCB, DSO, MC*. London: Brassey's, 1989.
Baxendale, John. '"You and I – All of Us Ordinary People": Renegotiating "Britishness" in Wartime.' In *'Millions Like Us'? British Culture in the Second World War*, edited by Nick Hayes and Jeff Hill, 295–322. Liverpool: Liverpool University Press, 1999.
Beck, Peter J. 'Locked in a Dusty Cupboard, Neither Accessible on the Policy-makers' Desks Nor Cleared for Early Publication: Llewellyn Woodward's Official Diplomatic History of the Second World War.' *English Historical Review* 127, no. 529 (2012): 1435–70.

Beevor, Antony. *Crete, The Battle and the Resistance*. London: John Murray, 1991.
Behrendt, Hans-Otto. *Rommel's Intelligence in the Desert Campaign, 1941–1943*. London: William Kimber Ltd, 1985.
Belchem, David. *All in the Day's March*. London: Collins, 1978.
Bell, Christopher M. *Churchill and Sea Power*. Oxford: Oxford University Press, 2013.
Bell, Rachel E. *Memory, History, Nation, War: The Official Histories of New Zealand in the Second World War 1939–45*. PhD diss., Massey University, Palmerston North, 2012.
Bell, Rachel E. 'Evidence and Interpretation in New Zealand's Official History: The Battle for Crete, May 1941.' *War in History* 22, no. 3 (2015): 364–81.
Benjamin, Walter. 'On the Concept of History.' In *Walter Benjamin, Selected Writings, Volume 4, 1938–1940*, edited by Howard Eiland and Michael W. Jennings, 389–400. Cambridge, MA: Belknap Press of Harvard University Press, 2006.
Bennett, Ralph. *Ultra and the Mediterranean Strategy*. New York: William Morrow, 1989.
Bidwell, Shelford, and D. Graham. *Fire-Power, The British Army Weapons and Theories of War, 1904–1945*. Barnsley, S. Yorkshire: Pen & Sword, 2004.
de la Billière, James. 'The Political-Military Interface: Friction in the Conduct of British Army Operations in North Africa 1940–1942.' *Defence Studies* 5, no. 2 (2005): 247–70.
Birkby, Carel. *Uncle George, The Boer Boyhood, Letters and Battles of Lieutenant-General George Edwin Brink*. Johannesburg: Jonathan Ball Publishers, 1987.
Blackburn, Kevin, and Karl Hack. *War Memory and the Making of Modern Malaysia and Singapore*. Singapore: NUS Press, 2012.
Bond, Brian, editor. *Chief of Staff, The Diaries of Lieutenant-General Sir Henry Pownall, Volume Two, 1940–1944*. London: Leo Cooper, 1974.
Brown, W. Sorley. *War Record of the 4th Bn. King's Own Scottish Borderers and Lothian and Border Horse*. Galashiels: John McQueen & Son, 1920.
Bryant, Arthur. *The Turn of the Tide*. Garden City, NY: Doubleday & Co., 1957.
Busvine, Richard. *Gullible Travels*. London: Constable, 1945.
Butcher, Harry C. *My Three Years with Eisenhower: The Personal Diary of Captain Harry C. Butcher, USNR, Naval Aide to General Eisenhower, 1942 to 1945*. New York: Simon and Schuster, 1946.
Butler, James R.M. *History of the Second World War. Grand Strategy, Volume II, September 1939–June 1941*. London: HMSO, 1957.
Butler, James R.M. 'The British Military Histories of the War of 1939–1945.' In *Official Histories, Essays and Bibliographies from around the World*, edited by Robin Higham, 511–14. Manhattan: Kansas State University, 1970.
Butterfield, Herbert. 'Official History: Its Pitfalls and Criteria.' In *History and Human Relations*, edited by H. Butterfield, 182–224. London: Collins, 1951.
Caddick-Adams, Patrick. *Monty and Rommel, Parallel Lives*. New York: Harry N. Abrams, 2013.

Calder, Angus. *The People's War, Britain 1939–1945*. London: Jonathan Cape, 1969.
Calder, Angus. *The Myth of the Blitz*. London: Jonathan Cape, 1991.
Carver, Michael. 'Desert Dilemmas.' *Royal Armoured Corps Journal* 2 (1948): 181–99.
Carver, Michael. *El Alamein*. London: Wordsworth, 1979.
Carver, Michael. *Dilemmas of the Desert War*. Bloomington: Indiana University Press, 1986.
Carver, Michael. *Out of Step, The Memoirs of Field Marshal Lord Carver*. London: Hutchinson, 1989.
Childs, David. *Britain Since 1945, A Political History*. London: Routledge, 1992.
Chung, Ong Chit. *Operation Matador: Britain's War Plans against the Japanese 1918–1941*. Singapore: Times Academic Press, 1997.
Churchill, Winston S. *The Grand Alliance*. New York: Houghton Mifflin, 1950.
Clarke, Peter. *The Last Thousand Days of the British Empire*. London: Bloomsbury, 2008.
Clifford, Alexander. *Crusader*. London: George G. Harrap, 1942.
Clifford, Alexander. *Three against Rommel, The Campaigns of Wavell, Auchinleck, and Alexander*. London: George G. Harrap, 1943.
Clifton, George. *The Happy Hunted*. London: Cassell, 1952.
Connell, John. *Auchinleck, A Critical Biography*. London: Cassell, 1960.
Cooper, Artemis. *Cairo in the War*. London: Hamish Hamilton, 1989.
Cox, Sebastian. '"The Difference between White and Black": Churchill, Imperial Politics, and Intelligence before the 1941 Crusader Offensive.' *Intelligence and National Security* 9, no. 3 (1994): 405–47.
Crang, Jeremy A. *The British Army and the People's War 1939–1945*. Manchester: Manchester University Press, 2000.
Crang, Jeremy A. 'The British Army as a Social Institution, 1939–45.' In *The British Army, Manpower and Society into the Twenty-First Century*, edited by Hew Strachan, 175–91. London: Frank Cass, 2000.
Crawford, Robert J. *I Was an Eighth Army Soldier*. London: Victor Gollancz, 1944.
Cronin, James E. *The Politics of State, Expansion War, State and Society in Twentieth-Century Britain*. London: Routledge, 1991.
Crisp, Robert. *Brazen Chariots: An Account of Tank Warfare in the Western Desert, November–December 1941*. London: Frederick Muller, 1959.
Curie, Eve. *Journey among Warriors*. New York: Doubleday, Doran and Company, 1943.
Danchev, Alex. *Alchemist of War, The Life of Basil Liddell Hart*. London: Weidenfeld & Nicolson, 1998.
Danchev, Alex, and D. Todman. *War Diaries, Field Marshal Lord Alanbrooke*. Berkeley: University of California Press, 2001.
Davidson, Jim. *A Three-Cornered Life: The Historian W. K. Hancock*. Kensington NSW: University of New South Wales Press, 2010.
Douglas, Keith. *Alamein to Zem Zem*. London: Faber and Faber, 1946.
Duncan, Andrew George. *The Military Education of Junior Officers in the Edwardian Army*. Unpublished PhD diss., University of Birmingham, 2016.

Eckert, Astrid. *The Struggle for the Files. The Western Allies and the Return of German Archives after the Second World War*. Washington, DC: German Historical Institute and Cambridge University Press, 2012.

Edgerton, David. 'The Prophet Militant and Industrial.' *Twentieth Century British History* 2, no. 3 (1991): 360-79.

Edgerton, Paul. *Britain's War Machine, Weapons, Resources, and Experts in the Second World War*. Oxford: Oxford University Press, 2011.

Elton, Geoffrey. *Modern Historians on British History, 1485-1945, A Critical Bibliography, 1945-1969*. London: Methuen & Co., 1970.

Etheridge, Brian C. 'The Desert Fox, Memory Diplomacy, and the German Question in Early Cold War America.' *Diplomatic History* 32, no. 2 (2008): 207-38.

Farrell, Brian P., editor. *Churchill and the Lion City, Shaping Modern Singapore*. Singapore: NUS Press, 2011.

Ferris, John. 'The "Usual Source": Signals Intelligence and Planning for the Eighth Army "Crusader" Offensive, 1941.' *Intelligence and National Security* 14, no. 1 (1994): 84-118.

Ferris, John. 'The British Army, Signals and Security in the Desert Campaign, 1940-1942.' In *Intelligence and Strategy, Selected Essays*, edited by J. Ferris, 181-238. London: Routledge, 2005.

Fielding, Sean. *They Sought out Rommel: A Diary of the Libyan Campaign, from November 16th to December 31st, 1941*. London: Issued for the War Office by the Ministry of Information, 1942.

Francis, Martin. *The Flyer, British Culture and the Royal Air Force, 1939-1945*. Oxford: Oxford University Press, 2008.

Frankland, Noble. 'Some Thoughts About and Experience of Official Military History.' *Journal of the Royal Air Force Historical Society* 17 (1997): 5-15.

Frankland, Noble. *History at War: The Campaigns of an Historian*. London: Giles de la Mare Publishers, 1998.

Fraser, David. *Alanbrooke*. New York: Atheneum, 1982.

Fraser, George MacDonald. *Quartered Safe Out Here: A Harrowing Tale of World War II*. London: Harvill, 1993.

French, David. '"An Extensive Use of Weedkiller": Patterns of Promotion in the Senior Ranks of the British Army, 1919-39.' In *The British General Staff, Reform and Innovation c. 1890-1939*, edited by D. French and B. H. Reid, 132-45. London: Frank Cass, 2002.

French, David. *Raising Churchill's Army, The British Army and the War against Germany 1919-1945*. Oxford: Oxford University Press, 2000.

French, David. 'Officer Education and Training in the British Regular Army, 1919-39.' In *Military Education: Past, Present, and Future*, edited by Gregory C. Kennedy and Keith Neilson, 105-28. Westport, CT: Praeger, 2002.

French, David. *Military Identities, The Regimental System, the British Army, & the British People c. 1870-2000*. Cambridge: Cambridge University Press, 2005.

French, David. *Army, Empire, and Cold War, The British Army and Military Policy, 1945-1971*. Oxford: Oxford University Press, 2012.

Fussell, Paul. *Wartime. Understanding and Behavior in the Second World War*. Oxford: Oxford University Press, 1988.

Gervasi, Frank. *War Has Seven Faces*. Garden City, NY: Doubleday, Doran, and Company, 1942.

Gladman, Brad W. 'Air Power and Intelligence in the Western Desert Campaign, 1940-43.' *Intelligence and National Security* 13, no. 4 (1998), 144-62.

Graecen, Lavinia. *Chink, A Biography*. London: Macmillian London, 1989.

Greenwood, Alexander A. *Auchinleck*. Aldershot: Pentland, 1990.

Grey, Jeffrey. 'A Commonwealth of Histories: The Official Histories of the Second World War in the United States, Britain and the Commonwealth.' *Trevor Reese Memorial Lecture*. London: Sir Robert Menzies Centre for Commonwealth Studies, Institute of Commonwealth Studies, 1998.

Grey, Jeffrey. '"Standing Humbly in the Ante-chambers of Clio": The Rise and Fall of the Union War Histories.' *Scientia Militaria* 30, no. 2 (2000): 253-66.

Grey, Jeffrey, editor. *The Last Word, Essays on Official History in the United States and the British Commonwealth*. Westport, CT: Praeger, 2003.

de Guingand, Francis. *Operation Victory*. London: Hodder & Stoughton, 1947.

de Guingand, Francis. *Generals at War*. London: Hodder and Stoughton, 1964.

Gwyer, James M.A., and J.R.M. Butler. *Grand Strategy*, vol III, June 1941-August 1942. London: Her Majesty's Stationary Office, 1964.

Hack, Karl, and Kevin Blackburn. *Did Singapore Have to Fall? Churchill and the Impregnable Fortress*. London: RoutledgeCurzon, 2004.

Hall, David I. *Strategy for Victory: The Development of British Tactical Air Power, 1919-1943*. Westport, CT: Greenwood, 2008.

Hamilton, Nigel. *Monty, The Making of a General, 1887-1942*. New York: McGraw-Hill, 1981.

Hamilton, Nigel. *Monty, Final Years of a Field Marshal, 1944-1976*. New York: McGraw-Hill, 1987.

Hancock, Keith. 'British Civil Histories of the Second World War.' In *Official Histories, Essays and Bibliographies from around the World*, edited by Robin Higham, 518-25. Manhattan, KS: Kansas State University, 1970.

Hannon, Brian P.D. *The Story behind the Stories, British and Dominion War Correspondents in the Western Theatres of the Second World War*. Unpublished PhD diss., University of Edinburgh, 2015.

Harper, Glyn. *Kippenberger, An Inspired New Zealand Commander*. Auckland: HarperCollins, 1997.

Harrison, Mark. *Medicine & Victory, British Military Medicine in the Second World War*. Oxford: Oxford University Press, 2004.

Hasluck, Paul. *The Government and the People, 1939-1941*. Canberra: Australian War Memorial, 1952.

Hayes, Nick. 'An "English War," Wartime Culture and "Millions Like Us."' In *'Millions Like Us'? British Culture in the Second World War*, edited by Nick Hayes and Jeff Hill, 18–22. Liverpool: Liverpool University Press, 1999.

Hermione, Countess of Ranfurly. *To War with Whitaker: The Wartime Diaries of the Countess of Ranfurly 1939–1945*. London: William Heinemann, 1994.

Higham, Robin. *Diary of a Disaster*. Lexington: University of Kentucky Press, 1986.

Higham, Robin. 'Duty, Honor and Grand Strategy: Churchill, Wavell and Greece, 1941.' *Balkan Studies* 8 (2012): 145–84 (Written in 2005).

Hill, Russell J. *Desert War*. New York: A.A. Knopf, 1942.

Hinsley, Frederick H. et al. *British Intelligence in the Second World War*, vol 2. New York: Cambridge University Press, 1981.

Hodson, James Lansdale. *War in the Sun*. London: Victor Gollancz, 1942.

Hohenberg, John. *Foreign Correspondence: The Great Reporters and Their Times*. New York: Columbia University Press, 1964.

Holton, Matthew. *Ten Years to Alamein*. Toronto: S.J. Reginald Saunders, 1944.

Horn, Karen, and David Katz. 'The Surrender of Tobruk in 1942: Press Reports and Soldiers' Memories.' *Scientia Militaria* 44, no. 1 (2016): 190–208.

Houghton, Frances. *The Veterans' Tale: British Military Memoirs of the Second World War*. Cambridge: Cambridge University Press, 2019.

Howard, Michael E. *Captain Professor: A Life in War and Peace*. New York: Continuum, 2006.

Ismay, Hastings. *The Memoirs of Lord Ismay*. New York: Viking Press, 1960.

Jackson, William G.F. *The North African Campaign, 1940–43*. London: B.T. Batsford, 1975.

Jacob, Alaric. *A Traveller's War*. New York: Dodd, Mead, 1944.

James, Clive. *Cultural Amnesia: Necessary Memories from History and the Arts*. New York: W. W. Norton, 2006.

Jeffreys, Kevin. *The Churchill Coalition and Wartime Politics, 1940–1945*. Manchester: Manchester University Press, 1995.

Jenner, Christopher J. 'Turning the Hinges of Fate: "Good Source" and the UK–US Intelligence Alliance, 1940–1942.' *Diplomatic History* 32, no. 2 (2008): 165–205.

Joffe, Alexander H., and Asaf Romirowsky. 'A Tale of Two Galloways: Notes on the Early History of UNRWA and Zionist Historiography.' *Middle Eastern Studies* 46, no. 5 (2010): 655–75.

Jones, Edgar, and Simon Wessely. '"Forward Psychiatry" in the Military: Its Origins and Effectiveness.' *Journal of Traumatic Psychiatry* 16, no. 4 (2003): 411–19.

Jones, Edgar, and Simon Wessely. *Shell Shock to PTSD, Military Psychiatry from 1900 to the Gulf War*. New York: Psychology Press, 2005.

Katz, David. 'A Case of Arrested Development: The Historiography Relating to South Africa's Participation in the Second World War.' *Scientia Militaria* 40, no. 3 (2012): 280–317.

Katz, David. 'The Greatest Military Reversal of South African Arms: The Fall of Tobruk 1942, an Avoidable Blunder or an Inevitable Disaster?' *Journal for Contemporary History* 37, no. 2 (2012): 71–104.

Kedourie, Elie. *The Chatham House Version and Other Middle Eastern Studies*. London: Weidenfeld & Nicolson, 1970.

Kennedy, Edward. *Ed Kennedy's War: V-E Day, Censorship, and the Associated Press*, edited by Julia Kennedy Cochran. Baton Rouge: Louisiana State University Press, 2012.

Kennedy, John Noble. *The Business of War*. New York: William Morrow and Company, 1958.

Kippenberger, Howard. *Infantry Brigadier*. London: Oxford University Press, 1949.

Knott, Richard. *The Trio, Three War Correspondents of World War II*. The Mill, Brimscombe Port, The History Press, 2015.

Kynaston, David. *Austerity Britain, 1945–1951*. London: Bloomsbury, 2007.

Hart, Basil H. Liddell. *The Other Side of the Hill: Germany's Generals, Their Rise and Fall, with Their Own Account of Military Events, 1939-1945*. London: Cassell, 1948.

Hart, Basil H. Liddell. *The Rommel Papers*. New York: Harcourt Brace, 1953.

Hart, Basil H. Liddell. *The Tanks, A History of the Royal Tank Regiment and Its Predecessors*, Volumes I and II. New York: Praeger, 1959.

Long, Gavin. *Greece, Crete and Syria*. Canberra: Australian War Memorial, 1953.

Lyttelton, Oliver. *The Memoirs of Lord Chandos*. London: Bodley Head, 1962.

Mandler, Peter. *The English National Character: The History of an Idea from Edmund Burke to Tony Blair*. New Haven, CT: Yale University Press, 2006.

Marshall-Cornwall, James. *Wars and Rumours of Wars*. London: Leo Cooper, 1984.

Maughan, Barton. *Tobruk and El Alamein*. Canberra: Australian War Memorial, 1966.

Maurer, John. "'Winston Has Gone Mad': Churchill, the British Admiralty, and the Rise of Japanese Naval Power." *Journal of Strategic Studies* 35, no. 6 (2012): 775–97.

McCamish, Thornton. *Our Man Elsewhere: In Search of Alan Moorehead*. Melbourne: Black, 2017.

McClymont, W.G. *To Greece*. Official History of New Zealand in the Second World War. Wellington: Department of Internal Affairs, 1959.

McGibbon, Thornton. "'Something of Them Is Here Recorded': Official History in New Zealand." In *The Last Word, Essays on Official History in the United States and the British Commonwealth*, edited by Jeffrey Grey, 53–68. Westport, CT: Praeger, 2003.

McIntire, Carl T. *Herbert Butterfield, Historian as Dissenter*. New Haven, CT: Yale University Press, 2004.

Mead, Richard. *Churchill's Lions, A Biographical Guide to the Key British Generals of World War II*. Stroud, Gloucestershire: Spellmount Press, 2007.

Mearsheimer, John. *Liddell Hart and the Weight of History*. Ithaca: Cornell University Press, 1988.

von Mellenthin, Frederick. *Panzer Battles*. Norman: University of Oklahoma Press, 1956.

Messenger, Charles. *Rommel, Leadership Lessons from the Desert Fox*. New York: Palgrave Macmillan, 2009.

Milligan, Spike. *Adolf Hitler: My Part in His Downfall*. London: Michael Joseph Ltd., 1971.

Milligan, Spike. *'Rommel?' 'Gunner Who?' A Confrontation in the Desert*. London: Penguin, 1976.
Montgomery, Bernard Law *The Memoirs of Field Marshal the Viscount Montgomery*. New York: World Publishing Company, 1958.
Montgomery, Brian. *Shenton of Singapore: Governor and Prisoner of War*. London: Leo Cooper, 1984.
Moorehead, Alan. *Mediterranean Front*. London: Hamish Hamilton, 1941.
Moorehead, Alan. *The End in Africa*. New York: Harper, 1943.
Moorehead, Alan. *A Year of Battle*. London: Hamish Hamilton, 1943 (Published originally as *Don't Blame the Generals*).
Moorehead, Alan. *African Trilogy*. London: Hamish Hamilton, 1945.
Moorehead, Alan. *Eclipse*. London: Hamish Hamilton, 1946.
Moorehead, Alan. *Montgomery, A Biography*. London: Hamish Hamilton, 1946.
Moorehead, Alan. *A Late Education*. London: Soho Press, 2003 (originally published 1970).
Mosse, George. *The Image of Man, The Creation of Modern Masculinity*. Oxford: Oxford University Press, 1996.
Moyal, Ann. *Alan Moorehead, A Rediscovery*. Canberra: National Library of Australia, 2005.
Murphy, Walter E. *The Relief of Tobruk*. Wellington: War History Branch, 1961.
Namier, Lewis B. 'Symmetry and Repetition.' In *Conflicts: Studies in Contemporary History*, 69–70. London: Macmillan, 1942 (originally published in the *Manchester Guardian*, 1 January 1941).
Nelis, Tina. *Northern Ireland in the Second World War*. Unpublished M. Phil thesis, University of Manchester, 2012.
Ollard, Richard. *Fisher and Cunningham, A Study in the Personalities of the Churchill Era*. London: Constable and Company, 1991.
Orange, Vincent. *Tedder, Quietly in Command*. London: Frank Cass, 2004.
Otley, Christopher B. *The Origins and Recruitment of the British Army Elite, 1870–1959*. Unpublished PhD diss., University of Hull, 1965.
Playfair, I.S.O. *The Mediterranean and the Middle East, Volume III-British Fortunes Reach Their Lowest Ebb*. London: HMSO, 1960.
Pollock, Andrew M. *Pienaar of Alamein: The Life Story of a Great South African Soldier*. Cape Town: Cape Times Limited, 1943.
Postan, Michael M. *British War Production*. London: HMSO, 1952.
Quail, Sarah. *Portsmouth in the Great War*. Barnsley, South Yorkshire: Pen & Sword Books Ltd, 2014.
Reynolds, David. *In Command of History: Churchill, Fighting and Writing the Second World War*. New York: Random House, 2005.
Reynolds, David. 'Official History: How Churchill and the Cabinet Office Wrote *The Second World War*.' *Historical Research* 78, no. 201 (2005): 400–22.

Reynolds, Quentin. *Only the Stars Are Neutral*. Garden City, NY: Blue Ribbon Books, 1943.

Richards, Denis, and Hilary St. George Saunders. *Royal Air Force 1939–1945, Volume 2, The Fight Avails*. London: HMSO, 1953.

Rose, Sonya O. *Which People's War? National Identity and Citizenship in Wartime Britain*. Oxford: Oxford University Press, 2003.

Roskill, Stephen. *Churchill and the Admirals*. New York: William Morrow, 1977.

Sheffield, Gary D. *Leadership in the Trenches: Officer-Man Relations, Morale and Discipline in the British Army in the Era of the First World War*. London: Macmillan, 2000.

Simpson, Michael. *A Life of Admiral of the Fleet Andrew Cunningham, A Twentieth Century Naval Leader*. London: Frank Cass, 2004.

Sixsmith, Eric K.G. *British Generalship in the Twentieth Century*. London: Arms and Armour Press, 1970.

Sixsmith, Eric K.G. 'Lieut. General Sir Alexander Galloway, K.B.E., C.B., D.S.O., M.C.' *The Covenanter* Summer Number (1977): 3–4.

Southey, Nicholas, and F.A. Mouton. '"A Volksvreemde Historian": J.A.I. Agar-Hamilton and the Production of History in an Alien Environment.' *South African Historical Journal* 44, no. 1 (2001): 72–98.

Stacey, Charles P. *A Date with History, Memoirs of a Canadian Historian*. Ottawa: Deneau Publishers, 1980.

Stewart, Andrew. '"The Klopper Affair": Anglo-South African Relations and the Surrender of the Tobruk Garrison.' *Twentieth Century British History* 17, no. 4 (2006): 516–44.

Stewart, Andrew. 'The "Atomic" Despatch: Field Marshal Auchinleck, the Fall of the Tobruk Garrison and Post-War Anglo-South African Relations.' *Scientia Militaria* 36, no. 1 (2008): 78–94.

Summerfield, Penny. 'Dunkirk and the Popular Memory of Britain at War, 1940–1958.' *Journal of Contemporary History* 45, no. 4 (2010): 788–811.

Tedder, Arthur. *With Prejudice: The War Memoirs of Marshal of the Royal Air Force*. London: Cassell, 1966.

Thompson, Leonard. *A History of South Africa*. New Haven, CT: Yale University Press, 2001.

Thompson, Reginald W. *The Montgomery Legend*. London: George Allen & Unwin, 1967.

Titmus, Richard. *Problems of Social Policy*. London: HMSO, 1950.

Tomlinson, Jim. *The Politics of Decline, Understanding Post-War Britain*. New York: Routledge, 2014.

Travers, Tim. 'The Hidden Army: Structural Problems in the British Officer Corps 1900–1918.' *Journal of Contemporary History* 17, no. 3 (1982): 523–44.

Tuker, Francis. *Approach to Battle, A Commentary, Eighth Army, November 1941 to May 1943*. London: Cassel, 1963.

van der Waag, Ian. 'Contested Histories: Official History and the South African Military in the 20th Century.' In *The Last Word? Essays on Official History in the United States*

and British Commonwealth, edited by Jeffrey Grey, 27–52. Westport, CT: Praeger, 2003.
van der Waag, Ian, and D. Visser. 'Between History, Amnesia and Selective Memory: The South African Armed Forces, a Century's Perspective.' *Scientia Militaria* 40, no. 3 (2012): 1–12.
Warner, Philip. *Auchinleck, The Lonely Soldier*. London: Buchan and Enright, 1981.
Waugh, Evelyn. *Unconditional Surrender*. London: Penguin Books, 1964.
Wilmot, Chester. *Tobruk 1941: Capture, Siege, Relief*. Sydney: Angus and Robertson, 1944.
Wilson, Cat. *Churchill on the Far East in World War II*. London: Palgrave Macmillan, 2014.
Wilson, Charles McMoran (Lord Moran). *The Anatomy of Courage*. Boston: Houghton Mifflin, 1967.
Woolbert, Robert Gale. Review of Q. Reynolds, *Only the Stars Are Neutral*. *Foreign Affairs*, October 1942, 177.
Yapp, Malcolm E. 'Elie Kedourie and the History of the Middle East.' *Middle Eastern Studies* 41, no. 5 (2005): 665–87.
Young, Desmond. *Rommel: The Desert Fox*. New York: Harper & Brothers, 1950.

Newspaper and Magazine Items

'Alexander Galloway.' *The Times*, 1 February 1977, 16.
Mr. Andrew, B. 'Acheson.' *The Times*, 13 May 1959, 13.
Buckley, Christopher, 'A Modern Blenheim in the Desert.' *Daily Telegraph and Morning Post*, 24 November 1941, 1.
'C.I.G.S. Appeals for Full Alamein Reunion.' *Sunday Times*, 5 October 1947, 6.
'Eighth Army Spirit.' *The Times*, 23 October 1948, 3.
Fowler, A. Keith, '"Anon." – Britain's Favorite Author.' *Saturday Review*, 19 June 1943, 13–14.
'Germans' Heavy Losses: 500 Bayoneted.' *Daily Telegraph*, 3 July 1942, 6.
Letter from Alexander Galloway, *Daily Telegraph*, 10 October 1960, 12.
'Libya Army Change'. *Sydney Morning Herald*, 12 December 1941, 8.
'Stop Arguing over the Last War.' *The Times*, 20 October 1962, 8.
A Student of War. 'Swift Success in Libya Tank Battle Would Have Decisive Effects.' *Daily Telegraph and Morning Post*, 24 November 1941, 4.
'Thrilling Stories Done by Foreign Correspondents.' *Chicago Tribune*, 7 December 1941, 61.
'"Tommy" and "Jerry" Bury Hatchet.' *The Sunday Times*, 29 October 1978, 1.

House of Commons

Hansard, House of Commons debate, 9 July 1941, vol 373, cc165-7. http://hansard.millbanksystems.com/commons/1941/jul/09/minister-of-state-duties-middle-east (accessed 5 April, 2017).

Hansard, House of Common debate, 11 December 1941, vol 376, cc1686-700. http://hansard.millbanksystems.com/commons/1941/dec/11/war-situation#S5CV0376P0_19411211_HOC_283 (accessed 5 April, 2017).

Hansard, House of Commons debate, 8 January 1942, col 377, cc43-174. http://hansard.millbanksystems.com/commons/1942/jan/08/war-situation#S5CV0377P0_19420108_HOC_398 (accessed 5 April, 2017).

Hansard, House of Commons debate, 27 January 1942. http://hansard.millbanksystems.com/commons/1942/jan/27/lieut-general-sir-alan-cunningham#S5CV0377P0_19420127_HOC_117 (accessed 5 April, 2017).

Hansard, House of Commons debate, 10 February 1942, vol 377, cc1370-1. http://hansard.millbanksystems.com/commons/1942/feb/10/military-operations-libya#S5CV0377P0_19420210_HOC_43 (accessed 5 April, 2017).

Hansard, House of Commons debate, 10 March 1942, vol 378, c912. http://hansard.millbanksystems.com/commons/1942/mar/10/lieut-general-sir-alan-cunningham#S5CV0378P0_19420310_HOC_84 (accessed 5 April, 2017).

Hansard, House of Commons debate, 19 May 1942, vol 380, cc43-204. http://hansard.millbanksystems.com/commons/1942/may/19/war-situation#S5CV0380P0_19420519_HOC_449 (accessed 5 April, 2017).

Hansard, House of Commons debate, 1 July 1942, vol 381, cc224-476. http://hansard.millbanksystems.com/commons/1942/jul/01/central-direction-of-the-war-1#S5CV0381P0_19420701_HOC_371 (accessed 5 April, 2017).

House of Commons, Papers by Command, vol 3 (London: HMSO, 1942), 29.

Internet Sources

Dennis, Peter. 'Leonard Charles Frederick Turner.' *Australian Dictionary of Biography*. http://adb.anu.edu.au/biography/turner-leonard-charles-frederick-15565

Dobbie, Ian. 'Lieutenant General Sir Arthur Smith (1890–1977).' http://www.evangelical-times.org/archive/item/7060/Historical/Lieutenant-General-Sir-Arthur-Smith–1890-1977-/

Farrar-Hockley, Anthony. 'Sir Alexander Galloway.' *Oxford Dictionary of National Biography*. https://www-oxforddnb-com.i.ezproxy.nypl.org/view/10.1093/odnb/9780192683120.001.0001/odnb-9780192683120-e-31135

Ferris, John. 'Assessing the Impact of Intelligence: The "Good Source" and Anglo-American Intelligence in the Second World War and After.' H-Diplo. https://issforum.org/reviews/PDF/Ferris-Jenner.pdf (4 November 2008).

The Goon Show, Rommel's Treasure, Series 6, Episode 6. First Broadcast 25th October 1955. http://www.thegoonshow.net/scripts_show.asp?title=s06e06_rommels_treasure

Howard, Michael. *The Uses of Military History*. Shedden Paper, No. 1. Canberra: Australian Defence College, 2008. http://www.defence.gov.au/ADC/Publications/Shedden/2008/Publctns_ShedPaper_050310_TheUse ofMilitaryHistory.pdf

Lieutenant-Colonel J. Cunningham, C.I.E., M.D., F.R.S.ED., I.M.S. (RET.). *British Medical Journal*, 1968, 503. https://www.bmj.com/content/3/5616/503

University of Edinburgh, Faculty of Medicine, Official List of Passes. *Scottish Medical and Surgical Journal*, vol 20, January to June (1907): 485. https://babel.hathitrust.org/cgi/imgsrv/download/pdf?id=mdp.39015074801104;orient=0;size=100;seq=513;num=485;attachment=0

University of Edinburgh, Degrees. *The British Medical Journal* 2, no. 2795 (25 July 1914): 208. https://www.ncbi.nlm.nih.gov/pmc/articles/PMC2299591/pdf/brmedj07293-0047.pdf

Official Publications and Pamphlets

Auchinleck, Claude J. 'Operations in the Middle East from 1st November 1941 to 15th August 1942.' *Supplement to the London Gazette* Number 38177, 309–400, Thursday, 15 January 1948.

The Battle for Egypt. London: Issued for the War Office by the Ministry of Information, 1943.

The Eighth Army, September 1941 to January 1943. London: His Majesty's Stationary Office, 1944.

Eighth Army: El Alamein to the River Sangro. Printing and Stationery Services, British Army of the Rhine, 1946.

Index

Acheson, Andrew B. 134, 136–9, 226 n.183
Agar-Hamilton, John A. I. 90, 104–5, 127, 129–30, 132–5, 138–9, 174
Alamein Reunion 3, 171
Alexander, Harold 3, 173, 199
armoured warfare 8, 12, 28, 31, 103, 131–3, 136, 167, 178, 180, 182
Auchinleck, Claude 3, 7, 12, 36, 73–9, 82, 89, 100–1, 113, 135, 182
   and Andrew B. Cunningham 35
   and Churchill 31, 33–4, 44–6, 98–9
   conference with commanders 29–30
   and Cunningham (Alan) 15, 29, 31–2, 33–5, 38–9, 43–5, 47–8, 56, 58–61, 71, 104, 114, 118, 122–3, 128, 154–5, 164, 185–6, 196
   despatch 98, 101, 103–5, 117, 120, 124–6
   education and experiences of 22
   and Galloway 39, 79, 88, 185
   in Indian Army 8, 22
   letter from Ismay 189
   letter from Smith 52–5, 208–9 n.2
   letters with Cunningham 49–51
   Liddell Hart and 140
   memoirs of *Crusader* 103–4
   and Montgomery 174
   Moorehead on 152–4
   political pressures on 13–14, 16, 105
   strategic perspective of 102
Australia 97
   Official History 120, 123

Barnett, Correlli 20, 125, 127, 154, 181, 193, 205 n.57, 217 n.15
   on Cunningham (Alan) 182–6
   decline thesis 96
   The Desert Generals 175, 186
   on Galloway 183, 185
   on Montgomery 181–2
'battle stress' 24

Belchem, David 140–1
   accounts of Cunningham's supersession 179–81
Ben Gurion, David 234 n.18
Benjamin, Walter 192
Beveridge, William 17
Birkby, Carel 218–19 n.45
Blackburn, Kevin 120
Blewitt, Guy 39, 63
Blewitt, James 35, 52, 55, 71, 131
   and Cunningham (Alan) 39–41, 43–4, 49, 63, 131, 208 n.35
Blewitt, Ralph 39, 63
Blewitt, William E. 63
Bower, Robert Tatton 69–70
Bradley, Omar 99
Brewer, Sam 112, 168
Brink, George 75, 218 n.45
Britain/British 1–4, 43, 51, 147, 152, 192
   and Commonwealth defence 97
   economic crisis 93
   evacuation of civilians 148
   labour demands 147–8
   'national character' 19–20, 193
   Official History 5, 107, 125, 129, 197
   postwar (*see* postwar Britain)
   restriction on home front 17–18
   version of *Crusader* 122
British Army/forces 1, 3, 12, 19, 21, 27, 65–6, 68, 113, 127, 184–5
   and Commonwealth forces 11
   despatches of commanders 106
   in Egypt 6–7, 9–10
   historical documents 111
   Labour government and 94
   lessons learned 197–9
   medical services of 12
   military psychiatry in 23
   political pressures on 8, 10
   soldiers 93, 151–2, 229 n.11
   Ultra intelligence 12, 32, 102, 108
British Empire 93–4, 97, 120, 216–17 n.15

British Nationality Act of 1948 97
Brooke, Alan 15, 21, 47, 61, 71–2, 90, 99, 153, 172, 194, 232 n.101, 235 n.18
  Cunningham's (Alan) report to 57–60, 64–5, 115–16
Brooke-Popham, Robert 66
Brook, Norman 110, 137
Buckley, Christopher 149–50, 230 n.45
Busvine, Richard 150, 167
  Gullible Travels 166
Butcher, Harry, *My Three Years with Eisenhower* 99
Butler, J. R. M. 108–9, 121, 131
Butterfield, Herbert 109, 121

CAB 106/655, supersession file of Cunningham (Alan) 60, 116–19, 127, 143, 207 n.15
Calder, Angus 95, 230 n.37
'campaign neurosis' 24
Carver, Michael 29, 125, 141, 226–7 nn.194–5
Chamberlain, Neville 13
Churchill, Randolph 156, 158, 160–1, 164, 169–70, 219 n.45
Churchill, Winston 3, 6, 8, 10, 13–14, 33, 56, 67, 69–71, 76, 84, 93, 98, 104, 120, 137, 171, 173, 190
  and Auchinleck 31, 33–4, 44–6, 98–9
  criticism of 13, 66, 68
  and Cunningham (Alan) 15, 45–7, 61, 65, 98
  Dill's clash with 15, 204 n.36
  The Grand Alliance 98
  Lyttelton to 207 n.8
  speech of 46, 147
  support for 148
  and Tedder 16
Clifford, Alexander 5, 30, 150, 155, 163
  Auchinleck's instruction 157
  Crusader 155
  operation disintegration 156
  on supersession of Cunningham 157
  Three Against Rommel 155
Clifton, George 125, 129
combat stress reaction 23
command, military 19–25
  amateurism/professionalism 20–1, 25
  codes of behaviour 20–1

education/experiences of notable figures 21–2
  Moran on courage of 24–5
  officer education 20
  regimental system 19–20
Commonwealth nations 4, 6, 97, 104
  forces 6, 11, 119
  leaders/commanders 16
  Official History 174
Coningham, Arthur ('Mary') 29, 36, 73–4, 81–2, 85, 164
Crang, Jeremy A. 229 n.11
Crawford, Robert John, *I Was an Eighth Army Soldier* 106
Creagh, Michael 175, 182
Crisp, Robert, *Brazen Chariots: An Account of Tank Warfare in the Western Desert, November–December 1941* 106
Crusader battle
  attack on November 21 27
  engagement and crisis (22–23 November) 28–32
  map 27
  November 18 27
  plan 11–13, 58–9, 78, 83, 115, 131–6, 158, 164–5, 167, 183–4, 202 n.11
  politics of 13–19
  progression (25 November) 32–6
Cunningham, Alan 3–4, 9, 11–12, 16, 32, 66, 69, 75–6, 85–6, 135–6, 138–9, 190, 195–6
  and Andrew B. Cunningham 60–1
  and Auchinleck 15, 31, 33–5, 38–9, 43–5, 49–52, 58–61, 71, 104, 118, 154–5, 164, 185–6, 196
  Barnett on 182–6
  and Blewitts 39–41, 43–4, 49, 63, 131, 208 n.35
  and Brooke 57–60, 64–5, 115–16, 235 n.18
  and Churchill 15, 45–7, 61, 65, 98
  conference with commanders 29–30
  'defensive minded' 3, 45–6
  East Africa Command 8, 173
  education and experiences of 22
  Fielding on 112
  and Haining 63–4
  Hill on 159

Hodson on 158–9
illness of 43–5, 55, 160
  medical explanation/reports 47–9, 89, 118, 133
  and Kennedy 114–16
  letter to solicitor (1943) 77–9, 88
  mental state of 89–92
  Moorehead on 154
  parliament members on issue of 65–71
  personal diary of (perceptions of *Crusader*) 37–9
  rehabilitation of 65, 71–2, 196
  Reynolds on 161–2
  and Smith 52, 54
  and Smuts 14, 61–2, 71
  supersession of 5–6, 16, 25, 33–5, 41, 43–7, 49, 56, 62, 73, 79, 95, 112, 116–19, 122–4, 143–4, 200
  in 8th Army 3, 8, 14, 28–31, 113–15, 128, 130
  and Weymss 114
  Wilmot on 168
Cunningham, Andrew B. ('ABC') 3, 8, 11, 15, 22, 49, 60–1, 89, 161
Cunningham, Daniel John 48
Curie, Eve 5, 77, 150, 185
  accounts of 164
  Journey among Warriors 163
Curie, Marie 156

Davies, Clement 69
Dean, Maurice 110
decolonization 4, 93–4
definitions of military failure 2, 13, 18–19, 22, 198
de Guingand, Francis 79, 88, 126, 129, 134, 138
  Latham on account of 134
  memoirs of 100–1, 123, 175–6
  Operation Victory 100, 175
demobilization 4, 93–4
Dill, John 13–14, 44, 51
  clash with Churchill 15, 204 n.36
documentaries/films on war 170
Dorman-Smith, Eric 14, 21, 134, 139–40, 153, 173, 182, 186–7, 211 n.42, 226 n.187
Douglas, Keith 20, 191, 230 n.40
  Alamein to Zem Zem 106

Eden, Anthony 14, 151
Egypt 3, 31, 112, 151–2, 166
  British Army in 6–7, 10, 156
  El Alamein 1, 33, 169–71, 173–5, 187, 190–2
  journalists in 150
Eisenhower, Dwight, *Crusade in Europe* 99
Ellenberger, George F. 124, 129, 133
Elton, Geoffrey 108–9
'exhaustion' 24, 36, 44–5, 48, 51

Fielding, Sean 111–12, 114, 150, 165
First World War 10, 18, 21–3, 91, 121, 198
Frankland, Noble 108–9, 137, 220 n.66
Fraser, George MacDonald 149
Freedom of Information Acts 110–11
French, David 19–20
Freyberg, Bernard 16, 128, 132–3, 174
Fussell, Paul 190–1

Galloway, Alexander 'Sandy' 3, 9–10, 33, 36, 73–5, 101, 117, 123, 174, 176, 193–5
  action on Cunningham 126–9, 135, 138–9, 144
  and Auchinleck 39, 79, 88, 185
  Barnett on 183, 185
  conference with Corps 29–30
  early/personal life 214 n.11
  education and experiences of 22, 214–15 n.11
  to Sixsmith 89, 198
  historical concerns 199
  letter to O'Connor 215–16 n.1
  Montgomery's final note to 200
  records and documents (1968) 80–8
Gatehouse, Alec 133
Germans/Germany 1, 8, 18, 81–2, 141–2, 159–60, 162, 171, 182
  attack on Tobruk 12, 83
  at borders of Egypt 3
  British Army against 2–3, 11–12, 32, 102–3, 112, 170
  forces 28, 31–2, 156, 159, 167, 169
  generals 142, 175
  invasion of Greece 6–7
  against Soviet Union 8, 142, 169
  weapon capabilities 12, 61–2, 184, 229 n.31

Godwin-Austen, Alfred Reade 11, 29–30, 37, 65, 127, 130, 153, 175, 208 n.35
Gordon-Finlayson, James R. 125
Greece 6–7, 9, 16, 87, 119–21, 196
Grigg, Edward 67, 194

Hack, Karl 120
Haining, Robert Hadden 63–4, 71
Hall, George H. 118
Halliday, Corrie Alexander 208 n.35
Halton, Matthew 112, 150
Hambro, Patricia 78–9
Hancock, Keith 107–8
Harding, John 181, 214
Harris, Arthur 110
Harrison, Mark 24
Higham, Robin 119, 207 n.8
Hill, Russell
   and Cunningham (Alan) 159
   Desert War 159
   and Ritchie 160
historiography 6, 28, 32–6, 120–1, 123, 190
   problems in 5–6, 106–11
history (writing) 1–2, 5, 71–2, 98–106, 196. *See also* Official History
   elements of 98–106
   journalists and first draft of 149–70
   and memory 95, 97–8, 191
Hodson, James Lansdale 157–9, 230 n.37, 230 n.42, 230 n.45
Holton, Matthew 166
   on issue of Cunningham (Alan) 165
   Ten Years to Alamein 165
home front 18, 147–9, 230 n.37
Howard, Michael 5, 109

interwar period 19–20
Ismay, Hastings 98–9, 173, 189

Jacob, Alaric 5, 112
   accounts of 164–5
   A Traveller's War 164
Jacob, Ian 124, 137
Japan 15, 43, 45, 120, 150
Johnston, George R. 124, 129–30
journalism 4, 97–8, 100, 149–50
   journalists 1–2, 111–12, 148–70
   public perceptions 170–2

Kedourie, Elie 216–17 n.15
Kennedy, Edward 162
   accounts of 162–3
   and Shearer 163
Kennedy, John Noble 44, 60
   Cunningham (Alan) and 114–16
Keyes, Roger 13, 68
Kippenberger, Howard 127, 131, 133–4, 136, 140, 174, 190
   Infantry Brigadier 132
   and Latham 224 n.166
   memoirs of 132
Klopper, Hendrik 104–5

Labour government 94
Labour Party, rise of 4, 93, 110
Lampson, Miles 14
Latham, Harry B. 117, 135–6, 138, 190
   and Cunningham (Alan) 138
   on de Guingand's account 134
   and Galloway 126–7, 129–31
   on Johnston 124
   and Kippenberger 224 n.166
   letter from Agar-Hamilton 90
Leese, Oliver 60–1
Libya 11, 27, 46–7, 66, 102. *See also* Tobruk, Libya
Liddell Hart, Basil H. 6, 14, 82, 90, 109, 130, 139, 170, 172–3, 186
   and Belchem 180–1
   as historian 139–42
   letter from Tedder 190
   Pile's reports to 140, 194
   to Playfair 226 n.187
Lord Gort 234–5 n.18
Lund, Otto Marling 39, 41, 63, 71
Lyttelton, Oliver 13, 16, 34, 68, 151
   to Churchill 207 n.8
   memoirs of 177–8
   report to Margesson 75–6, 177–8

Malaya 43, 66, 88, 97, 120, 148, 195
Margesson, David 75–6, 177–8
Marshall-Cornwall, James
   Cunningham (Alan) and 90–1
   memoirs of 91
masculinity 19, 205 n.50
Mearsheimer, John 228 n.199
Messervy, Frank 153, 175

Middle East 13, 24, 101–2, 136, 149, 151, 185
Middle East Defence Committee (MEDC) 13
military memoirs/memoirists 2, 5–6, 25, 44, 91, 94, 98–100, 103, 106, 125, 132, 149, 170, 172–87
  Crusader participants 5–6, 29, 98, 109, 119, 125–7, 131, 134, 140, 143
  Belchem 179–81
  de Guingand 100–1, 123, 175–6
  Harding 181
  Lyttelton 177–8
  Robertson 176–7
  Tedder 178–9
  purposes of 172–5
  revisionists 181–7
Miller, Charles 80–1, 85
Milligan, Spike 106, 192, 220 n.55
Molony, C. J. C. 144
Montgomery, Bernard Law 1, 3, 6, 21, 60, 104, 118–19, 140, 144, 171, 190, 196, 199
  and Auchinleck 174
  Barnett on 181–2
  documents 99
  El Alamein to the River Sangro 99, 173
  final note to Galloway 200
  memoirs of 100, 173–4
  Thompson on 186–7
Moorehead, Alan 6, 100, 157, 228 n.6
  accounts of 151
  African Trilogy 150
  on Auchinleck 152–4
  on Cunningham (Alan) 154
  relationship with Montgomery 218 n.34
Moorehead, Lucy 218 n.36
Moore, Thomas Cecil Russell 67, 70
Murphy, W. E. 133, 140

Namier, Lewis 192
narratives, historical 6, 94, 106, 111–13, 116, 119–22, 143, 145, 190
  Barnett's 183, 185
  Cunningham's medical condition 44–5, 55, 63, 88, 160
  Ellenberger's 124, 133
  Hodson's 230 n.42
  Johnston's 124–5
  South African 134, 141
  structure 31
  Wilmot's 167
National Health Service 70, 93, 95, 137
National Party, rise of 105
New Zealand 103, 119, 133, 171, 174
  Official History 120, 131–2, 143, 197
  version of *Crusader* 123
  War History Branch 131
Norrie, Willoughby 11, 28–9, 32, 78, 85, 141, 158
North Africa 1–3, 8, 102, 119, 131, 169, 174

O'Connor, Richard 10, 14, 81, 86, 88, 93, 168, 170, 182, 196, 200, 206 n.66, 215–16 n.1
Official History 4, 6, 35, 88, 95, 98, 101, 105, 175, 189–90, 197. *See also* historiography; history (writing)
  British 5, 107, 125, 129, 197
  categories of 5
  Commonwealth 174
  end of 143–5
  New Zealand 120, 131–2, 143, 197
  pamphlets 149
  problem of 106–11
  sources of 111–45
    British-led failures and narratives 119–22
    CAB 106/655 (supersession file of Cunningham) 116–19
    different versions of *Crusader* 122–4
    The Eighth Army, September 1941 to January 1943 113–17
    "flap (incident)" 124–6, 223 n.131
    South African 106, 134–5, 143, 176, 180, 182
Official Secrets Act 109
operational documents 2, 5–6, 30–1, 36, 123–5, 143

Peirse, Richard 110
"Piccadilly Jim" 230 n.40
Pienaar, Dan 133, 226 n.194
Pile, Frederick Alfred (Tim) 10, 90, 139–40, 194

Playfair, Edward 144
Playfair, I. S. O. 124, 129, 136, 140, 144, 174, 226 n.187, 227 n.195
Portal, Charles 110, 235 n.18
    Tedder's reports to 73–4
postwar Britain 4, 19
    crisis of returning soldiers 93
    'decline' 95–6, 193
    decolonization/demobilization 93–4
    deference 94–5
    economic crisis 93
    national identity 95, 97, 193
    politics and culture 95
    writing wartime history in 93–8
Pownall, Henry 66, 98–9, 203 n.35
psychiatric casualties
    'battle stress' 24
    'exhaustion' 24, 36
    'Neurasthenia' (nervous breakdown) 23
    psychiatric cases 24
    'shell shock' 23–4, 44

regimental system 19–20
Reynolds, Quentin 160–1, 168
    on Cunningham (Alan) 161–2
Ritchie, Neil 3, 33–4, 36, 40, 52, 65, 69, 72, 75, 77, 80–1, 84, 123, 153, 161, 163, 173, 175, 227 n.195
    Galloway on 128
    Hill on 160
    on supersession of Cunningham (1984) 88–9
Robertson, John Connell 60, 115, 117, 176–7
    Auchinleck, A Critical Biography 203 n.27
Rommel, Erwin 3, 6, 8, 11, 28–9, 31–3, 75, 77–8, 80–3, 98, 123, 129–30, 136, 140, 142, 158–9, 163, 169
Royal Air Force 19, 124
Royal Artillery 8, 16, 39
    and Blewitt family 63
Royal Tank Regiment 20, 142
Russia 147, 162

Sandys, Duncan 64, 67
Seagoon, Neddie 192
Second World War 1–2, 8, 23–4, 106, 110, 121, 149, 187, 190

Shearer, Ann 79
Shearer, Eric John 29, 32, 34, 61, 75, 77–9, 163–4, 169, 207 nn.8–9
Singapore 43, 66, 70, 119–21, 148, 197
Sirri Pasha, Hussein 14
Sixsmith, Eric 194, 198
    British Generalship in the Twentieth Century 80–8
Small, William Denton Douglas 47–9, 54, 59, 63, 89, 118
Smith, Arthur 33–6, 40, 43–4, 59, 88–9, 117–18
    and Cunningham (Alan) 52, 54
    letter to Auchinleck 52–5, 208–9 n.2
    religious faith of 56
Smuts, Jan 25, 65, 72, 104
    and Cunningham (Alan) 14, 61–2, 71
    Klopper and 105
    Theron's reports to 74–5
South Africa/South Africans 104–5, 119, 126–7, 133
    Apartheid 105–6
    5th Infantry Brigade 74, 103–4
    Official History 106, 134–5, 143, 176, 180, 182, 197
    and Tobruk 105–6
    version of *Crusader* 122, 128
Soviet Union 8, 97, 121, 142, 148, 169
Stacey, Charles Perry 220 n.59
Staff College 21–2
Stokes, Richard 65, 213 n.37
    criticism on Churchill 66
    on issue of Cunningham (Alan) 66–7, 70

Tedder, Arthur 29, 31–2, 34, 76, 79, 85, 88, 110, 118, 156, 177
    Churchill and 16
    letter to Liddell Hart 190
    memoirs of 178–9, 206–7 n.6
    reports to Portal 73–4
Theron, Frank 17, 62, 79
    reports to Smuts 74–5
Thompson, Reginald William 181, 186–7
Tobruk, Libya 2, 7–8, 11, 15, 105, 148
    British forces towards 27–8
    fall of 68, 112, 119–20, 219 n.49
    German attack on 3, 12, 28
    relief of 3, 16, 53, 128, 180

South African relationship to 106
surrender of 104
Tuker, Francis 175
Turner, Leonard Charles Frederick 134–5, 139, 224–5 n.166

United States 43, 62, 120, 147–8, 165

von Mellenthin, Frederick 134–5

Wardlaw-Milne, John 68
War Office 104–5, 110–12, 124, 227 n.195
Cunningham's file 30–1, 35, 67, 72, 136
pamphlet published by 61, 79, 111–12
Wavell, Archibald 8, 13, 64, 80, 100, 113, 119, 161–2, 169–70, 196–7

Webster, Charles 109–10
Western Desert Force 10
Weymss, Henry Colville 60, 71–2
and Cunningham (Alan) 114–15
Willink, Henry Urmston 68–70
Wilmot, Chester 150
on Cunningham (Alan) 168
The Struggle for Europe 167
Tobruk 1941 167
Wilson, Cat 120
Wilson, Charles McMoran (Lord Moran) 91
The Anatomy of Courage 24
Wilson, Henry Maitland 'Jumbo' 9, 14, 86

Young, Desmond 142, 170

www.ingramcontent.com/pod-product-compliance
Lightning Source LLC
Chambersburg PA
CBHW072136290426
44111CB00012B/1888